Judging and Emotion

Judging and Emotion investigates how judicial officers understand, experience, display, manage and deploy emotions in their everyday work, in light of their fundamental commitment to impartiality.

Judging and Emotion challenges the conventional assumption that emotion is inherently unpredictable, stressful or a personal quality inconsistent with impartiality. Extensive empirical research with Australian judicial officers demonstrates the ways emotion, emotional capacities and emotion work are integral to judicial practice. Judging and Emotion articulates a broader conception of emotion, as a social practice emerging from interaction, and demonstrates how judicial officers undertake emotion work and use emotion as a resource to achieve impartiality. A key insight is that institutional requirements, including conceptions of impartiality as dispassion, do not completely determine the emotion dimensions of judicial work. Through their everyday work, judicial officers construct and maintain the boundaries of an impartial judicial role which necessarily incorporates emotion and emotion work.

Building on a growing interest in emotion in law and social sciences, this book will be of considerable importance to socio-legal scholars, sociologists, the judiciary, legal practitioners and all users of the courts.

Sharyn Roach Anleu is Matthew Flinders Distinguished Professor, Judicial Research Project, College of Humanities, Arts and Social Sciences at Flinders University, Adelaide, Australia.

Kathy Mack is Emerita Professor of Law, Judicial Research Project, College of Business, Government and Law at Flinders University, Adelaide, Australia.

Judging and Emotion

A Socio-Legal Analysis

Sharyn Roach Anleu
and Kathy Mack

Routledge
Taylor & Francis Group
LONDON AND NEW YORK

First published 2021
by Routledge
2 Park Square, Milton Park, Abingdon, Oxon OX14 4RN

and by Routledge
52 Vanderbilt Avenue, New York, NY 10017

Routledge is an imprint of the Taylor & Francis Group, an informa business

British Library Cataloguing-in-Publication Data
A catalogue record for this book is available from the British Library

Library of Congress Cataloging-in-Publication Data
A catalog record has been requested for this book

ISBN: 978-1-138-89302-3 (hbk)
ISBN: 978-0-367-67868-5 (pbk)
ISBN: 978-1-315-18004-5 (ebk)

Typeset in Times New Roman
by MPS Limited, Dehradun

Contents

Illustrations

Figures

Table

Preface

Judging and Emotion is the latest outcome of the Judicial Research Project at Flinders University. Over the past two decades, the Project, led by Sharyn Roach Anleu and Kathy Mack, has undertaken sustained examination of the everyday work, experiences and attitudes of the judiciary. This research is the basis for the insights into the role of emotion and emotion work in judging discussed in this book.

The Judicial Research Project began in 2000 as the Magistrates Research Project, with substantial financial and practical commitment from the Association of Australian Magistrates (AAM), a professional association of judicial officers presiding in Australia's lower courts. Flinders University and the Australasian Institute of Judicial Administration (AIJA) provided additional early support. Issues of emotion, emotion work and judging were apparent from the outset of the Project. As it expanded to include all Australian courts, it was renamed the Judicial Research Project. The scope for investigating emotion and emotion work as part of judging deepened, with wider data collection and further conceptual development.

We are grateful to the many magistrates, judges, court staff and court administrators who contributed to all stages of this research. Their time, energy and engagement with the research have provided extensive and exceptionally valuable data on the Australian judiciary not otherwise obtainable. The ongoing engagement of AAM and its members and the Council of Chief Magistrates have been crucial to success throughout the research programme. The Judicial Conference of Australia (JCA), especially its Executive Officer Christopher Roper AM and various JCA presidents, the Council of Chief Justices and the Council of Chief Judges were helpful in many phases of the research. We also appreciate the financial and practical contributions of the AIJA, especially Professor Greg Reinhardt AM, the late Kathy Jarrett, Delwyn Gillan and Mary Young the AIJA librarian. Anne Wallace, now Adjunct Professor with La Trobe Law School, has been a close collaborator especially in relation to the workload study and our participation in and subsequent publications arising from the workshop:

'*Too Few Judges?' Regulating the Number of Judges in Society*, held at the International Institute for the Sociology of Law in 2016. We value her many contributions. Dr Andrew Cannon, formerly Deputy Chief Magistrate South Australia, has provided valuable guidance since the beginning of the research.

Generous funding has been received throughout these projects from the Australian Research Council (ARC):

Linkage Project Grant (LP0210306): *The Changing Role of the Magistrates Court* with the Association of Australian Magistrates and all chief magistrates and their courts as Industry Partners and support from Flinders University as the administering organisation.

Discovery Project Grant (DP0665198): *The Australian Judiciary: A National Socio-Legal Analysis.*

Linkage Project Grant (LP0669168): *Judicial Officers and Workload Allocation* with the Association of Australian Magistrates and the chief magistrates and magistrates courts of the Northern Territory, South Australia and Victoria, and the Australasian Institute of Judicial Administration as Collaborating Organisations.

Discovery Project Grant (DP1096888): *Courts, the Judiciary and Social Change.*

Discovery Project Grant (DP15010663): *Changing Judicial Performance: Emotion and Legitimacy* conducted with Partner Investigators from the US National Center for State Courts (Williamsburg, Virginia) Dr Jennifer Elek and Dr David Rottman.

The Project has received considerable support over many years from Flinders University and the home Colleges of the authors: the College of Humanities, Arts and Social Sciences (Sharyn Roach Anleu) and the College of Business, Government and Law (Kathy Mack). We thank the library staff and the Social and Behavioural Research Ethics Committee for assistance and advice. We appreciate financial assistance from the Deputy Vice Chancellor (Research) Professor Robert Saint AM; internal grant funding from the former School of Social and Policy Studies; and a publication support grant awarded by the College of Humanities, Arts and Social Sciences.

From the inception of the Judicial Research Project, we have been fortunate to have many capable and diligent research and administrative assistants who made valuable and sustained contributions to the various studies, data collection and analysis that underpin this book, in particular (in alphabetical order) Dr Russell Brewer, Carolyn Corkindale, Elizabeth Edwards, Ruth Harris, Lily Jacobs, Leigh Kennedy, Mary McKenna, Rose Polkinghorne, Mavis Sansom and Dave Wootton.

In relation to the development and production of this book, we thank Colleen deLaine, Jordan Tutton, Rae Wood and Dr Rhiannon Davies. Colleen deLaine provided the overall management of the many paper and electronic versions of interview and court transcripts as well as drafts of the chapters, cheerfully, rapidly and accurately typing and retyping and interpreting our own notes, even when we could not do so. Her oversight of the book project enabled all the different parts to come together smoothly. Jordan Tutton took primary responsibility for all legal research and referencing, imaginatively and thoroughly locating, clarifying and correcting substantive material. He contributed to all other phases of production of the book, including undertaking data analysis to prepare tables and figures as needed and typing of drafts. We thank Rae Wood particularly for her work locating emotion-related material in the court transcripts, the coding of interview transcripts and the associated NVivo analysis, and the identification and preliminary analysis of the Arizona discipline material. We appreciate her return from retirement to continue working with us. Dr Rhiannon Davies undertook intensive work coding court transcripts as well as providing critical analysis of the Australian bias cases.

We thank Dr Jennifer Elek (Senior Court Researcher) and Dr David Rottman (Principal Court Researcher, retired) of the US National Center for State Courts for their collaboration on our current joint project: *Changing Judicial Performance: Emotion and Legitimacy*. They have each provided essential comparative focus to our work and are enjoyable and effective collaborators. Sharyn appreciates the hospitality of the National Center for State Courts (NCSC) hosting her visits in 2015, 2017, 2018 and 2019, and she thanks President Mary McQueen; Dr Pam Casey, Vice President Research; Dr Nicole Waters, Director of Research Services; Paula Hannaford-Agor and Robert Phipps for their collegiality and local advice.

We especially thank our co-convenors of the workshop on *Judging, Emotion and Emotion Work* held at the International Institute for the Sociology of Law, Oñati, Spain, 2–4 May 2018, Associate Professor Stina Bergman Blix (Uppsala University, Sweden) and Professor Terry Maroney (Vanderbilt University, USA) for their collegiality and extended discussions on researching judging and emotion. We deeply value the insights that emerged from all the participants at that workshop. We thank the International Institute for the Sociology of Law, Malen Gordoa Mendizabal for all her assistance in organising the workshop and Leire Kortabarria for her careful editorial input and assistance coordinating authors, referees and editors across several countries as we prepared the resulting special issue of *Oñati Socio-Legal Studies,* entitled: 'Judging, Emotion and Emotion Work' (2019).

We thank the participants in, and organisers of, many academic and judicial conferences, workshops and public lectures for their questions and comments on presentations drawing on this research, and we thank those who provided comments and reviews of our publications. We have gained from involvement in Collaborative Research Networks (CRN) sponsored by the Law and Society Association, in particular CRN 32: Gender and Judging, CRN 42: Law and Emotion, and CRN 43: Innovations in Judging, and The Australia Sociological Association's Thematic Group: Sociology of Emotions and Affect.

Our work has been enriched through sustained intellectual interchange and collegiality with scholars and collaborators in Australia and beyond. We thank (in alphabetical order) Professor Gabrielle Appleby (University of New South Wales), Emerita Professor Susan Bandes (DePaul University), Professor Janeen Baxter (University of Queensland), Dr Katie Barclay (University of Adelaide), Dr Francesco Contini (Instituto di Informatica Giuridica e Sistemi Giudiziari, Consiglio Nazionale delle Ricerche/The Institute of Legal Informatics and Judicial Systems, National Research Council of Italy), Professor Margaret Davies (Flinders University), Professor Jill Hunter (University of New South Wales), Professor Rosemary Hunter (University of Kent), Professor Elena Marchetti (Griffith University), Professor Lorraine Mazerolle (University of Queensland), Emerita Professor Jessica Milner Davis (University of Sydney), Emeritus Professor Leslie Moran (Birkbeck College), Professor Linda Mulcahy (University of Oxford), Professor Brian Opeskin (University of Technology Sydney), Emeritus Professor Wilfrid Prest (Adelaide University), Associate Professor Heather Roberts (Australian National University), Associate Professor Kate Rossmanith (Macquarie University), Emerita Professor Ulrike Schultz (FernUniversität in Hagen), Ms Carly Schrever (University of Melbourne/Judicial College of Victoria), Professor Mark Western (University of Queensland) and Professor Åsa Wettergren (University of Gothenburg). We also wish to thank our discipline colleagues in law and sociology for corridor conversations and interest in our research over the years.

A period of study leave (Sharyn Roach Anleu) at the International Institute for the Sociology of Law in 2017 was invaluable in further developing links between humour and emotion. Thanks to Ainhoa Markuleta Letamendi and Susana Arrese Murguzur for making this visit possible and productive and to the library staff: Ainhoa Baños and Rakel Lizarralde for all their assistance. Professor João Paulo Dias and Dr Paula Casaleiro, Centro de Estudos Sociais (Centre for Social Studies), University of Coimbra, Portugal in 2019 provided new opportunities to elaborate ideas on emotions and judging. Sharyn also appreciates the opportunity to be a

Visiting Professor at the University of Cardiff in 2018 and the invitation to contribute to the workshop entitled *Remorse and Responsibility in Constructions of the 'Ideal' Defendant* during that visit. Thanks to Professor Jiří Přibáň, Professor Stewart Field, Emeritus Professor Phil Thomas, Editor of *Journal of Law and Society* and Dr Rachel Cahill-O'Callaghan for their collegiality and diverse discussions on socio-legal research. We particularly appreciate Professor Cyrus Tata's (Strathclyde University) engagement with our research and his valuable scholarship shared at several conferences and workshops.

A book is not possible without a publisher. We value the enthusiasm and encouragement from Dr Colin Perrin at Routledge. At the outset we worked with Hannah Lovelock, Editorial Assistant–Law, then her successor Nicola Sharpe; we value their advice, patience and guidance. We benefitted from the detailed comments and enthusiasm of the anonymous reviewers of the book proposal and hope they enjoy reading the book. We are grateful for the work of Ajanta Bhattacharjee, Editorial Assistant, Routledge and the thoroughness of those involved in the production process: Neema Sangmo Lama, Production Manager, the copyeditors and the production team.

Sharyn especially wishes to thank Oliver, Tristan, Lucinda and Edmer. Our household life has always entailed me writing a book or a paper and collectively managing the domestic challenges that presents. Kathy gives special thanks to Rod for his steady support throughout the decades of Project work on which this book rests. And Sharyn and Kathy thank each other for a such a successful collaboration and friendship, and the pleasure shared in writing this book.

While many others have contributed to the research and findings reported in this book, any errors or omissions are our own.

*****

Glossary

ABA	American Bar Association
ABS	Australian Bureau of Statistics
AGPC	Australian Government Productivity Commission
AIJA	Australasian Institute of Judicial Administration
ALRC	Australian Law Reform Commission
ARC	Australian Research Council
COCJ	Council of Chief Justices
FamCA	Family Court of Australia
FCCA	Federal Circuit Court of Australia
DFV	Domestic/Family Violence
FCA	Federal Court of Australia
HCA	High Court of Australia
JCA	Judicial Conference of Australia
JCIO	Judicial Conduct Investigation Office
JCNSW	Judicial Commission of New South Wales
JCV	Judicial College of Victoria
JPE	Judicial Performance Evaluation
NCSC	National Center for State Courts (USA)
NJC	National Judicial College (USA)
NJCA	National Judicial College of Australia
NSWLRC	New South Wales Law Reform Commission
RCFV	Royal Commission into Family Violence
VIS	Victim Impact Statement

Chapter 1

Introduction

Introduction

Judging and Emotion aims to identify the place(s) of emotion in judicial work and to understand how emotion relates to the core judicial value of impartiality.[1] The central argument is that emotion and impartiality in judging and judicial work are not alternatives or necessarily in conflict; rather, emotion is integral to judicial work. The important questions are how and when emotion enters judicial work and the intersections among judging, emotion and impartiality. This approach contrasts with the typical treatment of emotion as something to be avoided, suppressed or as inevitably resulting in stress, compromising judicial performance and wellbeing.

Judging and Emotion challenges the assumption that emotion is inherently unpredictable, harmful or a personal quality inconsistent with impartiality. Using extensive empirical data—interviews, court observations and surveys—*Judging and Emotion* demonstrates how judicial officers[2] understand, experience, display, manage and deploy emotion as part of their everyday work.

1 A growing and broad body of scholarship addresses the role of emotion in law. See for example Abrams 2015; Abrams and Keren 2010; Amaya and Del Mar 2020; Bandes 2001; Bandes and Blumenthal 2012; Conway and Stannard 2016; Grossi 2015, 2019; Temple 2019. This book intersects with this wider research with a more specific focus on judicial experience and practice.

2 In this book, the terms 'judicial officer' and 'judiciary' are used generically to refer to any member of the judiciary, regardless of court level or type. Within Australia, the term 'magistrate' refers to members of the judiciary who preside in the lower state and territory courts, except in the Northern Territory where magistrates were given the title 'judge' in 2016. Australian magistrates are paid judicial officers, with legal qualifications, and are appointed until a fixed retirement age. The term 'judge' indicates those who preside in the intermediate and higher state and territory courts and all national courts. Jurisdictions outside Australia may use other labels for their judiciary or may use these terms, but the words may not have the same meanings as in Australia.

This chapter first outlines the distinctive role of judges, their core obligation of impartiality, and the conventional model of judicial authority which rejects emotion and requires judicial officers to display an emotionless demeanour. The next section addresses the growing scholarship on emotion and the approaches of different disciplines including history, psychology and sociology. A key theme is that context shapes the different feeling rules or norms that specify appropriate emotion experience and display. The chapter then investigates emotion work and feeling rules in occupations and professions and addresses the judiciary as a distinctive profession. It concludes with an overview of the remaining chapters and some comments on researching emotion.

Judges and judging

Judicial officers embody legal authority and are the nexus between formal abstract law and the practical tasks of everyday judicial work (Roach Anleu and Mack 2017). Judges must perform their judicial role impartially and without bias in relation to any party or issue and must be independent, especially of government, in rendering decisions (Barak 2006; Council of Chief Justices of Australia and New Zealand 2017; Geyh 2013; McIntyre 2019). Judicial officers are required to apply existing law to proven facts within set procedures, 'without fear or favour, affection or ill-will'.[3] These are obligations of judicial attitude, role and practice (Lucy 2005).

The conventional model of the impartial judge casts judging as without emotion, emphasising reason over feeling and legal rules over emotion. 'Ideally, judges reach their decisions utilizing facts, evidence, and highly constrained legal criteria, while putting aside personal biases, attitudes, emotions, and other individuating factors' (Nugent 1994: 4, also see Bybee 2010; Epstein, Landes and Posner 2013; Moran 2009, 2010).

Dichotomisation of reason and emotion has persisted across post-Enlightenment Western knowledge systems, including law (Patulny and Olson 2019; Reddy 2009; Weber 1978). Emotion is regarded as reactive, irrational, unpredictable, associated with the body not the mind, and with private sentiment rather than public obligation. This concept of emotion has:

[3] The full text of the oath used for the High Court of Australia: 'I, [name], do swear that I will bear true allegiance to Her Majesty Queen Elizabeth the Second, Her Heirs and Successors according to law, that I will well and truly serve Her in the Office of Chief Justice [or Justice] of the High Court of Australia and that I will do right to all manner of people according to law without fear or favour, affection or ill-will. So Help me God!': *High Court of Australia Act 1979* (Cth) s 11 and sch 1.

> long functioned as a catchall category for much of what law aspires to avoid or counteract: that which is subjective, irrational, prejudicial, intangible, partial, and impervious to reason (Bandes and Blumenthal 2012: 162).

These characterisations of law, reason and emotion treat emotion as incompatible with, and even potentially destructive of, impartiality and so threatening the legitimacy of judicial authority and the rule of law (see Krygier 2016; Tamanaha 2010). Maroney points out that this 'insistence on emotionless judging—that is, on judicial dispassion—is a cultural script of unusual longevity and potency' (2011b: 630).

Dispassion in judging has come to mean the absence of emotion in decision making and in demeanour (Goffman 1956). The incursion of emotion into judicial decision making can be a source or indicator of bias for or against a party or a claim. A judicial decision influenced by emotion, as a non-legal value or attitude, may be, or appear to be, biased and therefore illegitimate (Rachlinski and Wistrich 2017; Wistrich and Rachlinski 2017; Wistrich, Rachlinski and Guthrie 2015; *Ebner v Official Trustee in Bankruptcy* (2000) 205 CLR 337). Conduct indicating loss of impartiality can be the basis for complaint and possible discipline of a judicial officer (Appleby and Le Mire 2014; Geyh, Alfini, Lubet et al. 2013; Roach Anleu, Mack and Tutton 2014).

The cultural script of dispassion requires that judicial performance be accompanied by appropriate judicial demeanour; conventionally, this would be emotionless, impersonal, detached and affectively neutral (Bandes 2009; Bandes and Blumenthal 2012; Maroney 2011a, 2011b). The judicial oath, ethics guidelines, codes of judicial conduct, appeal cases and disciplinary proceedings convey expectations relating to impartiality, judicial dispassion, emotion and its expression. The frequently expressed obligation for judicial officers to be courteous, patient and maintain decorum necessarily implies emotion and its management. A judicial officer's experience, management and expression of emotion, or lack thereof, is sometimes framed as judicial temperament (Maroney 2020). Norms about judging, emotion and emotion display are also communicated through occupational socialisation such as professional training, continuing education and formal and informal interaction among judicial officers (Wharton 2009).

Legal requirements that prescribe emotionless judging and demeanour, along with the cultural script of judicial dispassion, are not the only forces influencing judicial practice. In common law adversarial systems, institutional and structural factors include the delineated judicial role as a passive arbiter and guarantees of judicial independence (Geyh 2014). Legal language, prescribed procedures and courthouse or courtroom design express ideas about judicial authority, impartiality, justice and the rule of law and so have significant symbolic and practical impact on judicial work (Mulcahy 2010; Mulcahy and Rowden 2020).

An extreme positivist conception of judging and legal authority constructs judges as operating only according to formal roles within the court and legal system and cannot readily accommodate a view of the judge as a human or social actor. Despite extensive challenge, from the legal realists in the early twentieth century and continuing through the critical legal studies movement, critical race theorists and feminist legal scholarship, the conventional formalist construction remains a powerful image and benchmark (Davies, M. 2017; Gey and Rossi 2005; Goodman 2013; Green and Roiphe 2008; Tamanaha 2010).

Nonetheless, judicial practice itself constitutes the institutional structure and legal values, including impartiality. Structures both empower and constrain social action and the capacity for change or routinisation. In certain circumstances, human agents can (or are forced to) improvise or innovate in structurally shaped ways that can significantly reconfigure the very structures that constitute them (Sewell 1992). This conception of structure and action as mutually constitutive and transformative can be applied to judging and emotion. To conceive of judicial officers as human agents 'implies that those agents are capable of putting their structurally formed capacities to work in creative or innovative ways' (Sewell 1992: 4). This means that judicial officers may have the capacity to alter or transform the social-legal relations of which they are a part. Recognising that judicial work is more interrelational, interactional and social than anticipated by the conventional image of judicial authority opens the possibility of investigating emotion and judging. This in turns allows scope to transform the conventional model of the judge.

Experience and display of emotion are embedded in the physical settings and institutional obligations in which judicial officers work—courtrooms, legal procedure, legal requirements—creating a constellation of relationships and interactions. While these structures construct and constrain the judiciary and judging, they also create opportunities and expectations for experience, expression and management of emotion. Despite the formal disavowal of emotion and attempts to erase and contain emotion, emotions are increasingly recognised as essential, though not uncontroversial, for judicial practice in everyday work (Bergman Blix and Wettergren 2018; Maroney 2011a, 2019; Roach Anleu and Mack 2013).

Judging and Emotion examines the interplay among impartiality, judicial authority and emotion in the social and institutional context of judicial work. In order to do this, it is first necessary to map out the conception of emotion that the book adopts and the related concept of emotion work.

Conceptualising emotion

Scholarship on emotion is vast, multidisciplinary and growing. Despite extensive research and writing on emotion(s), '[t]here is no commonly agreed-upon definition of emotion in any of the disciplines that study this phenomenon' (Mulligan and Scherer 2012: 345). Not surprisingly, different disciplines define emotion differently.

Historians document the diversity and complexity of emotion and emotion concepts across different eras and societies and show how 'knowledge of emotions and their classification have altered over time' (Frevert 2014: 10; also see Schnädelbach 2019). The term emotion assimilated and displaced previous words: 'Today we no longer talk of feeling, passion, fervour, affect, sensibility, sentiment, appetite, changes of temper, and its inclination, but for the most part simply of emotion' (Frevert 2014: 16). This displacement can be attributed to the increasing dominance of the natural science paradigm, instead of metaphysics or philosophy, to explain emotion.

The idea that emotion is basic, innate, human and therefore universal dominated the psychology of emotions from the 1970s to the 1990s (Wetherell 2015). This paradigm characterised emotion as spontaneous and involuntary, a physiological reaction to external stimuli (Ekman and Cordaro 2011). Contemporary psychological approaches generally agree that cognition and emotion are intertwined and a rigid separation between cognition and affect is artificial (Barrett 2017; Frevert 2014; Scheer 2014). Emotion underlies all action; sharp distinctions between rational and irrational, between reason and emotion, cannot be made (Barbalet 2008; Bennett and Broe 2007, 2010; Damasio 1994).

Another challenge in conceptualising emotion is to delineate the relationships among emotion, affect and feeling. Generally, affect is used as an umbrella term that includes emotions as well as stress responses and moods (Gross 2015). Some emotion researchers view affect as prior to and independent of intentions, meanings, interpretations, reasons and beliefs (Leys 2011). Others choose not to use the term affect because it is only one component of the 'physiological-psychological-social complex of emotion', and identifying or interpreting affect requires cultural and social input (Scheer 2012: 198 fn 26). Some researchers do not define emotion at all, and many use the term collectively—emotion—rather than referring to discrete emotions (Stets 2012). Others use the terms emotion and feeling interchangeably (Hochschild 1979; Scheer 2012).

A comprehensive conception of emotion encompasses interpretation and meaning given to experience and display comprising motor expression, bodily symptoms and subjective experiences (Mulligan and Scherer 2012). Though emphases differ, most current conceptualisations of emotion:

- acknowledge physiological change in response to an event or situation that generates the emotion (Gross 2015);
- view emotion as the product of social interactions and embedded in interpersonal relations rather than a primarily individual phenomenon (Burkitt 2018);

- agree that emotion requires cultural categorisation using available language, discourses and narratives (Bericat 2015; Illouz, Gillon and Shachak 2014; Robinson 2014);
- acknowledge that concepts shape perceptions and experiences of emotion (Barrett 2017; Holmes 2015; Ng and Kidder 2010); and
- recognise that norms (informal and formal) specify, regulate and shape the experience and display of emotions: their type, quantity and intensity (Lively 2008; Lively and Weed 2014).

Judging and Emotion adopts a composite approach to emotion. Emotion is interactive, interdependent and context specific as well as subjective, internal and personal. Emotion is psychobiological (recognising instinct or impulse) and individual. It is also a social practice performed in, emergent from and embedded in social settings and situations. The terms emotion and feeling will be used interchangeably, and display is used to describe outward bodily manifestations including demeanour. Affect will generally not be used.

This book does not seek to classify or distinguish emotions—for example fear, frustration, happiness, joy, sadness—as discrete, separate or easily identifiable phenomena. Nonetheless, in emotion research, participants may use specific emotion words such as sadness, anger, frustration, pride and happiness to describe their feelings, or those they observe in others. As a result, despite ambiguity in distinguishing separate and identifiable emotions, a specific emotion or different emotions may be discussed rather than the broader, omnibus, singular concept of emotion.

Emotion as social practice

Several key insights follow from conceptualising emotion as culturally and historically embedded rather than primarily biologically or naturally given. Feelings that emerge in a social situation may engender multiple interpretations and be experienced or identified as several emotions. Emotions overlap and bleed into each other, making them difficult to disentangle. Feelings and emotions may be ambivalent, in tension or in conflict and may not be easily or immediately identifiable or describable (Burkitt 2018).

Emotion has to be realised in performance; it 'is not a material thing to be possessed and then displayed … [it is] something that must be enacted and portrayed, something that must be realized' (Goffman 1959: 75). Emotion as practice is not just about the body and mind, physiology and cognition. It necessarily involves language, material artefacts, other people and the environment, all of which are historically and culturally specific.

The language of emotion affects the ways emotions are experienced and expressed or performed. The images and metaphors that 'English speakers routinely draw upon to think about "anger" as, for example, hot fluid in a container (boiling, steaming, bursting, etc)', affect the experience of anger (Lutz and White

1986: 419). This image of anger, which perpetuates the notion of emotion as irrational and uncontrollable, has 'surprising traction in the common law' (Sorial 2019: 129) and has significance in understanding judging and emotion.

Observable bodily presentation, including posture, facial expression, gestures and tone of voice are often used to identify or suggest particular emotions, though they are unstable markers and heavily context dependent (Barrett 2017). Observers may assess and interpret certain movements or sounds in emotion terms, but accuracy is not guaranteed, and scope for multiple interpretations of the same observations is wide.

Understanding emotion as a social practice recognises that emotive performance is oriented toward others in the social setting and implies an audience, even multiple audiences.

> [T]he *doing* of emotion is an interactive performance that constantly shapes, develops, and alters the meanings of the emotion expressed … [participants] not only display emotion through their bodily manifestations; they also perform emotion through narratives (Ng and Kidder 2010: 197, emphasis in original).

It is these interrelations and interactions that form the context for emotion experience, display and management.

Formal and informal norms specify expected or appropriate emotion—experience, performance, expression, management—in particular settings or contexts. Ideally, these norms are distinctive, shared and acquired through training and experience. They also change and are negotiated in social settings. Participants in any setting must, to some extent, be aware of, share and comply with the formal and informal norms relating to emotion (Rimé 2007). Not surprisingly, scholars from different disciplines adopt different concepts to describe these norms which vary historically, culturally, situationally and in levels of abstraction and visibility. These concepts include emotional standards (Reddy 2009), emotional communities (Rosenwein 2006), emotionology (Stearns and Stearns 1985), emotional styles (Gammerl 2012), emotional regimes (Bergman Blix and Wettergren 2016) and feeling rules (Hochschild 1979).

The social context or social setting itself can also have an emotion dimension. Terms such as emotional climate, emotional landscape, emotional environment, emotional ecology or emotional atmosphere refer to emotion that exists and endures beyond individuals, their feelings and actions. The emotional climate or emotional atmosphere is a quality or characteristic of a collectivity, for example a workplace, a classroom, a courtroom, an organisation or a community. Psychologists distinguish between emotional atmosphere—a transitory mood—and emotional climate which is a more enduring environment (Conejero and Etxebarria 2007; de Rivera 1992). These collective terms are used non-specifically in this book to refer to emotion that exists at the organisational or workplace level as distinct from the emotion that individuals experience, display and manage. Even so, the collective and the individual levels are inextricably linked through the social sharing of emotions and conformity with, or deviation from, appropriate feeling rules (Karstedt 2019; Rimé 2007).

Judging and Emotion investigates the ways emotion is constituted, experienced, manifested, displayed and managed in judicial work. It addresses how judicial officers approach and perform emotion. The focus is on everyday judicial work in its legal and social setting, in which emotion is disavowed yet essential. This setting is integral to understanding the constraints on and capacities for emotion and the ways in which emotion is experienced, performed and displayed.

Situationally specific norms pertaining to the courtroom regulate appropriate feelings and behaviour. Conforming to those feeling rules will entail emotion work. However, courtroom settings are complex; not all judicial officers feel the same things; not all connect bodily responses, sensations or feelings with emotion concepts; and not all will express or display their feelings in the same ways. Some of this variation will be personal and biographical, moulded by experiences, training and socialisation, others will be shaped by social institutions such as gender and social class, as well as by judicial and legal institutional norms. The emotions experienced and expressed by judicial officers, the management of those emotions and judicial perception, interpretation and management of others' emotions constitute and can potentially alter the emotional standards.

Emotion work and feeling rules

One conclusion that sits across much discussion of emotion is that 'emotions are considered a domain of effort, and individuals are expected to conform to norms and strive for ideals' (Reddy 2009: 311). The level and kind of effort has been calibrated in different concepts, sometimes used interchangeably: emotional labour (Hochschild 1983; Wharton 1999, 2009); emotion work (Hochschild 1979); emotion management (Bolton and Boyd 2003; Lively and Weed 2014); emotion regulation (Gross 2015; Maroney and Gross 2014); affective practice (Wetherell 2015); affective work (Craciun 2018); and emotional capital (Cottingham 2016: Heaney 2019).[4]

[4] Other concepts such as service emotions (White 2014, 2019), emotional granularity (Barrett 2017; Gendron and Barrett 2019) and background emotion (Barbalet 2011; Bergman Blix and Wettergren 2018) suggest that some kinds of emotion-related work may not require conscious effort or even awareness. Backgrounded emotions can be part of a general routine or professional orientation experienced (or perceived) as taken for granted, natural, automatic, effortless even intuitive with low expressivity and not consciously experienced (Barbalet 2011).

Each of these terms suggests some level of agency. Emotion is something that someone does, implying a capacity and situational or social expectation to control, even use, one's own emotional experience and display and perhaps also to manage the emotions of others. Emotion work is oriented to expectations or norms that 'inform the sense of what is "proper" feeling in the performance and reading of emotional expression' (Scheer 2012: 216). Feeling rules are 'guidelines for the assessment of fits and misfits between feeling and situation' (Hochschild 1979: 566). This raises the prospect of deviation from appropriate emotion experience and display (Roach Anleu 2006).

Conceptions of emotion work all imply interaction, interdependence and social relations. The capacity, need or motivation to manage emotion does not occur independently of institutional or social contexts. The interdependence and interaction that occur in social settings, in turn, constrain the amount and type of emotion permitted. 'How specific emotions like grief, happiness or affection are generated, handled and expressed depends to a large degree on *where* they occur' (Gammerl 2012: 164, emphasis in original). Assessing the meaning or significance of emotion depends on the context (Bandes 2017; Gross 2015). In one situation, anger can be disruptive; in a different one, it can remind participants of their responsibilities and enhance compliance (Maroney 2012). Instances of emotion regarded as unhelpful can motivate consideration of emotion regulation to bring non-normative feelings and expressions back in line with the norms operating in the setting (Lively and Weed 2014). This account links emotion regulation, whether of one's own emotions or others, to the idea of feeling rules, emotion standards or styles, or to other conduct norms and the context in which the emotion occurs. Managing one's own emotions and emotion display can function to manage others' felt and displayed emotions. Both are necessarily intertwined: 'emotion management involves the simultaneous attention to one's own as well as others' emotion' (Bergman Blix and Wettergren 2016: 34).

Another facet of emotion management is the distinction between deep and surface acting. Surface acting describes the process of managing one's outward expression, typically to conform with situational feeling rules. This can entail suppressing one's actual feelings. Deep acting involves individuals actually experiencing the socially or institutionally expected feelings (Lively and Weed 2014). However, in some circumstances, experiencing such feelings may not entail acting. Because of the potential dissonance between the display and experience of emotion, surface acting is often associated with emotional exhaustion, stress, impaired wellbeing, burnout and depression (Grandey 2003; Humphrey, Ashforth and Diefendorff 2015; Lively and Powell 2006; Ozcelik 2013; Schrever, Hulbert and Sourdin 2019). Research suggests that the negative impact of emotion work occurs when employees have to fake their feelings and engage in 'false face acting' (Hsieh, Jin and

Guy 2012: 383). Display rules that require suppressing negative emotions seem to be the most emotionally demanding (Hsieh 2014). Hochschild (1983; also see Williams 2003) identifies emotional labour that is neither explicitly compensated nor considered compensable work as especially damaging or alienating. Professional occupations in which incumbents typically exercise more autonomy than employees in the service sector also engage in emotion work, but may avoid some of the negative experiences (Craciun 2018).

The concept of emotion work explicitly ties emotion—experience, display and management—to paid work, as a requirement of many occupations where employees directly interact with others, typically face-to-face. Hochschild coined the term emotion work to 'refer to the act of trying to change in degree or quality an emotion or feeling' (Hochschild 1979: 561). It 'can be done by the self upon the self, by the self upon others, and by others upon oneself' (Hochschild 1979: 562). In *The Managed Heart* (1983), she further develops the idea that emotion can be commodified by introducing the concept of emotional labour to emphasise the relational and hierarchical nature of occupations found typically in the service sector. Emotional labour is work that 'requires one to induce or suppress feeling in order to sustain the outward countenance that produces the proper state of mind in others' (Hochschild 1983: 7). It involves managing feeling to create a publicly observable facial and bodily display for the benefit of another person and is subject to supervision and evaluation.

Emotion work and professions

While not strictly conforming to Hochschild's original concept of emotional labour, the work of professional occupations entails emotion management.[5] The suppression of emotion and personal feelings is a key attribute of traditional conceptions of the profession, implying emotion management as part of detached professional service (Abbott 1988; Wilensky 1964). The professions are characterised by 'disinterestedness' (Parsons 1954: 35). The requirement to be '*impersonal* and *objective*' limits the relationship with

[5] The research on professions is vast with significant differences in the interpretation of professional attributes. Functionalist approaches acknowledge such traits as entry requirements, credentials, licensing and the service ideal as intrinsic to certain kinds of work. Critical approaches take the same attributes as evidence of monopolisation, exclusion and maintenance of prestige and status. Social constructionists examine the ways in which professional tasks and boundaries are maintained and negotiated in everyday work (Abbott 1988; Macdonald 1995; Roach Anleu 2010). A newer literature uses broader and more inclusive terms such as 'knowledge-based work' (Gorman and Sandefur 2011: 276). These occupations (many relatively recent) are characterised by expert knowledge, autonomy, a normative orientation to service and high status with associated financial and other rewards—all characteristics relevant to the traditional professions and to the judiciary.

clients ‘to the technical task at hand, avoid[ing] emotional involvement’ (Wilensky 1964: 140, emphasis in original). Professional ethics oblige members to maintain social distance and prohibit expression of unregulated or inappropriate emotions, especially in the relationship with clients (Abbott 1983). Members of a profession typically ‘supervise their own emotional labor by considering informal professional norms and client expectations’ (Hochschild 1983: 153).

Three strong themes emerge from research on emotion work in professional occupations:

1 The occupational culture, organisational context, professional-client relationship and interprofessional relations generate feeling rules that direct emotion work. While professions may not have supervisors in the same way as front-line service workers, they experience strong pressures to engage in emotion work.
2 The nature of the interactions, the organisational setting and professional norms all shape the kinds of emotion available, the experience and display of emotion, which in turn can reinforce or challenge what is appropriate emotion experience and display.
3 Emotion—display and experience—is embedded in the performance of professional tasks and can be a practical strategy or tool for influencing feelings or emotional expression of the self and others.

The judiciary is a distinctive professional occupation. Unlike other professions, judicial officers do not have a client relationship; their service ideal is abstract: to justice and the wider society (Roach Anleu and Mack 2005). The judiciary also has a constitutional role as an arm of government. Typically, courts are publicly accessible and their decisions publicly available. Although decisions are reviewable by appellate courts, the principles of judicial independence and security of tenure guarantee extensive autonomy in everyday work, in judicial decision making and in courtroom practice.

More importantly, the judiciary shares several characteristics of professions that are relevant to the demand for and the limits on their feelings, emotion expression and emotion work. For judicial officers, especially in court, ‘authority is made concrete through practices of speaking, dressing, and feeling—in other words, through orchestrated performances’ (Craciun 2016: 365). As with other professions, the judiciary can use their own feelings and emotion displays to accomplish their daily tasks and professional goals. Judicial officers can adopt a certain demeanour to evoke particular emotions as a way to foster trust, or as an attempt to induce certain feeling states among participants in their workplaces. They can ‘make use of what they perceive to be their internal states as they attempt to understand and treat … problems’ (Craciun 2018: 973).

Emotion and emotion work can have important positive effects on accomplishing professional work, including judicial work, without undermining professional authority. These empowering dimensions of emotion work have not received as much attention as the disempowering consequences.

Judging, emotion and emotion work

The human experience presented in legal cases entails a wide range of emotions. Courts can be places of considerable emotion, often deemed to be negative, for judicial officers as well as for other participants. Court users may experience fear, uncertainty, embarrassment, shame or anger, which will affect their emotional displays (Booth 2012; Davies, R. 2017; Jacobson, Hunter and Kirby 2015; Karstedt 2002; Roach Anleu and Mack 2005; Schuster and Propen 2010; Toy-Cronin 2019). Other feelings might include grief (Booth 2016), frustration (Tutton, Mack and Roach Anleu 2018) or remorse (Rossmanith 2013, 2015). The judicial officer must anticipate, perceive, interpret and/or manage these emotions experienced or displayed by others in the courtroom. Indeed, Hochschild (1983) includes judges in a list of some 15 occupations that involve substantial amounts of emotional labour.

The explicit recognition of a place for emotion in judicial work is especially evident in concepts such as procedural justice or procedural fairness and therapeutic jurisprudence (King 2003, 2006; Lens 2016). A key dimension of psychological models of procedural justice is that court users are more likely to comply with court decisions, even where they go against their interests, if they feel they have been listened to and treated with respect by authority figures (Burke and Leben 2007–2008; Hunter, Roach Anleu and Mack 2016; Tyler 1990, 2006).

Other recent scholarship on the judiciary and judicial practice in diverse legal systems points to the importance of emotion, emotional experiences, emotion management and emotion display (Bandes 2009; Bandes and Blumenthal 2012; Bergman Blix and Wettergren 2016, 2018; Elek 2019; Maroney 2011a, 2011b; Maroney and Gross 2014; Roach Anleu and Mack 2005, 2013; Scarduzio 2011; Tata 2020; Toy-Cronin 2019; Wojciechowski, Dowgiałło and Rancew-Sikora 2015; also see *Oñati Socio-Legal Series* (2019) 9(5), special issue on 'Judging, Emotion and Emotion Work'). Much of the research to date tends to focus on the emotions experienced and displayed by the judicial officer, which the judicial officer must manage, for example, anger (Maroney 2012) or disgust (Conway and Stannard 2019) or emotional capacities which judges may deploy such as empathy or compassion (Bandes 2009; Bergman Blix and Wettergren 2016).

One emerging theme, in mass media as well as scholarship, is judicial stress, vicarious trauma and burnout (see, for example, Pelly 2018; Thompson 2018). A recent Australian study finds that judicial officers report levels of psychological distress higher than those of the general population, and symptoms of burnout and secondary trauma are prominent features of their work (Schrever 2018; Schrever, Hulbert and Sourdin 2019). In Australia, recent judicial suicides have brought wider public attention to the extreme stress which can be generated by judicial work (see, for example, *Myall: Finding Into Death Without Inquest* [2020] VicCorC (COR 2018 1210)). Strategies that address judicial wellbeing and resilience are now more visible, especially in professional development programmes (see, for example, Judicial College of Victoria [JCV] 2019; National Judicial College of Australia [NJCA] 2019). In some jurisdictions, the head of jurisdiction's responsibilities for judicial health and wellbeing are explicit and statutory (for example *Federal Circuit Court of Australia Act 1999* (Cth) s 12(1)).

While the language of emotion is rarely used in descriptions of the institutional role of the judge, concepts implicitly related to emotion exist. Formal judicial guides consistently exhort judges to display qualities such as courtesy, dignity and patience, which necessarily imply interaction and therefore emotion. Examples include the American Bar Association (ABA) *Model Code of Judicial Conduct* (2011), the Australasian Institute of Judicial Administration (AIJA) *Guide to Judicial Conduct* (Council of Chief Justices of Australia and New Zealand 2017), the England and Wales *Guide to Judicial Conduct* (Courts and Tribunals Judiciary 2020) and the *Bangalore Principles of Judicial Conduct* (United Nations Office on Drugs and Crime 2002). This suggests the feeling rules and norms applicable to the judicial role entail considerable work to manage the experience and performance of judicial officers' own emotions and to elicit or suppress feelings or emotional displays in others (Mack and Roach Anleu 2010; Roach Anleu, Rottman and Mack 2016). Important emotion-related qualities and the capacity for emotion work are part of the notion of judicial temperament, often identified as a qualification for appointment (see, for example, AIJA 2015). Indeed, Maroney (2020) makes this link explicit by proposing that a lack of judicial temperament can be understood as poor emotion regulation skills.

Institutional changes within courts, sometimes building on scholarship about judging, emotion and judicial practice, and related development of professional norms and regulation, expand the circumstances in which judicial officers are expected to be more emotionally engaged and expressive than anticipated by the conventional model of judicial authority. Judicial officers are now expected to recognise, and even manage, some of the social and emotional needs of courtroom participants (Booth 2016; Maroney and Gross 2014; McIvor 2009) or to adopt a judicial approach that conveys care, support, empathy and compassion (Bergman Blix and Wettergren 2016; Lens 2016). Problem-oriented courts such as drug treatment or family violence courts may be based on a philosophy of therapeutic jurisprudence which explicitly anticipates engagement between a judicial officer and court users, especially defendants (King, Freiberg, Batagol et al. 2014). This engagement entails emotion. 'While traditional judges strike a passive, neutral pose, the ideal problem-solving judge is active and engaged, displaying compassion and empathy' (Lens 2016: 703; also see Fay-Ramirez 2015).

In many jurisdictions, the judiciary is becoming more diverse along a range of dimensions, including professional background, gender and race. Judicial officers bring with them different cultural, social and individual approaches to emotional experiences, display and regulation (Cahill-O'Callaghan 2013, 2020). Feeling rules are not only driven by the occupation; they are also affected by the incumbents of the job. Different emotions can be expected of men and women in the same occupation, and emotion experiences or display by men or women may be perceived and interpreted differently. Feeling rules and emotion work expectations are also shaped by race and ethnicity (Wingfield 2010). Such research signals the complexity of gender or race or ethnicity as explanations for differences in judicial attitudes, values and approaches, reinforcing the importance of context for understanding judicial emotion and emotion work. It also signals caution in inferring too quickly that observed differences in emotion, emotion display or emotion work among judicial officers of different genders, races or other social characteristics are solely or primarily attributable to those differences (Harris and Sen 2019).

Increased attention to formal processes of judicial performance evaluation and discipline exposes gaps in the guidance available and regulation of judicial conduct in relation to emotion. Framing the question of emotion and judging as relying on individual judicial qualities such as temperament, or enforcing these norms through individual performance evaluation or discipline, also reinforces the idea that judicial emotion and regulation are personal rather than embedded in the social relations of the institutional context.

Judging and Emotion demonstrates that judicial emotion and emotion work are more than individual experience and conduct and include a much wider range of experiences than negative ones. As with other professions and occupations, emotion work can have many positive implications (Humphrey, Ashforth and Diefendorff 2015). While some emotionally-laden judicial behaviours could indicate that the judicial officer is not sufficiently detached and so raise questions about impartiality, judicial behaviour which effectively incorporates human personality and feeling may enhance public confidence in the courts and the judiciary (ABA 2011; Council of Chief Justices of Australia and New Zealand 2017; Tyler 2003, Tyler 2007–2008; Tyler and Huo 2002).

Outline of chapters

Judging and Emotion relies on extensive empirical findings to understand emotion as a dimension of judicial work, situated in an interactional social context and bounded by rules and norms. It demonstrates the utility of emotion as a judicial resource to achieve the core value of impartiality.

Chapter 2: Emotion and everyday judicial work: the context

This chapter describes the contexts of judicial work, including the pace and volume of work, the varied interactions and the emotion which judicial officers and other court participants may experience and display. Dimensions of the judicial work context include court level, kinds of judicial work including trials, particular court participants such as unrepresented parties, legal representatives, jurors, or witnesses and specific case types, for example, sexual assault, domestic/family violence and family law. This chapter documents the interconnectedness among formal court structures, context, judging and emotion.

Given the relational nature of emotion and emotion work, distinguishing management of emotion and display to maintain and communicate impartiality in Chapter 3 from management of the judicial officer's own emotion in Chapter 4 and from managing the emotion of others in Chapter 5 is somewhat arbitrary. Judicial emotion work may be directed towards self or others. Judicial self-management can be inextricably linked to managing others, and similar approaches may be used for multiple purposes. A brief quote from interviews or court transcripts can raise several issues, belonging in different chapters. Nonetheless, it is helpful to address these three dimensions of emotion work in separate chapters.

Chapter 3: Judicial impartiality, emotion and empathy

This chapter investigates how judicial officers frame and perform impartiality in the legal context where feelings and the need for emotion work are embedded but formally disavowed. Impartiality, and its performance as dispassion, is the touchstone for judicial officers' reflexive monitoring of the myriad emotions they experience. At the same time, their commitment to impartiality entails emotion work which requires recognising, not denying, a place for emotion. Judicial officers describe different conceptions of impartiality and several conscious strategies for maintaining impartiality as an internal state and its appearance through their demeanour. They understand that, while empathy is typically considered a challenge to impartiality, it also has an important, though circumscribed, place in judicial work.

Chapter 4: Judicial emotion: experience, display and management

By examining what judicial officers say and do about their own feelings and emotion experiences, this chapter shows how emotion and emotion work are integral to the performance of judicial work. Empirical findings document the ways judicial officers manage their own emotion, especially when confronted with challenging cases or difficult face-to-face behaviour from other participants. As well as self-management, judicial emotion is also perceived, interpreted and managed by others, such as judicial colleagues and court staff.

Chapter 5: Judicial emotion work: others' emotions

This chapter shows how emotion and emotion work are essential to the strategies judicial officers adopt to manage the emotions and conduct of other participants, especially in the courtroom. These approaches include anticipating, assessing or responding to others' emotions. Judicial officers may be able to avert an anticipated feeling or display, or they may choose to allow an expression of emotion within limits, or they may exert control after an emotional expression. Chapter 5 also maps the boundaries of the judicial role in relation to emotion management.

Chapter 6: Professional regulation of judicial emotion

Emotion experience, display and emotion work can be regulated in many ways. This chapter considers forms of professional regulation of judging and emotion, somewhat distinct from the self-management judicial officers undertake discussed in previous chapters. Regulatory mechanisms considered include judicial ethics or conduct guidelines, judicial performance evaluation programmes, complaint and disciplinary processes, challenges on the ground of bias, and professional socialisation, such as judicial education, mentoring and other forms of judicial communication. Although these mechanisms are rarely framed in the explicit language of emotion or emotion work, they implicitly anticipate emotion from the judicial officer or others in the court, and they communicate standards which regulate judging and emotion.

Chapter 7: Conclusion

The conventional norms of judicial behaviour are often interpreted as requiring feelings and emotional display to be repressed. As the research findings and analysis in this book demonstrate, judicial officers experience complex and sometimes intense emotion in their everyday work. They must deploy a wide range of emotion-related skills and qualities to accomplish their work within the institutional framework of the judicial role and the core value of impartiality (Roach Anleu and Mack 2013, 2017). This book demonstrates how emotion is a resource for impartial judging, as well as affirming the power of conventional norms linking dispassion with impartiality to anchor judicial emotion work.

Researching emotion

For the empirical researcher, a key question is how to identify and collect reliable, valid data on emotion and emotion work. Scheer asks: 'How do we know when a source is talking about an emotion?' (2012: 218). A 'source' could be interviewees; individuals observed in their natural, everyday settings; respondents to a social survey; or historical or contemporary texts. A related research question is: 'How do we know what they feel?' (Wettergren 2015: 115). Emotion can be suggested by or interpreted from specific emotion language (sad or angry), a description of something as a feeling (upset), language that links the body and the mind (blood boiling) or observable conduct or physical states (raised/lowered voices, smiles). Similarly, when a judicial officer describes or displays emotion, whether in the courtroom or in interviews, these same kinds of language or conduct can be the basis for an inference about emotion (Bericat 2015; Gammerl 2012; Rossmanith 2015). In her focussed ethnography of a family court, Lens reports observing what she describes as 'obvious states of emotion (for example, anger, crying, laughter)' (2016: 707). However, such signs may not accurately indicate felt emotion or can be misinterpreted (Barrett 2017).

While some emotion states may be more obvious or readable than others, and some words or actions may appear to relate directly to feelings, problems of observational and interpretive error exist. What is obvious to some participants may not be obvious to others. The emotion words and/or display may not align with actual feelings. The display may be an outcome of deep or surface acting, a part of emotion work (Hochschild 1983) or may be generated by other internal or relational factors. Trying to infer a specific emotion from observed bodily signs is difficult. Barrett cautions: 'You cannot recognize or detect anger, sadness, remorse, or any other emotion in another person—you can only guess, and some guesses are more informed than others' (2017: 246; also see Bandes 2001). When investigating emotion that suffuses the practice of law and judicial work, it is essential to consider taken-for-granted emotions that may be unnoticed or assumed as normal, as well as emotions like anger and remorse which are typically more obvious and observable (Bandes 2001).

A third question is 'how do they make use of their internal states and emotional displays' to accomplish the work of an occupation or organisation (Craciun 2018: 960 fn 3). Much research attention emphasises the ways employees or members of a profession display emotion in an attempt to evoke certain feeling states or attitudes in others, such as trust, confidence, happiness, guilt or fear. Emotion display can be a positive resource or strategy, which can enhance job satisfaction or lead to alienation, depending in part on the type of occupation or organisation and the level of autonomy.

This book focusses on the ways judicial officers manage their feelings, or express emotion, or convey emotion-related qualities such as empathy, to facilitate their everyday work, especially in the courtroom.

To meet the challenge of researching emotion in judicial work, *Judging and Emotion* draws on and synthesises several kinds of data obtained primarily through interviews, court observations and transcripts, surveys and publicly available data, including appeal court judgments. This multi-method approach enables deciphering emotion from different angles (Flam and Kleres 2015).

The different projects and studies providing the data for this book include:

- the *National Court Observation Study*, including transcriptions of court proceedings, 2004–2005;
- the *National Survey of Australian Magistrates* 2007;
- the *National Survey of Australian Judges* 2007;
- interviews with judges, magistrates and court staff conducted as part of the *Judicial Officers and Workload Allocation* project, 2007–2012;
- interviews with judges and magistrates undertaken nationally as part of the *Courts, the Judiciary and Social Change* project, 2012–2015; and
- materials relating to judicial ethics, discipline and performance evaluation in Australia, the USA and the United Kingdom collected as part of the *Changing Judicial Performance: Emotion and Legitimacy* project, 2015–2020.

Research design and research methods are described in detail in the Appendix. When material from any of these projects or studies is discussed in the text, it is clearly identified. Anonymisation and data presentation are explained in each chapter in a footnote where the data is first discussed.

References

Abbott, Andrew, 1983, 'Professional Ethics', *American Journal of Sociology 88*: 855–885.

Abbott, Andrew, 1988, *The System of Professions: An Essay on the Division of Expert Labor*. Chicago, IL: University of Chicago Press.

Abrams, Kathryn, 2015, 'Seeking Emotional Ends with Legal Means', *California Law Review 103*: 1657–1678.

Abrams, Kathryn and Hila Keren 2010, 'Who's Afraid of Law and the Emotions?', *Minnesota Law Review 94*: 1997–2074.

Amaya, Amalia and Maksymilian Del Mar, eds. 2020, *Virtue, Emotion and Imagination in Law and Legal Reasoning*. Chicago, IL: Hart Publishing.

American Bar Association 2011, *ABA Model Code of Judicial Conduct*. Retrieved 9 May 2020, from http://www.americanbar.org/groups/professional_responsibility/publications/model_code_of_judicial_conduct.html.

Appleby, Gabrielle and Suzanne Le Mire 2014, 'Judicial Conduct: Crafting a System That Enhances Institutional Integrity', *Melbourne University Law Review 38*: 1–67.
Australasian Institute of Judicial Administration 2015, *Suggested Criteria for Judicial Appointments*. Melbourne: Australasian Institute of Judicial Administration.
Bandes, Susan A., ed. 2001, *The Passions of Law*. New York and London: New York University Press.
Bandes, Susan A., 2009, 'Empathetic Judging and the Rule of Law', *Cardozo Law Review De Novo*: 133–148.
Bandes, Susan A., 2017, 'Compassion and the Rule of Law', *International Journal of Law in Context 13*: 184–196.
Bandes, Susan A. and Jeremy A. Blumenthal 2012, 'Emotion and the Law', *Annual Review of Law and Social Science 8*: 161–181.
Barak, Aharon, 2006, *The Judge in a Democracy*. Princeton, NJ: Princeton University Press.
Barbalet, Jack, 2008, *Weber, Passion and Profits: 'The Protestant Ethic and the Spirit of Capitalism' in Context*. Cambridge and New York: Cambridge University Press.
Barbalet, Jack, 2011, 'Emotions Beyond Regulation: Backgrounded Emotions in Science and Trust', *Emotion Review 3*: 36–43.
Barrett, Lisa Feldman, 2017, *How Emotions Are Made: The Secret Life of the Brain*. Boston, MA: Houghton Mifflin Harcourt.
Bennett, Hayley and G. A. Broe 2007, 'Judicial Neurobiology, Markarian Synthesis and Emotion: How Can the Human Brain Make Sentencing Decisions?', *Criminal Law Journal 31*: 75–90.
Bennett, Hayley and G. A. Broe 2010, 'Judicial Decision-Making and Neurobiology: The Role of Emotion and the Ventromedial Cortex in Deliberation and Reasoning', *Australian Journal of Forensic Sciences 42*: 11–18.
Bergman Blix, Stina and Åsa Wettergren 2016, 'A Sociological Perspective on Emotions in the Judiciary', *Emotion Review 8*: 32–37.
Bergman Blix, Stina and Åsa Wettergren 2018, *Professional Emotions in Court: A Sociological Perspective*. Abingdon: Routledge.
Bericat, Eduardo, 2015, 'The Sociology of Emotions: Four Decades of Progress', *Current Sociology 64*: 491–513.
Bolton, Sharon C. and Carol Boyd 2003, 'Trolley Dolly or Skilled Emotion Manager? Moving on from Hochschild's Managed Heart', *Work, employment & society 17*: 289–308.
Booth, Tracey, 2012, '"Cooling out" Victims of Crime: Managing Victim Participation in the Sentencing Process in a Superior Sentencing Court', *Australian & New Zealand Journal of Criminology 45*: 214–230.
Booth, Tracey, 2016, *Accommodating Justice: Victim Impact Statements in the Sentencing Process*. Annandale: Federation Press.
Burke, Kevin and Steve Leben 2007–2008, 'Procedural Fairness: A Key Ingredient in Public Satisfaction', *Court Review 44*: 4–15.
Burkitt, Ian, 2018, 'Decentring Emotion Regulation: From Emotion Regulation to Relational Emotion', *Emotion Review 10*: 167–173.
Bybee, Keith J, 2010, *All Judges Are Political—except When They Are Not: Acceptable Hypocrisies and the Rule of Law*. Stanford, CA: Stanford Law Books.

Cahill-O'Callaghan, Rachel J., 2013, 'The Influence of Personal Values on Legal Judgments', *Journal of Law and Society 40*: 596–623.
Cahill-O'Callaghan, Rachel J., 2020, *Values in the Supreme Court: Decisions, Division and Diversity*. Oxford: Hart Publishing.
Conejero, Susana and Itziar Etxebarria 2007, 'The Impact of the Madrid Bombing on Personal Emotions, Emotional Atmosphere and Emotional Climate', *Journal of Social Issues 63*: 273–287.
Conway, Heather and John Stannard, eds. 2016, *Emotional Dynamics of Law and Legal Discourse*. Oxford and Portland, OR: Hart Publishing.
Conway, Heather and John Stannard 2019, 'Deconstructing Judicial Expressions of Disgust', *Oñati Socio-Legal Series 9*: 636–658.
Cottingham, Marci D., 2016, 'Theorizing Emotional Capital', *Theory and Society 45*: 451–470.
Council of Chief Justices of Australia and New Zealand 2017, *Guide to Judicial Conduct*. 3rd ed. Melbourne: Australasian Institute of Judicial Administration. Available from https://aija.org.au/publications-introduction/guidelines/guide-to-judicial-conduct/.
Courts and Tribunals Judiciary (England and Wales) 2020, *Guide to Judicial Conduct*. 30 March. Retrieved 9 May 2020, from https://www.judiciary.uk/publications/guide-to-judicial-conduct/.
Craciun, Mariana, 2016, 'The Cultural Work of Office Charisma: Maintaining Professional Power in Psychotherapy', *Theory and Society 45*: 361–383.
Craciun, Mariana, 2018, 'Emotions and Knowledge in Expert Work: A Comparison of Two Psychotherapies', *American Journal of Sociology 123*: 959–1003.
Damasio, Antonio R., 1994, *Emotion, Reason and the Human Brain*. New York: Avon Books.
Davies, Margaret, 2017, *Asking the Law Question*. 4th ed. Sydney: Lawbook.
Davies, Rhiannon, 2017, *Stories of Pervasive Uncertainty: A Victim-Focused Analysis of Victim Impact Statements and Sentencing in Sexual Offence Cases*. PhD Thesis, Faculty of Law, University of Tasmania. Retrieved 9 May 2020, from https://eprints.utas.edu.au/28673/.
de Rivera, Joseph, 1992, 'Emotional Climate: Social Structure and Emotional Dynamics'. In *International Review of Studies on Emotion*: *Volume 2*, ed. K T Strongman, 197–218. New York: John Wiley & Sons.
Ekman, Paul and Daniel Cordaro 2011, 'What Is Meant by Calling Emotions Basic', *Emotion Review 3*: 364–370.
Elek, Jennifer K., 2019, 'Judicial Perspectives on Emotion, Emotion Management, and Judicial Excellence in the USA', *Oñati Socio-Legal Series 9*: 865–879.
Epstein, Lee, William M. Landes and Richard A. Posner 2013, *The Behavior of Federal Judges: A Theoretical and Empirical Study of Rational Choice*. Cambridge, MA: Harvard University Press.
Fay-Ramirez, Suzanna, 2015, 'Therapeutic Jurisprudence in Practice: Changes in Family Treatment Court Norms over Time', *Law & Social Inquiry 40*: 205–236.
Flam, H. and J. Kleres, eds. 2015, *Methods of Exploring Emotions*. Abingdon and New York: Routledge.
Frevert, Ute, 2014, 'Defining Emotions: Concepts and Debates over Three Centuries'. In *Emotional Lexicons: Continuity and Change in the Vocabulary of Feeling 1700–2000*, eds.. J. Kleres, Ute Frevert, Monique Scheer, Anne Schmidt,

Pascal Eitler, Bettina Hitzer, Nina Verheyen, Benno Gammerl, Christian Bailey and Margrit Pernau, 1–31. Oxford: Oxford University Press.
Gammerl, Benno, 2012, 'Emotional Styles—Concepts and Challenges', *Rethinking History 16*: 161–175.
Gendron, Maria and Lisa Feldman Barrett 2019, 'A Role for Emotional Granularity in Judging', *Oñati Socio-Legal Series 9*: 557–576.
Gey, Steven G. and Jim Rossi 2005, 'Empirical Measures of Judicial Performance: An Introduction to the Symposium', *Florida State University Law Review 32*: 1001–1014.
Geyh, Charles Gardner, 2013, 'The Dimensions of Judicial Impartiality', *Florida Law Review 65*: 493–551.
Geyh, Charles Gardner, 2014, 'Judicial Independence as an Organizing Principle', *Annual Review of Law and Social Science 10*: 185–200.
Geyh, Charles Gardner, James J. Alfini, Steven Lubet and Jeffrey M. Shaman 2013, *Judicial Conduct and Ethics*. 5th ed. Newark, NJ: Lexis.
Goffman, Erving, 1956, 'The Nature of Deference and Demeanor', *American Anthropologist 58*: 473–502.
Goffman, Erving, 1959, *The Presentation of Self in Everyday Life*. New York: Doubleday Anchor.
Goodman, Maxine, 2013, 'Three Likely Causes of Judicial Misbehavior and How These Causes Should Inform Judicial Discipline', *Capital University Law Review 41*: 949–997.
Gorman, Elizabeth and Rebecca L. Sandefur 2011, '"Golden Age," Quiescence, and Revival: How the Sociology of Professions Became the Study of Knowledge-Based Work', *Work and Occupations 38*: 275–302.
Grandey, Alicia, 2003, 'When "the Show Must Go On": Surface Acting and Deep Acting as Determinants of Emotional Exhaustion and Peer-Rated Service Delivery', *Academy of Management Journal 46*: 86–96.
Green, Bruce A. and Rebecca Roiphe 2008, 'Regulating Discourtesy on the Bench: A Study in the Evolution of Judicial Independence', *New York University Annual Survey of American Law 64*: 497–558.
Gross, James J. 2015, 'Emotion Regulation: Current Status and Future Prospects', *Psychological Inquiry 26*: 1–26.
Grossi, Renata, 2015, 'Understanding Law and Emotion', *Emotion Review 7*: 55–60.
Grossi, Renata, 2019, 'Law, Emotion and the Objectivity Debate', *Griffith Law Review 28*: 23–36.
Harris, Allison P. and Maya Sen 2019, 'Bias and Judging', *Annual Review of Political Science 22*: 241–259.
Heaney, Jonathan G., 2019, 'Emotion as Power: Capital and Strategy in the Field of Politics', *Journal of Political Power 12*: 224–244.
Hochschild, Arlie Russell, 1979, 'Emotion Work, Feeling Rules and Social Structure', *American Journal of Sociology 85*: 551–575.
Hochschild, Arlie Russell, 1983, *The Managed Heart: Commercialization of Human Feeling*. Berkeley, CA: University of California Press.
Holmes, Mary, 2015, 'Researching Emotional Reflexivity', *Emotion Review 9*: 61–66.
Hsieh, Chih-Wei, 2014, 'Burnout among Public Service Workers: The Role of Emotional Labor Requirements and Job Resources', *Review of Public Personnel Administration 34*: 379–402.

Hsieh, Chih-Wei, Myung H. Jin and Mary E. Guy 2012, 'Consequences of Work-Related Emotions: Analysis of a Cross-Section of Public Service Workers', *American Review of Public Administration 2012*: 39–53.
Humphrey, Ronald H., Blake E. Ashforth and James M. Diefendorff 2015, 'The Bright Side of Emotional Labor', *Journal of Organizational Behavior 36*: 749–769.
Hunter, Rosemary, Sharyn Roach Anleu and Kathy Mack 2016, 'Judging in Lower Courts: Conventional, Procedural, Therapeutic and Feminist Approaches', *International Journal of Law in Context 12*: 337–360.
Illouz, Eva, Daniel Gillon and Mattan Shachak 2014, 'Emotions and Cultural Theory'. In *Handbook of the Sociology of Emotions: Volume II*, eds. Jan E. Stets and Jonathan H. Turner, 221–244. Dordrecht: Springer.
Jacobson, Jessica, Gillian Hunter and Amy Kirby 2015, *Inside Crown Court: Personal Experiences and Questions of Legitimacy*. Bristol: Policy Press.
Judicial College of Victoria 2019, *Annual Report 2018/19*. Retrieved 9 May 2020, from https://www.judicialcollege.vic.edu.au/sites/default/files/2019-11/JCV_Annual%20Report%202018-2019_FINAL_web.pdf.
Karstedt, Susanne, 2002, 'Emotions and Criminal Justice', *Theoretical Criminology 6*: 299–317.
Karstedt, Susanne, 2019, 'Emotions and Criminal Law: New Perspectives on an Enduring Presence'. In *Emotions in Late Modernity*, eds., Roger Patulny, Alberto Bellocchi, Rebecca E. Olson, Sukhmani Khorana, Jordan McKenzie and Michelle Peterie, 101–113. Abingdon and New York: Routledge.
King, Michael, 2003, 'Applying Therapeutic Jurisprudence from the Bench', *Alternative Law Journal 28*: 172–175.
King, Michael, 2006, 'Therapeutic Jurisprudence in Australia: New Directions in Courts, Legal Practice, Research and Legal Education', *Journal of Judicial Administration 15*: 129–141.
King, Michael, Arie Freiberg, Becky Batagol and Ross Hyams 2014, *Non-Adversarial Justice*. 2nd ed. Annandale: Federation Press.
Krygier, Martin, 2016, 'The Rule of Law: Pasts, Presents, and Two Possible Futures', *Annual Review of Law and Social Science 12*: 199–229.
Lens, Vicki, 2016, 'Against the Grain: Therapeutic Judging in a Traditional Family Court', *Law & Social Inquiry 41*: 701–718.
Leys, Ruth, 2011, 'The Turn to Affect: A Critique', *Critical Inquiry 37*: 343–472.
Lively, Kathryn J., 2008, 'Status and Emotional Expression: The Influence of "Others" in Hierarchical Work Settings'. In *Social Structure and Emotion*, eds. Jody Clay-Warner and Dawn T. Robinson, 287–305. New York: Elsevier/Academic Press.
Lively, Kathryn J. and Brian Powell 2006, 'Emotional Expression at Work and at Home: Domain, Status, or Individual Characteristics?', *Social Psychology Quarterly 69*: 17–38.
Lively, Kathryn J. and Emi A. Weed 2014, 'Emotion Management: Sociological Insight into What, How, Why, and to What End?', *Emotion Review 6*: 202–207.
Lucy, William, 2005, 'The Possibility of Impartiality', *Oxford Journal of Legal Studies 25*: 3–31.
Lutz, Catherine and Geoffrey M. White 1986, 'The Anthropology of Emotions', *Annual Review of Anthropology 15*: 405–436.

Macdonald, Keith M., 1995, *The Sociology of the Professions*. London: SAGE Publications.

Mack, Kathy and Sharyn Roach Anleu 2010, 'Performing Impartiality: Judicial Demeanor and Legitimacy', *Law & Social Inquiry 35*: 137–173.

Maroney, Terry A., 2011a, 'Emotional Regulation and Judicial Behavior', *California Law Review 99*: 1485–1555.

Maroney, Terry A., 2011b, 'The Persistent Cultural Script of Judicial Dispassion', *California Law Review 99*: 629–682.

Maroney, Terry A., 2012, 'Angry Judges', *Vanderbilt Law Review 65*: 1207–1284.

Maroney, Terry A., 2019, 'Empirically Investigating Judicial Emotion', *Oñati Socio-Legal Series 9*: 799–830.

Maroney, Terry A., 2020, '(What We Talk About When We Talk About) Judicial Temperament', *Boston College Law Review 61*: 2085–2153

Maroney, Terry A. and James J. Gross 2014, 'The Ideal of the Dispassionate Judge: An Emotion Regulation Perspective', *Emotion Review 6*: 142–151.

McIntyre, Joe, 2019, *The Judicial Function*. Singapore: Springer.

McIvor, Gill, 2009, 'Therapeutic Jurisprudence and Procedural Justice in Scottish Drug Courts', *Criminology & Criminal Justice 9*: 29–49.

Moran, Leslie J., 2009, 'Judging Pictures: A Case Study of Portraits of the Chief Justices, Supreme Court of New South Wales', *International Journal of Law in Context 5*: 295–314.

Moran, Leslie J., 2010, 'In Conversation with Lord Justice Etherton: Judicial Legitimacy, Diversity and the Representation of Judicial Authority', *Public Law 4*: 662–671.

Mulcahy, Linda, 2010, *Legal Architecture: Justice, Due Process and the Place of Law*. New York: Routledge.

Mulcahy, Linda and Emma Rowden 2020, *The Democratic Courthouse: A Modern History of Design, Due Process and Dignity*. London: Routledge.

Mulligan, Kevin and Klaus R. Scherer 2012, 'Toward a Working Definition of Emotion', *Emotion Review 4*: 345–357.

National Judicial College of Australia 2019, *Conference 2019: Judges: Angry? Biased? Burned Out?* Retrieved 9 May 2020, from https://njca.com.au/njca-anu-joint-conference-2019-judges-angry-biased-burned-out/.

Ng, Kwai Hang and Jeffrey L. Kidder 2010, 'Toward a Theory of Emotive Performance: With Lessons from How Politicians Do Anger', *Sociological Theory 28*: 193–214.

Nugent, Donald, 1994, 'Judicial Bias', *Cleveland State Law Review 42*: 1–59.

Ozcelik, Hakan, 2013, 'An Empirical Analysis of Surface Acting in Intra-Organizational Relationships', *Journal of Organizational Behavior 34*: 291–309.

Parsons, Talcott, 1954, *Essays in Sociological Theory*. New York: Free Press.

Patulny, Roger and Rebecca E. Olson 2019, 'Emotions in Late Modernity'. In *Emotions in Late Modernity*, eds. Roger Patulny, Alberto Bellocchi, Rebecca E. Olson, Sukhmani Khorana, Jordan McKenzie and Michelle Peterie, 8–24. Abingdon and New York: Routledge.

Pelly, Michael, 2018, 'Stressed-out Judges Turn to the Drink', *Australian Financial Review*. 7 May. Retrieved 9 May 2020, https://www.afr.com/companies/professional-services/stressed-out-judges-turn-to-the-drink-20190506-p51kly.

Rachlinski, Jeffrey J. and Andrew J. Wistrich 2017, 'Judging the Judiciary by the Numbers: Empirical Research on Judges', *Annual Review of Law and Social Science 13*: 203–229.
Reddy, William M., 2009, 'Historical Research on the Self and Emotions', *Emotion Review 1*: 302–315.
Rimé, Bernard, 2007, 'The Social Sharing of Emotion as an Interface between Individual and Collective Processes in the Construction of Emotional Climates', *Journal of Social Issues 63*: 307–322.
Roach Anleu, Sharyn, 2006, *Deviance, Conformity and Control*. 4th ed. Frenchs Forest: Pearson Longman.
Roach Anleu, Sharyn, 2010, *Law and Social Change*. 2nd ed. Thousand Oaks, CA: SAGE Publications.
Roach Anleu, Sharyn and Kathy Mack 2005, 'Magistrates' Everyday Work and Emotional Labour', *Journal of Law and Society 32*: 590–614.
Roach Anleu, Sharyn and Kathy Mack 2013, 'Judicial Authority and Emotion Work', *The Judicial Review 11*: 329–347.
Roach Anleu, Sharyn and Kathy Mack 2017, *Performing Judicial Authority in the Lower Courts*. London: Palgrave.
Roach, Anleu, Sharyn, Kathy Mack and Jordan Tutton 2014, 'Judicial Humour in the Australian Courtroom', *Melbourne University Law Review 38*: 621–665.
Roach Anleu, Sharyn, David Rottman and Kathy Mack 2016, 'The Emotional Dimension of Judging: Issues, Evidence, and Insights', *Court Review 52*: 60–71.
Robinson, Dawn T., 2014, 'The Role of Cultural Meanings and Situated Interaction in Shaping Emotion', *Emotion Review 6*: 189–195.
Rosenwein, Barbara H., 2006, *Emotional Communities in the Early Middle Ages*. Ithaca NY: Cornell University Press.
Rossmanith, Kate, 2013, 'Getting into the Box: Risky Enactments of Remorse in the Courtroom', *About Performance* (*12*): 7–26.
Rossmanith, Kate, 2015, 'Affect and the Judicial Assessment of Offenders: Feeling and Judging Remorse', *Body & Society 21*: 167–193.
Scarduzio, Jennifer A., 2011, 'Maintaining Order through Deviance? The Emotional Deviance, Power, and Professional Work of Municipal Court Judges', *Management Communication Quarterly 25*: 285–310.
Scheer, Monique, 2012, 'Are Emotions a Kind of Practice (and Is That What Makes Them Have a History)? A Bourdieuan Approach to Understanding Emotion', *History and Theory 51*: 193–220.
Scheer, Monique, 2014, 'Topographies of Emotion'. In *Emotional Lexicons: Continuity and Change in the Vocabulary of Feeling 1700-2000*, eds. Ute Frevert, Monique Scheer, Anne Schmidt, Pascal Eitler, Bettina Hitzer, Nina Verheyen, Benno Gammerl, Christian Bailey and Margrit Pernau, 32–61. Oxford: Oxford University Press.
Schnädelbach, Sandra, 2019, 'The Voice Is the Message: Emotional Practices and Court Rhetoric in Early Twentieth Century Germany', *Oñati Socio-Legal Series 9*: 615–635.
Schrever, Carly, 2018, 'Australia's First Research Measuring Judicial Stress and Wellbeing: A Preview of the Findings', *Australian Law Journal 92*: 858–862.
Schrever, Carly, Carol Hulbert and Tania Sourdin 2019, 'The Psychological Impact of Judicial Work: Australia's First Empirical Research Measuring Judicial Stress and Wellbeing', *Journal of Judicial Administration 28*: 141–168.

Schuster, Mary Lay and Amy Propen 2010, 'Degrees of Emotion: Judicial Responses to Victim Impact Statements', *Law, Culture and the Humanities 6*: 75–104.
Sewell, William H., 1992, 'A Theory of Structure: Duality, Agency and Transformation', *American Journal of Sociology 98*: 1–29.
Sorial, Sarah, 2019, *Anger and the Defence of Provocation*. Abingdon and New York: Routledge.
Stearns, Peter N. and Carol Z. Stearns 1985, 'Emotionology: Clarifying the History of Emotions and Emotional Standards', *American Historical Review 90*: 813–836.
Stets, Jan E., 2012, 'Current Emotion Research in Sociology: Advances in the Discipline', *Emotion Review 4*: 326–334.
Tamanaha, Brian Z., 2010, *Beyond the Formalist-Realist Divide: The Role of Politics in Judging*. Princeton, NJ and Oxford: Princeton University Press.
Tata, Cyrus, 2020, *Sentencing as a Social Process: Re-thinking Research and Policy*. Cham: Palgrave.
Temple, Kathryn, 2019, *Loving Justice: Legal Emotions in William Blackstone's England*. New York: New York University Press.
Thompson, Angus, 2018, *'I Fear for My Colleagues': Judge Warns NSW Judiciary Workload Could Have Tragic Consequences*. 5 October. Retrieved 9 May 2020, from https://www.smh.com.au/national/nsw/i-fear-for-my-colleagues-judge-warns-nsw-judiciary-workload-could-have-tragic-consequences-20181004-p507tv.html.
Toy-Cronin, Bridgette, 2019, 'Leaving Emotion Out: Litigants in Person and Emotion in New Zealand Civil Courts', *Oñati Socio-Legal Series 9*: 684–701.
Tutton, Jordan, Kathy Mack and Sharyn Roach Anleu 2018, 'Judicial Demeanor: Oral Argument in the High Court of Australia', *Justice System Journal 39*: 273–299.
Tyler, Tom R., 1990, *Why People Obey the Law*. New Haven, CT: Yale University Press.
Tyler, Tom R., 2003, 'Procedural Justice, Legitimacy and the Effective Rule of Law', *Crime and Justice 30*: 283–357.
Tyler, Tom R., 2006, 'Psychological Perspectives on Legitimacy and Legitimation', *Annual Review of Psychology 57*: 375–400.
Tyler, Tom R., 2007–2008, 'Procedural Justice and the Courts', *Court Review 44*: 26–31.
Tyler, Tom R. and Yuen J. Huo 2002, *Trust in the Law: Encouraging Public Cooperation with the Police and Courts*. New York: Russell Sage Foundation.
United Nations Office on Drugs and Crime 2002, *The Bangalore Principles of Judicial Conduct*. Retrieved 9 May 2020, from https://www.unodc.org/pdf/crime/corruption/judicial_group/Bangalore_principles.pdf.
Weber, Max, 1978, *Economy and Society: An Outline of Interpretive Sociology*. Berkeley, CA: University of California Press.
Wetherell, Margaret, 2015, 'Trends in the Turn to Affect: A Social Psychological Critique', *Body & Society 21*: 139–166.
Wettergen, Åsa, 2015, 'How Do We Know What They Feel?' In *Methods of Exploring Emotions*, eds. Flam Helen and Kleres Jochem, 115-24. London: Routledge.
Wharton, Amy S., 1999, 'The Psychosocial Consequences of Emotional Labor', *Annals of the American Academy of Political and Social Science 561*: 158–176.

Wharton, Amy S., 2009, 'The Sociology of Emotional Labor', *Annual Review of Sociology 35*: 147–165.
White, Emily Kidd, 2014, 'Till Human Voices Wake Us: The Role of Emotion in the Adjudication of Dignity Claims', *Journal of Law, Religion and State 3*: 201–239.
White, Emily Kidd, 2019, 'Replaying the Past: Roles for Emotion in Judicial Invocations of Legislative History, and Precedent', *Oñati Socio-Legal Series 9*: 577–594.
Wilensky, Harold L., 1964, 'The Professionalization of Everyone?', *American Journal of Sociology 70*: 137–158.
Williams, Claire, 2003, 'Sky Service: The Demands of Emotional Labour in the Airline Industry', *Gender, Work and Organization 10*: 513–550.
Wingfield, Adia Harvey, 2010, 'Are Some Emotions Marked "Whites Only"? Racialized Feeling Rules in Professional Workplaces', *Social Problems 57*: 251–268.
Wistrich, Andrew J., Jeffrey J. Rachlinski and Chris Guthrie 2015, 'Heart Versus Head: Do Judges Follow the Law of Follow Their Feelings?', *Texas Law Review 93*: 855–923.
Wistrich, Andrew J. and Jeffrey J. Rachlinski 2017, 'Implicit Bias in Judicial Decision Making: How It Affects Judgment and What Judges Can Do About It'. In *Enhancing Justice*, ed. Sarah E. Redfield, 87–130. Chicago, IL: American Bar Association.
Wojciechowski, Maciej, Bogna Dowgiałło and Dorota Rancew-Sikora 2015, 'Emotional Labour of Judges', *Archiwum Filozofii Prawa i Filozofii Społecznej 9*: 97–110.

Cases

Ebner v Official Trustee in Bankruptcy (2000) 205 CLR 337. Available from http://www.austlii.edu.au/cgi-bin/viewdoc/au/cases/cth/HCA/2000/63.html.
Myall: Finding Into Death Without Inquest [2020] VicCorC (COR 2018 1210). Available from https://www.coronerscourt.vic.gov.au/sites/default/files/2020-08/COR%202018%201210%20-%20Stephen%20Myall%20finding.pdf.

Legislation

Federal Circuit Court of Australia Act 1999 (Cth)
High Court of Australia Act 1979 (Cth)

Chapter 2

Emotion and everyday judicial work

The context

Introduction

The central obligation of the judicial role is to 'make reasoned decisions based on the facts and the law' (Wistrich, Rachlinski and Guthrie 2015: 856–857; also see Barak 2006; French 2010). While this statement appears to exclude emotion, the contexts in which judicial officers work necessarily generate emotion experience, display and expectations of judicial emotion work. These contexts encompass different court levels and legal institutional structures, myriad tasks and activities in and out of court, various cases, and the many interactions cases and tasks entail, constituting what can be called an emotion environment for judicial officers and other court participants. This environment generates opportunities for emotion experience and expression, affects judicial emotion and emotion engagement, and determines the ways judicial norms of dispassion and impartiality are realised in practice. Understanding different court contexts is integral to understanding the capacities for and constraints on emotion and the ways judging and emotion are experienced, performed and displayed.

This chapter describes key structural and organisational features of judicial work at different court levels, involving varied participants, tasks and case types. All these features shape the emotions experienced and displayed by the judicial officer and others, and the emotion work which may be undertaken.

Court organisation

The primary empirical research on which this book is based has been undertaken in Australia which has a common law, adversarial legal system. In this system, opposing parties control proceedings with little input from the passive, detached judicial officer (Australian Law Reform Commission [ALRC] 2000). These parties comprise prosecution versus defence in criminal cases, plaintiff versus defendant in civil cases or, in some case types or jurisdictions or on appeal, applicant versus respondent.

A multi-tier court structure is typical of many common law countries and of state or province subdivisions within a country (Abadinsky 2014; Darbyshire 2011; Jacobson, Hunter and Kirby 2015; McCormack and Buekckert 2013; Roach Anleu and Mack 2017; Ward 2017). First is a lower court, hearing less serious criminal and civil matters, usually without juries, and the early stages of more serious criminal cases. Specialist jurisdictions such as family or childrens/youth or domestic/family violence (DFV) can be located at any court level but are frequently at the first level. The next level comprises primarily trial courts, hearing more serious criminal and civil cases, often with juries, especially in criminal cases. Non-criminal matters may be the subject of special lists or even separate or specialist courts, such as commercial, administrative or constitutional law. The final level is a court with a largely and sometimes exclusively appellate jurisdiction.

Australia's court system follows the multi-tier model within a federal political and legal structure. Judicial officers[1] at all court levels are required to have specific legal qualifications, are appointed by the executive government and serve until they reach a fixed retirement age, unless removed for cause (Appleby and Le Mire 2016; Lee and Campbell 2013).

Each state[2] and two territories[3] has a magistrates court[4] and a supreme court. Five states have an intermediate trial court.[5] Magistrates courts are courts of first instance, exercising general criminal and civil jurisdiction, limited in length of sentence (usually up to two years), amount of fine, offence types and value of claim in civil matters (Australian Government Productivity Commission [AGPC] 2020c). Magistrates sit alone, without juries, in civil and criminal matters, dominated by criminal cases. About two-thirds of all lodgements in these courts from 2013 to 2019 were criminal, and one-third were civil (excluding childrens/youth courts) (AGPC 2020b). About 90 percent of adult criminal matters across all Australian courts are initiated and finalised in magistrates courts, an average of about 540,000 finalised cases per year (Australian Bureau to Statistics [ABS] 2020). The

1 In this book, the terms 'judicial officer' and 'judiciary' are used generically to refer to any member of the judiciary, regardless of court level or type. Within Australia, the term 'magistrate' refers to members of the judiciary who preside in the lower state and territory courts, except in the Northern Territory where magistrates were given the title 'judge' in 2016. Australian magistrates are paid judicial officers, with legal qualifications, and are appointed until a fixed retirement age. The term 'judge' indicates those who preside in the intermediate and higher state and territory courts and all national courts. Jurisdictions outside Australia may use other labels for their judiciary or may use these terms, but the words may not have the same meanings as in Australia.

2 New South Wales, Victoria, Queensland, South Australia, Western Australia and Tasmania.

3 The Northern Territory and the Australian Capital Territory.

4 Called the Local Court in New South Wales and the Northern Territory.

5 The intermediate court is known as the District Court in New South Wales, Queensland, South Australia and Western Australia, and is known as the County Court in Victoria.

most common types of offences are driving related, including driving under the influence of drugs or alcohol or more than an allowable amount of alcohol; varieties of assault; possession or use of illegal drugs; theft and minor property crimes; and breaches of various court orders, including protection orders (ABS 2020). The most frequent principal penalty is a fine imposed on about two-thirds of defendants proven guilty in these lower courts. The fine may be accompanied by some other order or conditions such as community supervision or work orders. Just over one in ten (12 percent) of convicted defendants received a custodial sentence, usually served in a correctional institution, though some sentences are suspended. In civil cases, the upper limit for case value in magistrates courts ranges between $75,000 and $125,000 (Bamford and Rankin 2017). There is no national information for outcomes in civil cases in magistrates courts, as there is for criminal cases, but most resolve without a trial (AGPC 2014; Cashman 2015). Debt collection and default judgments are common (Bamford and Rankin 2017) as are applications for protection orders (AGPC 2020a).

The great bulk of intermediate trial court work is serious criminal cases, similar to the Crown Courts in England and Wales (Jacobson, Hunter and Kirby 2015), as well as some civil cases. Criminal cases in these courts are usually heard by a judge and jury. The jury, traditionally composed of 12 jurors chosen from members of the public, hears the evidence at trial, is instructed in the applicable law by the judge and collectively renders a verdict of guilty or not guilty (Hans 2008; Marder and Hans 2016). In Australia, the most common crimes heard at this court level are serious assaults, sexual assault, armed robbery, property crimes and drug trafficking. For example, the County Court of Victoria indicates that in the financial year 2018–2019, 77 percent of matters go into the 'general list', while the remaining 23 percent go into the 'sexual offences list' (County Court of Victoria 2019). Among the 'general list', 19 percent are drug offences, 21 percent are offences against the person, 42 percent are property and dishonesty, three percent are driving and the remaining 15 percent were 'other offences' (County Court of Victoria 2019: 17).

The most serious criminal charges and higher value civil cases are tried in the supreme courts, which also hear appeals, generally constituted as a separate division of the court (Bamford and Rankin 2017). Criminal cases are mainly murder, manslaughter or other charges which may carry a life sentence. Supreme courts may also hear serious drug offences and sexual assault, especially in those jurisdictions with no intermediate trial court (ABS 2020). Appeals may come from magistrates courts, intermediate trial courts, in those states where they exist, and from a decision of a single judge in the supreme court itself (AGPC 2020c). Civil jurisdiction is generally unlimited in amount, although typically there are cost deterrents from bringing smaller claims to a supreme court (see, for example, *Uniform Civil Procedure Rules 2005* (NSW) r 42.34).

Another way to describe the relative size and workload of the different levels of the state/territory courts is to note that magistrates courts have 93 percent of the caseload, compared with district courts which have 3.5 percent and supreme courts which have 4.5 percent (AGPC 2020b). Of the approximately 950 judicial officers in the state/territory courts, magistrates make up about 54 percent while supreme court judges account for about 20 percent, and judges in the intermediate courts account for around 26 percent (Australasian Institute of Judicial Administration [AIJA] 2019; also see Opeskin 2013).

National courts include the Federal Court of Australia (approximately 55 judges), the Family Court of Australia (approximately 33 judges), the Federal Circuit Court of Australia (approximately 70 judges) and the High Court of Australia (seven justices). The Federal Court has original and appellate jurisdiction under Australian federal law, mainly administrative law, corporations and trade practices, industrial law, native title and migration, with about 4500–6000 cases initiated and finalised per year (Federal Court of Australia [FCA] 2020). The Family Court[6] has original and appellate jurisdiction over 'matrimonial causes' including marriage, divorce and related issues such as children and property (*Family Law Act 1975* (Cth) s 31). About 20,000 applications are filed and finalised per year, nearly three-quarters resolved by agreement between the parties, entered as consent orders, and about 375 appeals (Family Court of Australia [FamCA] 2020). The Federal Circuit Court shares the jurisdictions of the Federal Court and the Family Court but about 90 percent of its nearly 100,000 matters annually are family law. More serious matters, and appeals, are heard in the Family or Federal Court (Federal Circuit Court of Australia [FCCA] 2020).[7]

The High Court of Australia is the final court of appeal from all state and national courts, with original jurisdiction in some constitutional matters. About 40–70 appeals are heard and determined annually, drawn from about 500 special leave applications per year (High Court of Australia [HCA] 2019).

Everyday work

A range of structural factors drives many of the emotional aspects of the work for the judicial officer and for other participants. These include the dominance of criminal cases, high volume, time pressure and unpredictability, and court architecture.

[6] Western Australia has a separate family court with five judges, administering the national *Family Law Act 1975* (Cth) (also see the *Family Court Act 1997* (WA)). These judges are not included in these figures.

[7] In 2018, the federal government proposed a structural merger of the Family Court and Federal Circuit Court, but the legislation to implement this has not yet been enacted and is unlikely to be considered until 2021.

Criminal proceedings make up nearly 70 percent of the caseload in the lower courts and over half in the intermediate courts (AGPC 2020b; Opeskin 2013). Though the most serious criminal cases are heard at the higher court levels, they are a smaller proportion of the overall caseload—about 15 percent (AGPC 2020b; Opeskin 2013). In a national survey, over half of Australian magistrates (52 percent) report always sitting in the criminal jurisdiction in the previous year, compared with 15 percent of intermediate court judges and only three percent of supreme court judges (Mack, Wallace and Roach Anleu 2012).

Considering all Australian courts, nearly all criminal charges (about 88 percent) are resolved by a guilty plea, and civil claims are resolved without trial (AGPC 2020b; Bamford and Rankin 2017; New South Wales Law Reform Commission [NSWLRC] 2014). However, there is still considerable judicial processing apart from a trial. In criminal cases, non-trial matters include issues such as bail, hearing guilty pleas and imposing sentence. Non-criminal cases may involve directions hearings and interlocutory applications for various orders such as for discovery or costs orders after resolution.

Case volume, time pressure and unpredictability

A key feature of everyday work in the lower courts is the sheer volume of cases processed (in Australia, see AGPC 2020b; Opeskin 2013; Roach Anleu and Mack 2017; compare, for example, Kohler-Hausmann 2018; McConville and Marsh 2016; Smith and Maddan 2011, 2019). This volume, whether of inputs (lodgements) or outputs (finalisations), generates the demand for the rapid pace of decision making characteristic of lower courts. The *National Court Observation Study* of the non-trial criminal list days in Australian magistrates/local courts found that the median time for each matter was two minutes and 20 seconds, with an average of four minutes and 20 seconds (Roach Anleu and Mack 2017; also see Carlen 1976; Hunter 2005; Mack and Roach Anleu 2007; Mileski 1971; Smith and Maddan 2011).

A related feature of judicial work is unpredictability. It is not possible for the judicial officer to know whether or when a guilty plea or settlement will occur, or in which cases, and the judicial officer has no or little influence on this. This unpredictability reflects the social, interactive and interdependent nature of judicial work. Much everyday judicial work in all courts depends on the actions of others, such as parties, police or legal representatives. In the courtroom, several participants must 'coordinate and shape their behavior in relation to others' (Ridgeway 2006: 5). Sometimes the expected and essential actions may not occur.

This unpredictability can continue until the date set for trial and even throughout it. In New South Wales, 29 percent of matters committed for trial result in a guilty plea on the day of trial (NSWLRC 2014). Darbyshire, in her UK research, describes the trial as 'fragile', with factors such as late settlements, guilty pleas or failure of a necessary participant to appear causing delay or cancellation of scheduled trial proceedings (2011: 191). This can be frustrating for the judicial officer, who wants to move cases along, and especially emotionally demanding for the non-judicial participants in the legal process, who face delays and uncertainty in having their cases heard, as well as the emotions generated by the experience giving rise to the case and their anticipation of the trial itself (Jacobson, Hunter and Kirby 2015; Toy-Cronin 2019).

One consequence of this unpredictability, and a source of the pressure experienced by judicial officers, is overlisting—scheduling more cases than can be heard in the time allowed. This practice is based on the expectation that many matters will require little or no judicial attention, because they will be adjourned or resolved. Overlisting is needed to ensure that as many cases as possible are heard on the day set and that scarce judicial resources are not wasted. The result is that many judicial officers are faced, every day, with more cases than are possible to be heard in the time available, with no way to know in advance who will appear (or not appear) or be prepared (or not prepared) and whether any particular case will need considerable judicial effort.

This unpredictability results in 'moments of bewildering activity, in which cases are dealt with as a matter of routine … interspersed with passive periods when the [judge] … waits' (Cowan and Hitchings 2007: 364). As in lower courts, 'delays and periods of tedium giving way to bursts of tense and even frantic action' are a feature of the pre-trial procedures in trial courts, such as the English Crown Court (Jacobson, Hunter and Kirby 2015: 111). The judicial officer's capacity to manage such unpredictability, resulting delays and consequential emotion is a central component of judgecraft (Carlen 1976; Darbyshire 2011; Kritzer 2007; Mack and Roach Anleu 2007; Metcalfe 2016; Roach Anleu and Mack 2018; Tata 2007).

Court design and (in)formality

A significant factor for all participants is the courtroom and courthouse design, and related formality or lack thereof (Henderson and Duncanson 2018; Mulcahy and Rowden 2020; Tait 2018). Conventional courtrooms have the judicial officer on a raised bench at one end of the room, with court staff below. Legal representatives sit or stand at tables facing the judicial bench, with their backs to the public gallery. In Australia and some other Commonwealth countries, judicial officers are usually robed, sometimes quite elaborately, though robes are not always worn in lower courts. Wigs are not worn by Australian magistrates or in the federal courts, and only occasionally in the higher state courts, perhaps for delivery of judgment or sentencing. Legal practitioners are robed in higher courts though not in lower courts, and wigs are rare in all Australian courts (Moran 2009; Supreme Court of New South Wales 2007; Yazdani 2019). A criminal defendant is often in the dock (a confined space within the courtroom) (Mulcahy 2010; Rossner, Tait and McKimmie et al. 2017; Tait 2011). In the USA, judges are robed but not wigged, legal practitioners do not robe and there is no dock (Resnik and Curtis 2011). Video link appearances, especially by defendants in custody, are increasingly common (Rowden, Wallace and Goodman-Delahunty 2010; Wallace, Roach Anleu and Mack 2017). These factors affect perceptions of the formality of the process and opportunities for communication, emotion and engagement (McKay 2018; Rowden and Wallace 2019; Wallace, Roach Anleu and Mack 2019). Some features emphasise the detachment of the judicial officer and the power of judicial authority, while others may facilitate engagement, emotion and emotion work (Jacobson, Hunter and Kirby 2015; Mulcahy 2007; Roach Anleu and Mack 2017; Tait 2018).

These structural factors—the dominance of criminal cases, high volume, time pressure, unpredictability and formal courtroom design—drive many of the emotions in the courtroom. Criminal cases inevitably contain distressing facts of loss, injury and often deliberate violence, as well as offenders who are themselves deeply disadvantaged. Such cases can entail considerable felt emotion and emotion work for the presiding judicial officer, as well as for other participants. This constant exposure to 'the very worst that humanity does to itself' can lead to what has been called secondary or vicarious trauma for judicial officers (Schrever, Hulbert and Sourdin 2019: 151; also see Miller, Edwards and Reichert et al. 2018; Rossouw and Rothmann 2020). Judicial officers may experience frustration, perhaps leading to anger, with the extreme time pressures and inevitable delays. Court users, who have waited for hours, with little understanding of the processes, will find the pattern of haste and delay bewildering, frustrating or even frightening, also contributing to the emotion environment of judicial work (Jacobson, Hunter and Kirby 2015; Ward 2017).

Court and trial participants

Although relatively few cases proceed to trial at any court level (AGPC 2020b; Bamford and Rankin 2017), presiding at trial takes up a considerable amount of judicial time at all court levels, more so for the intermediate and higher courts (Mack, Wallace and Roach Anleu 2012). The emotional experiences and display generated by court participants (whether parties, witnesses, jurors or legal representatives) all contribute to an emotion environment which the judicial officer will experience and must manage. In the lower courts, interacting directly with defendants and litigants, even when they have legal representation, can engender emotion and the need for emotion work. In the higher courts, the emotion environment may be intensified by the more serious nature of the criminal charges or the complexity and length of civil matters, or it may become less immediate as distressing facts are translated into legal categories and formal presentations. Because of the highly interactive nature of court proceedings, the circumstances, behaviour, characteristics and needs of many of the participants are significant in understanding judging and emotion.

Parties, litigants and criminal defendants

For parties, being involved in any kind of litigation, and particularly a criminal trial, can be a demanding experience:

> it may be the most traumatic occasion in the whole of their lives. The conclusion of the judge or the verdict of the jury … could be the prelude to ruin or disgrace (Gilbert 1986: xii).

Every case, even the most apparently trivial small claim, debt or traffic matter, involves one or more individuals, organisations or public officials for whom the judicial decision can matter a great deal. Emotions of parties may be apparent in the facts of the case, conveyed by documentary material or by evidence during a trial or in other proceedings such as bail or sentencing.

UK research, drawing on interviews with court participants, identifies many emotions experienced by criminal defendants. These include being 'acquiescent observers', demonstrating 'disengagement and alienation', experiencing 'anger and cynicism', 'apathy, resignation, or detachment' and feeling 'belittled by aspects of the process, certainly excluded and often confused … and sometimes frustrated' (Kirby, Jacobson and Hunter 2014: 6, 10, 11).

In civil matters, it is rare for plaintiffs to express positive feelings towards their court experience, in part because their expectations about respect, dignity and vindication are not met (Relis 2009; Stewart and Wood 2013). Unfamiliar language, loss of control of their story and relegation to a passive role can all result in plaintiffs feeling 'uncomfortable or alienated' (Stewart and Wood 2013: 136). Similarly, a defendant's involvement in civil litigation—ordinarily slow, expensive and public—will often be stressful, distressing or generally unpleasant, especially where proceedings allege some personal or professional failing. Active participation in the trial process by any party, such as a witness undergoing direct and cross-examination, can be experienced as 'degrading and deeply humiliating' leading to feeling hurt, angry and victimised (Stewart and Wood 2013: 137–138).

The circumstances of court users, especially in lower courts, may reflect deep social inequalities. Those who are present in lower courts may be there, in part, as a consequence of social, political and economic circumstances beyond their control and beyond the control of the courts (Gray 2002; King, Freiberg and Batagol et al. 2014; Roach Anleu and Mack 2007; Pleasence, Balmer and Buck et al. 2004; Roach Anleu and Mack 2005). Magistrates, district judges and their courts in England and Wales also deal with court users who experience considerable disadvantage (Darbyshire 2011; Genn 2019; Jacobson, Hunter and Kirby 2015). 'Many are disadvantaged by poverty, low intelligence, homelessness, ill health, mental illness, learning difficulties, immigrant or asylum status, lack of English, or a combination' (Darbyshire 2011: 142).

In Australia, the overrepresentation of Indigenous Australians as victims and defendants is stark (ALRC 2018; Cunneen 2014). The obstacles Indigenous Australians experience when confronting the court system is the culmination of centuries of colonisation, dispossession, cultural destruction and resulting disadvantage (ALRC 2018; Marchetti 2019). The capacity of a judicial officer, at any court level, to address the causes and consequences of Indigenous disadvantage is necessarily very limited (Bennett 2016; also see ALRC 2018; Marchetti 2019). One initiative is specialist sentencing courts for Indigenous Australians operating in some jurisdictions. By engaging the 'participation of … Elders and other Aboriginal community members in a sentencing dialogue' (Bennett 2016: 98), these courts aim to address an offender's long-term 'psychological and emotional wellbeing' (Marchetti and Ransley 2014: 21).

Unrepresented litigants

A distinctive aspect of judicial work, especially but not only in the lower courts, is the prevalence of unrepresented parties. Nearly six in ten magistrates in the *National Survey of Australian Magistrates* report that their time is always or often taken up by explaining things to unrepresented litigants (Roach Anleu and Mack 2017). In contrast, judges in other courts do so much less frequently; only five percent of judges in the intermediate courts find that their time is always or often taken up explaining things to unrepresented litigants, and just ten percent of supreme court judges report this. Other data confirms that a larger proportion of participants in lower courts are unrepresented compared with higher courts and that there may be some increase in some settings, such as in migration appeals (Richardson, Grant and Boughey 2018).

The perception that unrepresented participants require more time can generate frustration for the judicial officer and for other court users when it is not possible to deal with the allotted cases in a reasonable time on the date set. In the higher courts, the lack of representation may present particular problems in a complex case or trial, especially when only one side is represented (Toy-Cronin 2015; see, for example, *Barmettler v Greer & Timms* [2007] QCA 170).

While any court user may experience anxiety and frustration resulting from delay or apparent unfairness of legal proceedings, unrepresented participants can feel special distress from their own lack of understanding of court processes (see, for example, Toy-Cronin 2015). New Zealand research shows that unrepresented litigants struggle to understand legal rules, legal terminology and courtroom practices (Toy-Cronin 2019). They report feeling nervous about when to speak and how to address the judge, anxiety about how to pronounce legal words and embarrassment about their cases. This lack of understanding, and the feelings generated and expressed, must be managed by the judicial officer.

Witnesses

Witnesses may be parties to the case; have an interest in the parties, the case or its outcome; may be professional witnesses such as police or experts; or may be unrelated to and disinterested in the parties or the case outcome. Regardless, most witnesses will approach the courtroom with a range of emotions, such as anxiety, nervousness, fear, determination or other feelings, creating part of the emotional context for the judicial officer (Fielding 2013; Jacobson, Hunter and Kirby 2015; Vaisman and Barrera 2020). Witnesses, including those who are giving evidence as victims of a crime or wrong, can feel frustrated and angry by cross-examination. They will resent any imputation that they are not telling the truth and feel 'a sense of unfairness' (Fielding 2013: 292) at counsel's attempts to (intentionally) manipulate their emotions and make them appear not credible. They may also experience intense emotions arising from having to give an account of traumatic events in front of strangers and in a public space.

Many of the emotions experienced by adult witnesses are intensified for children, whose understanding and agency are likely to be less (Rush, Quas and McAuliff 2013). A visibly distressed child witness will also generate emotional impact on the judge and jury, if there is one. Jurors may feel sympathy, so the judge must undertake difficult emotion management to meet the judicial duty to ensure that the trial proceeds fairly. Particular issues relating to witnesses testifying about sexual assault are discussed in the 'Case types' section below.

Another category of potentially emotionally vulnerable witnesses are eyewitnesses who are asked to identify the perpetrator in a criminal case (Bornstein, Hullman and Miller 2013). The events observed may themselves have been traumatic, and the responsibility for making the identification in court will generate emotion as well. The visibility of this emotion will impact, perhaps positively or negatively, on credibility. Anger and fear are each emotions which could affect judge or juror evaluation. Research suggests that, while anger may generate confidence, confidence does not necessarily equate to accuracy (Wells, Memon and Penrod 2006; also see Bornstein, Hullman and Miller 2013; Brewer and Wells 2011).

The special vulnerabilities and needs of witnesses, victims, adults and children present significant occasions for emotion work. The judicial officer's emotion capacities and conduct may alleviate some of the trauma experienced by the court participants, or can increase their pain and distress (Davies 2017; Smith 2018; Smith and Skinner 2017).

Jurors

Another key group of courtroom participants is jurors, who are members of the public (Hans 2008). In research drawing on surveys and interviews conducted in the Australian states of Tasmania and Victoria, Davis (2015) finds that:

> Across the process of a trial … jurors experience a range of positive and negative emotions. … [A]s they go through the process of reporting for jury duty, being selected and sworn in, listening to the lawyers and witnesses, taking in the judge's directions, deliberating on the verdict and then delivering the verdict (also see Warner and Davis 2011; Warner, Davis and Spiranovic et al. 2016).

Research in New South Wales, South Australia and Victoria finds that '[m]ore empanelled than non-empanelled jurors were satisfied with their overall experience of jury service (67 percent vs 48 percent)' (O'Brien, Goodman-Delahunty and Clough et al. 2008: 3).

Jurors may experience a wide variety of feelings as part of their service. 'Jurors are often surprised when they realise that a real trial is nothing like the version that is presented on television' (Davis 2015; also see Rossner 2019). They may be upset about the practical aspects of jury duty such as the inconvenience and disruption to their daily life and work and the inability to discuss the case with others, or they may be concerned about media interest in the trial or even their own safety (National Center for State Courts [NCSC] 1998; also see Miller and Bornstein 2004, 2013).

A range of juror emotions, whether related to the trial itself or from extrinsic sources, may affect outcomes (Feigenson 2016; Simon 2019). While it is often asserted in the media that the public, from whom juries are drawn, are angry about crime and criminals, Australian research into the attitude of jurors finds that anger towards the defendant is rare, with sorrow and compassion more frequent (Davis 2015).

An aspect of trials that can generate strong emotion for judicial officers as well as jurors is grisly or gruesome evidence (Flores, Miller and Chamberlain et al. 2009; Miller, Edwards and Reichert et al. 2018). 'A common theme … is the concern that some types of evidence can prejudicially impact juror decision-making, especially when that evidence induces emotional responses in jurors' (Bright and Goodman-Delahunty 2006: 184; also see Bandes and Salerno 2014). There is legislation and case law in Australia and in other jurisdictions designed to manage juror emotion in relation to such evidence, by excluding or limiting material where there is 'a risk that the evidence will damage the defence case in some unacceptable way, such as provoking some irrational, emotional or illogical response' (*R v Dirani (No 6)* [2018] NSWSC 891 at [31], citing *Evidence Act 1995* (NSW) s 137 and *BJS v R* [2013] NSWCCA 123). However, it may be necessary for the judicial officer to review such material, either to implement the evidentiary rules at trial or in relation to sentencing, such as where a judicial officer must classify child exploitation material to determine an appropriate sentence (*R v Oliver* [2002] EWCA Crim 2766; Queensland Sentencing Advisory Council 2017).

Legal representatives

Barristers accept that 'emotional detachment' (Harris 2002: 571) is an aspect of the rationality required by law and is necessary to maintain the emotional regime of the courtroom (Richard 1993; also see Flower 2016). Such emotion compliance is a significant marker distinguishing professional participants from witnesses and defendants (Rock 1993). While commitment to detachment on the part of legal professionals may make the judicial task of emotion management easier in some ways, it could also result in insensitivity to emotion, limiting the capacity of lawyers to understand and manage their own and others emotions and so affect the emotional environment of the courtroom (Reed and Bornstein 2013).

On the other hand, in the courtroom, especially during trials and in particular before a jury, legal representatives use emotions and emotion management as resources or strategies to further professional or institutional legal objectives. For example, they may use 'feigned and exhorted emotional display during witness examinations and cross-examinations' (Harris 2002: 570; also see Vaisman and Barrera 2020). US research finds that lawyer behaviour during trial is among the most stressful situations for judges (Flores, Miller and Chamberlain et al. 2009). Darbyshire recounts some of the provocative conduct observed in her research: 'grossly inept advocacy and lack of preparation; impolite advocates who routinely did not take responsibility for their failure[s] … bombastic, aggressive or argumentative advocates who had to be warned repeatedly about their inappropriate behaviour' (2011: 127–128). In contrast, 'jovial camaraderie between the prosecution and defence lawyers' may be helpful in improving the emotion environment for the judge and legal representatives (Kirby, Jacobson and Hunter 2014: 11), though this 'can feel alienating and exclusionary for defendants (and, indeed, victims and witnesses)' (p. 11; also see Roach Anleu, Mack and Tutton 2014; Roach Anleu and Milner Davis 2018).

While unrepresented parties may be thought to be especially emotionally and practically demanding, the behaviour of legal representatives can generate considerable emotion for the judicial officer, as well as for other courtroom participants, and can require judicial emotion work, as discussed more fully in Chapters 4 and 5. Unprepared or inexperienced lawyers can present particular challenges. Fewer than four in ten magistrates report that legal representatives are always or often well prepared. In contrast, nearly half of intermediate court judges report that legal representatives are always/often well prepared. Even more striking, 70 percent of supreme court judges report legal representatives are always/often well prepared, demonstrating a substantial difference in the context of judicial work at each court level (Roach Anleu and Mack 2017). However, this still means that half of intermediate court judges and nearly one-third of supreme court judges must regularly deal with poorly prepared or inexperienced lawyers. Engaging with unprepared lawyers in any circumstance can affect a judicial officer's feelings and how emotion is managed and displayed.

Highest courts and appeals

In appeals, especially at the very highest final court level, it might be expected that occasions for emotion display and management would be reduced, as the justices deal primarily with lawyers, and because much of the 'human complexity', including feelings, have been removed, leaving 'a purely legal context with purely legal concerns' (Abbott 1981: 823–824). One consequence of this purification is abstraction and depersonalisation and, therefore, reduced opportunity and demand for emotion (Heimer 2001; Solove 1997).

A study of oral argument in the High Court of Australia finds that judicial performance contains very little perceptible emotional display from any of the justices, and their demeanour adheres strongly to formal, conventional norms of unemotional detachment, though achieving this appearance may require considerable emotion work (Tutton, Mack and Roach Anleu 2018). This judicial demeanour is maintained throughout a variety of appeal cases, even those involving distressing facts such as child sexual abuse.

In spite of the emphasis on detachment on the part of lawyers and the judiciary in the highest appeal courts, emotion language may be used in submissions to the court. However, research suggests this may not be a successful advocacy strategy and that 'measured, objective language' may be more effective (Black, Hall and Owens et al. 2016: 377).

In the Supreme Court of the United States, the final court of appeal in the USA, judges engage directly with each other during oral argument, sometimes involving fairly heated exchanges (Black, Sorenson and Johnson 2013; Johnson, Black and Wedeking 2009; Paterson 2013). Harsh or unpleasant language is sometimes used towards advocates appearing before the Court, perhaps signalling negative judicial views of the substance of the argument (Black, Treul and Johnson 2011).

A substantial part of judicial work in the higher courts is judgment writing, a relatively open-ended task, sometimes involving many decisions. Those judges who spend more time on judgment writing may find decision making slightly more difficult or stressful, though those who report the most time judgment writing also report higher rates of satisfaction with the intellectual challenge of their work (Mack, Wallace and Roach Anleu 2012). While judgment writing is a less frequent part of lower court work, it can be experienced as stressful in part because of the lack of time allowed for this work (Roach Anleu and Mack 2017).

There are other emotional positives in judgment writing. This work could engage background emotions such as pride (Bergman Blix and Wettergren 2018). The written judgment itself, through content and presentation, can engage the feelings of other court participants and can be an occasion to reduce the depersonalisation and abstraction which can strip out valuable emotion.

Judgment writing is an exercise in advocacy, to persuade the parties and other readers of the correctness of the decision, especially for those who have not succeeded (Barak 2006; Baum 2017; Gibson and Nelson 2014). Emotional rhetoric and imagery can be important in this persuasion. Lord Denning MR was known for his vivid prose, designed to evoke feelings and create a particular emotional atmosphere: 'In summertime, village cricket is the delight of everyone' (*Miller v Jackson* [1977] QB 966 at 976). 'It happened on April 19, 1964. It was bluebell time in Kent' (*Hinz v Berry* [1970] 2 QB 40 at 42).

Research tracking the sources, use and impact of 'emotive language' in US court decisions is becoming more frequent (Bryan and Ringsmuth 2016: 159; Budziak, Hitt and Lempert 2019). As with advocacy, emotive language in judgments is perhaps not always successful (see Blackshield 2007) and may be perceived as inconsistent with judicial norms (Ray 2002).

Sentencing

One especially visible and publicly contentious aspect of judicial decision making is determining a sentence in criminal cases. Sentencing is a central part of the work of all courts hearing criminal cases, at all levels, though the practical context and emotional circumstances vary. Australian research finds that a majority (57 percent) of magistrates regard sentencing as one of their most important judicial functions. In contrast, sentencing is identified as a most important function by only 28 percent of judges in the higher courts. These differing views may reflect the lesser emphasis on criminal law in the higher courts (Mack, Wallace and Roach Anleu 2012).

Sentencing can be an important site for emotional experience and expression for all participants, including the judicial officer (Hall 2016; Tata 2007, 2020).[8] Tata characterises sentencing as a 'social process' and as work

[8] There is substantial literature on emotion and other factors possibly affecting the outcomes or content of judicial decisions generally and sentencing in particular, which is beyond the scope of this book. See, for example, Epstein and Lindquist (2017), Howard and Randazzo (2017), Roach Anleu, Brewer and Mack (2017), Wandall (2010), Weimann-Saks, Peleg-Koriat and Halperin (2019) and research cited therein.

that is 'culturally reflective and instructive: it signals ideas about harm, authority, and community. It may offer emotional resolution and catharsis, or, it may be degrading' (2020: 2; also see Durkheim 1938, 1984).

While sentencing nearly always takes place in the presence of the defendant, there are important contextual differences. In the lower courts, sentencing is usually imposed immediately upon conviction (whether by trial or guilty plea) after hearing primarily oral submissions from prosecution and defence. The sentence is nearly always delivered orally and extemporaneously. A magistrate may sometimes delay until later in the day or another day to give time for reflection, or, less frequently, to seek further information, such as a pre-sentence report. In higher courts, sentencing will usually take place sometime after conviction in a separate proceeding, after consideration of pre-sentence reports and other documentation or representations, including victim impact statements (VIS) (discussed below). The judge may prepare written sentencing remarks which are read aloud.

Two aspects of sentencing have received substantial attention in the research literature on emotion and judging: assessment of a convicted offender's remorse and the role of the VIS.

Remorse, an emotion, is a mitigating factor in sentencing (Bandes 2016; Mackenzie 2005; Proeve and Tudor 2010; Roberts 2011; Weisman 2014). Judicial officers are legally required to assess remorse and take it into account when making sentence determinations. Therefore, a 'performance of remorse' (Rossmanith, Tudor and Proeve 2018: 380) or explicit 'expressions of remorse' (Weisman 2009: 48) can be appropriate, expected or even required.

In this legal context, remorse is framed as an internal, individual emotion, but one which the judicial officer can discern and distinguish from an insincere or strategic display (Johansen 2019). In the lower courts, a defendant's direct performance of remorse may be limited. An analysis of transcripts of sentencing proceedings in Australian lower courts finds that most references to remorse are from the defence representative to the magistrate, sometimes relaying information about the defendant's apology or other post-offence actions (Roach Anleu and Mack forthcoming).

The use of VIS is now a settled part of sentencing in Australia and elsewhere, for example, Canada, USA and the United Kingdom (Davies 2017). These may be presented orally by the victim personally, or in writing, or may be given through the prosecutor (Davies 2017). There was considerable public and legal debate about whether to allow VIS at all and what their legitimate use is, largely driven by concerns about emotion and emotionality in a legal space where emotion is conventionally inappropriate (Bandes 1996; Booth 2016; Davies 2017). In spite of these concerns, in most jurisdictions the judicial officer is legally required to permit, observe, assess and take into consideration the victim's emotion and emotion display (Bandes 1996; Booth, Bosma and Lens 2018). Several Australian jurisdictions publish guidelines for the preparation of VIS suggesting that victims detail the emotional impacts of, or emotional harm caused by, the offending (Davies 2017). As a result, judicial officers must manage emotions of victims and their expression without undermining the legitimate role of the VIS in the legal process.

Case types

Emotions may be intensely animated in any area of judicial work, though some case types may appear to be more emotionally demanding or satisfying than others. This chapter has concentrated on describing judicial work and tasks in criminal cases that form the bulk of the work of general jurisdiction courts in Australia and in similar courts in other common law countries. There are several areas of law which generate particularly or potentially emotionally laden contexts: sexual assault, DFV, childrens/youth, small claims, coroners, family law, and migration and refugee cases.

Sexual assault charges may be heard at any court level and may also arise in non-criminal cases such as family or migration. DFV, childrens/youth, small claims and coronial work are often located in lower courts, either as part of everyday judicial work or as specialist lists or separate courts and may have specialist judicial officers (AGPC 2020c). Family law and migration appeals are other specialised areas with particular emotional dimensions. In Australia, these are heard in the Federal Circuit Court, the Family Court and the Federal Court.

Locating these case types separately enables specialist judicial expertise in managing them, including managing their emotional aspects, but the demands of a specialist jurisdiction can be difficult for the judicial officer, possibly leading to secondary or vicarious trauma or compassion fatigue (Jaffe, Crooks and Dunford-Jackson et al. 2003). Judicial officers presiding in these kinds of matters also face high case volume and time pressure, evidence of violent and traumatic events and limited legal representation. All of these can be exacerbated by an intimate, personal or familial setting; the special vulnerabilities of some participants; and/or the repeated nature of the conduct or events.

Sexual assault

Trials involving charges of sexual assault against adults or children are particularly emotionally demanding for all participants because of the facts, the vulnerability and special needs of witnesses, and the complex and contested evidentiary issues of cross-examination (Davies 2017; Herlihy and Turner 2016; Smith 2018; Smith and Skinner 2017). Witnesses' court experiences have been described as 'terrifying', 'painful' and 'ritualised degradation' (van de Zandt 1998: 125–126; also see Victorian Law Reform Commission 2016). In one study of 150 sexual assault trials in New South Wales, two-thirds were stopped at least once during the complainant's evidence because of distress. At least one witness vomited in the witness box. Questioning about sexual matters ordinarily regarded as intensely intimate and private can be extensive. Even with considerable changes to legislation and court practice to alleviate such traumatic experiences, abusive cross-examination and re-traumatising sexual assault victims still occurs (Booth, Kaye and Wangmann 2019; Easteal 1998; Herlihy and Turner 2016; Smith and Skinner 2017; Smith 2018). In 2018 in Queensland, a woman testifying about having been raped by her then-husband was cross-examined for 12 hours over three days (Robertson 2018). These testimonial emotional difficulties can be further magnified by delay, repeated telling of the story and anxiety about the outcome. Whatever fear and confusion witnesses experience can make their testimony seem less consistent and less credible (Denne, Sullivan and Ernest et al. 2020; Epstein and Goodman 2013). The obligations on judges to manage the legal process as well as their own and others' emotions in this context are extraordinary. Research identifies sexual assault and crimes against children as the most stressful aspects of trial work for judges (Flores, Miller and Chamberlain et al. 2009).

Domestic/family violence

The most common form of gendered crime—DFV—appears regularly in lower courts (Douglas and Chapple 2019). It may present as criminal charges, usually a form of assault, applications for protection orders, proceedings related to breach of protection orders or sentencing after conviction. The Victorian Royal Commission into Family Violence (RCFV) (2016) notes that civil matters such as debt, residential tenancy or inheritance may involve family violence (also see Hunter 2008). Applications for protection orders, categorised as civil matters in Australian court statistics, amount to 35 percent of finalised civil cases in magistrates courts, about 120,000 matters nationally (AGPC 2020a). Three-quarters of magistrates report always or often sitting in the DFV jurisdiction (Mack, Wallace and Roach Anleu 2012).

The RCFV (2016) gives a picture of emotions involved in DFV processes in lower courts. For an applicant, seeking a protection order can be a time of extreme danger and escalating violence. The formalities of application can be bewildering; delay can intensify the uncertainty, fear, anxiety and danger. The courthouse may lack security features such as separate waiting rooms.

The court appearance itself can be terrorising and humiliating. One particularly difficult circumstance for an applicant is facing cross-examination in court conducted by the person against whom the order is sought, if he lacks legal representation. While most Australian jurisdictions have some legislative restrictions on this practice, there is a 'marked unevenness' in the actual protection available (Booth, Kaye and Wangmann 2019: 1106). Emotion is not confined to the applicants seeking protection. Those against whom an order is sought, most often men, may also experience and express strong emotion.

Australian and US research shows the emotional value of meaningful communication between the judicial officer and the parties in court (Hunter 2005; Ptacek 1999). Submissions to the RCFV emphasised the 'importance of a magistrate's language, manner and behaviour in court to ensuring that parties feel respected and heard [and] that they understand the court process' (2016: vol III, ch 16, 132). They described how compassionate responses from judicial officers can help alleviate anxiety as well as validate the applicant for engaging with the court. However, research shows considerable variability in judicial response (RCFV 2016; also see Hunter 2005; Ptacek 1999), even to the point of emotionally abusive conduct (Gray 2010). 'The conflict and intense emotions inherent in court proceedings involving allegations of domestic violence can challenge a judge's ability to demonstrate judicial temperament and convey impartiality' (Gray 2010: 1). Judicial officers may, for example, become frustrated when a woman refuses to leave an abusive relationship, failing to recognise the practical and even life-threatening obstacles her partner has created should she try to leave and the reasons she may have for not leaving (Epstein and Goodman 2013). Parents, especially mothers, can feel harshly judged and demeaned by judicial conduct and experience shame, embarrassment and anxiety (Lens 2016, 2017; Weisz, Beal and Wingrove 2013).

Childrens/youth

Courts with a special focus on young people, which may include youth offending and/or child protection, are often located in overburdened lower courts (AGPC 2020c; Borowski 2013; Sheehan 2013; Travers 2007). Almost half (47 percent) of magistrates report that they always or often preside in childrens/youth matters. In contrast, only six percent of judges of the intermediate or higher courts report this kind of work (Mack, Wallace and Roach Anleu 2012).

Cases involving young people accused of crime entail all the emotional elements of criminal law plus distinctive concerns about the vulnerability and welfare of the children, as well as their immediate or extended families. Parents of the children who are the direct subject of the proceedings may also experience or describe the court processes in negative terms (Pennington 2015). These courts often have the care and protection jurisdiction, dealing with children who are at risk in their homes and who may be subject to removal. These cases are 'heart-rending' (Darbyshire 2011: 288). Australian research on childrens/youth courts indicates that:

> [a]lthough dealing with youth offenders was seen [by interviewees] as being more time-consuming than dealing with similar adult cases, it was

> nevertheless 'more manageable'—much less emotionally taxing—than child protection matters (Borowski 2013: 275).

These features can result in 'an intimidating and complex environment' for all involved (Lens 2017: 132). Constant exposure to allegations of harm done by and to children, and concerns for their welfare, impose emotional burdens on the judicial officer. The intense emotions experienced and displayed by those appearing in these courts generates considerable need for emotion management. Hope for the potential of an intervention to alleviate harm or even significantly improve the course of a young person's life is also an important emotional feature of these courts. Australian research finds that:

> [M]agistrates considered Family Division work more demanding than work in other courts—time-consuming, emotionally 'intense', 'onerous', complex and often 'traumatic', with magistrates having to make 'difficult decisions' [under considerable time pressures] (Borowski and Sheehan 2013: 131).

Civil and small claims

Lower courts process a large number of general civil and small claims matters, about five times as many as the higher courts (AGPC 2020b; Bamford and Rankin 2017). However, these cases form a smaller part of everyday work of magistrates: about four in ten magistrates indicate always or often sitting in the civil jurisdiction, compared with over five in ten judges in the intermediate and higher courts (Mack, Wallace and Roach Anleu 2012).

Some civil matters can be lengthy or difficult. Flores, Miller and Chamberlain et al.'s (2009) US research identifies long boring trials as a particular feature which judges find stressful. Civil litigation can also be an area of considerable emotion for the parties. These feelings can occur at any stage of the legal process and may reflect the strong emotions that motivate some civil plaintiffs to bring their actions (Lind, Greenberg and Scott et al. 2000; Vincent, Young and Phillips 1994). US research finds that the decision to sue is influenced by factors including the plaintiff feeling poorly treated by the defendant (Lind, Greenberg and Scott et al. 2000; also see Vincent, Young and Phillips 1994; Stewart and Wood 2013) and wanting to feel 'heard and acknowledged' by the defendant (Relis 2009: 58).

Even in small claims, where the amount in issue is limited compared to other matters before the courts, the dispute itself can be very important to the parties, generating strong emotions similar to those for any civil action. Legal and factual issues can be complex, and individual litigants, whether plaintiff or defendant, are almost always unrepresented (Darbyshire 2011), either because of limited legal aid or because legal representation may not be allowed (see, for example, *Magistrates Court Act 1992* (SA) s 38(4)), perhaps adding to the emotion demands on the judicial officer.

A large proportion of these cases are debt collection proceedings, often brought by repeat player collection agencies against debtors with little or no capacity to pay, facing the social disadvantages confronting so many lower court users (Darbyshire 2011; Genn 2019) or finalised by default judgments (Bamford and Rankin 2017). As with criminal cases, the limited capacity of the magistrate to address the underlying social and economic inequities can lead to frustration.

Coroners

About a quarter of magistrates in Australia sit at least sometimes in the coronial jurisdiction investigating causes and circumstances of deaths, especially those that are sudden or unexpected (Mack, Wallace and Roach Anleu 2012; also see Scott Bray 2010). This jurisdiction presents a distinctive emotional context for judicial work. Coronial matters are handled through an inquisitorial rather than adversarial process, either as a specialist jurisdiction or, in regional areas, as part of a general caseload. Emotional needs, especially of survivors, can be challenging. Tait, Carpenter and Quadrelli et al. state that 'coroners are necessarily confronted with raw and pressing emotions' arising from the grief resulting from the unexpected death (2016: 572). The potential for emotional harm to families from the coronial process itself can be especially acute in cases of possible suicide (Biddle 2003; Chapple, Ziebland and Hawton 2012; Tait, Carpenter and Quadrelli et al. 2016).

Facts in these inquiries can be emotionally challenging for the coroner: '[d]eath investigations are understood by all coronial professions to be confronting emotional experiences which have the capacity to distress and disturb' (Tait et al. 2016: 576). One study of coroners in Australia finds that they are 'troubled by questions of emotion and how to therapeutically manage its expression in oneself and others' (Roper and Holmes 2016: 143). Tait, Carpenter and Quadrelli et al. indicate that coroners may draw on the 'cultural script of judicial dispassion' (Maroney 2011: 630) to manage the 'intensely emotional nature of a coroner's role' (2016: 581).

Family law

Family law addresses legal issues arising from marriage and divorce, including property division; spousal and child support; and arrangements for access to, custody of and parenting of children. Even in jurisdictions with 'no-fault' divorce, family courts must hear and determine allegations of DFV, sexual abuse of children or sexual assault, as these can become relevant to questions of safety of children or other family members or to court management issues such as ensuring safety during court proceedings (Darbyshire 2011). These cases can be emotionally wrenching for all the participants (Huntington 2016). Many litigants experience significant distress of various kinds, including violence (Harman 2017; Huntington 2016). The inherently and intensely human emotional experience central to divorce and related issues lead to stress and require judicial emotion work. In survey research conducted with US judges, 63 percent of the judges 'reported one or more symptoms that they identified as work-related vicarious trauma experiences' (Jaffe, Crooks and Dunford-Jackson et al. 2003: 1).

Family courts often face similar challenges as other lower courts, such as growing caseloads, time pressure and lack of legal representation (ALRC 2019; Barlow, Hunter and Smithson et al. 2017; Biland and Steinmetz 2017; NCSC 2018). US research suggests that legal representation in and of itself may not improve the emotional landscape in family law. A survey of US divorce attorneys finds that they perceived 'opposing counsel's actions … as increasing the emotional level of the dispute in about half of the cases' studied (Braver, Cookston and Cohen 2002: 332; also see Mather, McEwen and Maiman 2001; Weisz, Beal and Wingrove 2013). In contrast, research in Australia suggests that family lawyers may help ameliorate an adversarial mindset in their clients by maintaining a focus on the children's interests (Batagol 2008).

Migration and refugee

In most common law countries, decisions on migration matters, including refugee and asylum applications, are made in the first instance by a government official but can be challenged in various ways, eventually ending up in court. In Australia, these cases make up about five percent of all filings in the Federal Circuit Court (FCCA 2018), about 80 percent of the Federal Court appeals and 92 percent of all appeals commenced by unrepresented litigants (FCA 2018). These are mostly determined by a single judge, while appeals in other matters are heard by a panel of three or sometimes five judges (Federal Court of Australia 2018: 31). In many jurisdictions, migration cases may be heard in specialist courts or tribunals, which are the functional equivalent of lower courts in many respects, and share similar qualities of high caseloads, pressure for rapid case processing, limited resources, unrepresented litigants and distressing facts (Lustig, Karnik and Delucchi et al. 2008).

These cases can generate a range of emotions. Lustig, Karnick and Delucchi et al. (2008) describe the facts in migration matters as 'horrifying stories' (p. 58), 'perhaps the most disturbing stories of human suffering' (p. 75). Migration decisions, especially in asylum cases, can mean life or death for some applicants. The intense emotions of those seeking asylum, language barriers requiring interpreters, and the difficulty of making assessments which often turn on credibility, are experienced as 'emotionally draining' by the judicial officer (Lustig, Karnik and Delucchi et al. 2008: 74; also see Herlihy and Turner 2016; Hunter, Pearson and San Roque et al. 2013; Johannesson 2018; Westaby 2010; Wettergren 2010). The emotional qualities intrinsic to the cases themselves may be intensified for all participants, including the judicial officer, by the very public nature of particular cases and the wider public and political conflicts around immigration and asylum policy (Mack, Roach Anleu and Tutton 2018; Peterie and Neil 2020; Tomkinson 2018).

Conclusion

Although emotion is formally disavowed as a legitimate part of judicial practice and decision making, judicial officers are human and judicial work occurs in circumstances in which emotion is experienced and displayed and needs to be managed. Judicial officers at all court levels are constantly exposed to the traumatic experiences of others, whether in criminal matters, DFV, family law or any other area of human activity that ends up in court. The courtroom involves face-to-face interaction with many participants, each with their own feelings. Decision making entails exercising judgment which can demand empathy or compassion, or elicit anger, sadness or disgust. While some judicial emotional capacities can be valuable judicial resources, emotional openness can also lead to a kind of secondary or vicarious trauma resulting in complex emotion experience and management (Chamberlain and Miller 2008).

The nature of interaction across different court contexts produces contrasting emotion environments and varied experiences of emotion and emotion display for the judicial officer and other participants. This chapter reveals the interconnectedness among formal court structures, context, judging and emotion. This overview provides the basis for understanding the interactions and emotion experiences investigated in the next three chapters.

References

Abadinsky, Howard, 2014, *Law, Courts, and Justice in America*. 7th ed. Long Grove, IL: Waveland Press.

Abbott, Andrew, 1981, 'Status and Status Strain in the Professions', *American Journal of Sociology 86*: 819–835.

Appleby, Gabrielle and Suzanne Le Mire 2016, 'The Australian Judiciary: Resistant to Reform?'. In *Regulating Judges: Beyond Independence and Accountability*, eds. Richard Devlin and Adam Dodek, 35–54. Cheltenham and Northampton, MA: Edward Elgar.

Australasian Institute of Judicial Administration 2019, *AIJA Judicial Gender Statistics*. March. Retrieved 9 May 2020, from https://aija.org.au/research/judicial-gender-statistics/.

Australian Bureau of Statistics 2020, *4513.0 - Criminal Courts, Australia, 2018-19*. 27 February. Retrieved 9 May 2020, from https://www.abs.gov.au/AUSSTATS/abs@.nsf/DetailsPage/4513.02018-19

Australian Government Productivity Commission 2014, *Access to Justice Arrangements*. Inquiry Report No 72, available at https://www.pc.gov.au/inquiries/completed/access-justice/report.

Australian Government Productivity Commission 2020a, *Report on Government Services, Part C, Section 7, Courts, Context*. Retrieved 9 May 2020, from https://www.pc.gov.au/research/ongoing/report-on-government-services/2020/justice/courts.

Australian Government Productivity Commission 2020b, *Report on Government Services, Part C, Section 7, Courts, Data Tables*. Retrieved 9 May 2020, from https://www.pc.gov.au/research/ongoing/report-on-government-services/2020/justice/courts/rogs-2020-partc-section7-data-tables.xlsx.

Australian Government Productivity Commission 2020c, *Report on Government Services, Part C, Section 7, Courts, Interpretative Material*. Retrieved 9 May 2020, from https://www.pc.gov.au/research/ongoing/report-on-government-services/2020/justice/courts/rogs-2020-partc-7-courts-interpretative-material.pdf.

Australian Law Reform Commission 2000, *Managing Justice: A Review of the Federal Civil Justice System*. ALRC Report 89, available at http://www.austlii.edu.au/au/other/lawreform/ALRC/1999/89.html.

Australian Law Reform Commission 2018, *Pathways to Justice—Inquiry into the Incarceration Rate of Aboriginal and Torres Strait Islander Peoples*. ALRC Report 133, available at https://www.alrc.gov.au/publication/pathways-to-justice-inquiry-into-the-incarceration-rate-of-aboriginal-and-torres-strait-islander-peoples-alrc-report-133/.

Australian Law Reform Commission 2019, *Family Law for the Future - an Inquiry into the Family Law System*. ALRC Report 135, available at https://www.alrc.gov.au/inquiry/review-of-the-family-law-system/.

Bamford, David and Mark Rankin 2017, *Principles of Civil Litigation*. 3rd ed. Sydney: Lawbook.

Bandes, Susan A., 1996, 'Empathy, Narrative, and Victim Impact Statements', *University of Chicago Law Review 63*: 361–412.

Bandes, Susan A., 2016, 'Remorse and Criminal Justice', *Emotion Review 8*: 14–19.

Bandes, Susan A. and Jessica M. Salerno 2014, 'Emotion, Proof and Prejudice: The Cognitive Science of Gruesome Photos and Victim Impact Statements', *Arizona State Law Journal 46*: 1003–1056.

Barak, Aharon, 2006, *The Judge in a Democracy*. Princeton, NJ: Princeton University Press.

Barlow, Anne, Rosemary Hunter, Janet Smithson and Jan Ewing 2017, *Mapping Paths to Family Justice: Resolving Family Disputes in Neoliberal Times*. London: Palgrave Macmillan.

Batagol, Becky, 2008, 'Fomenters of Strife, Gladiatorial Champions or Something Else Entirely? Lawyers and Family Dispute Resolution', *Queensland University of Technology Law & Justice Journal 8*: 24–45.

Baum, Lawrence, 2017, 'Judges and Their Audiences'. In *The Oxford Handbook of US Judicial Behavior*, eds. Lee Epstein and Stefanie A Lindquist, 343–360. Oxford and New York: Oxford University Press.

Bennett, Paul, 2016, *Specialist Courts for Sentencing Aboriginal Offenders: Aboriginal Courts in Australia*. Annandale: Federation Press.

Bergman Blix, Stina and Åsa Wettergren 2018, *Professional Emotions in Court: A Sociological Perspective*. Abingdon: Routledge.

Biddle, Lucy, 2003, 'Public Hazards or Private Tragedies? An Exploratory Study of the Effect of Coroners' Procedures on Those Bereaved by Suicide', *Social Science & Medicine 56*: 1033–1045.

Biland, Émilie and Hélène Steinmetz 2017, 'Are Judges Street-Level Bureaucrats? Evidence from French and Canadian Family Courts', *Law & Social Inquiry 42*: 298–324.

Black, Ryan C., Matthew E. K. Hall, Ryan J. Owens and Eve M. Ringsmuth 2016, 'The Role of Emotional Language in Briefs before the US Supreme Court', *Journal of Law and Courts 4*: 377–407.

Black, Ryan C., Maron W. Sorenson and Timothy R. Johnson 2013, 'Toward an Actor-Based Measure of Supreme Court Case Salience: Information-Seeking and Engagement During Oral Arguments', *Political Research Quarterly 66*: 804–818.

Black, Ryan C., Sarah A. Treul, Timothy R. Johnson and Jerry Goldman 2011, 'Emotions, Oral Arguments, and Supreme Court Decision Making', *Journal of Politics 73*: 572–581.

Blackshield, Tony, 2007, 'Case Note: *New South Wales v Commonwealth*', *Melbourne University Law Review 31*: 1135–1160.

Booth, Tracey, 2016, *Accommodating Justice: Victim Impact Statements in the Sentencing Process*. Annandale: Federation Press.

Booth, Tracey, Alice K. Bosma and Kim M. E. Lens 2018, 'Accommodating the Expressive Function of Victim Impact Statements: The Scope for Victims' Voices in Dutch Courtrooms', *British Journal of Criminology 58*: 1480–1498.

Booth, Tracey, Miranda Kaye and Jane Wangmann 2019, 'Family Violence, Cross-Examination and Self-Represented Parties in the Courtroom: The Differences, Gaps and Deficiencies', *University of New South Wales Law Journal 42*: 1106–1142.

Bornstein, Brian H., Gwen Hullman and Monica K. Miller 2013, 'Stress, Trauma, and Wellbeing in the Legal System: Where Do We Go from Here?'. In *Stress, Trauma, and Wellbeing in the Legal System*, eds. Monica K. Miller and Brian H. Bornstein, 293–309. New York: Oxford University Press.

Borowski, Allan, 2013, 'Whither Australia's Children's Courts? Findings of the National Assessment of Australia's Children's Courts', *Australian & New Zealand Journal of Criminology 46*: 268–288.

Borowski, Allan and Rosemary Sheehan 2013, 'The Children's Court of Victoria'. In *Australia's Children's Courts Today and Tomorrow*, eds. Rosemary Sheehan and Allan Borowski, 123–142. Dordrecht: Springer.

Braver, Sanford, Jeffrey T. Cookston and Bruce R. Cohen 2002, 'Experiences of Family Law Attorneys with Current Issues in Divorce Practice', *Family Relations 51*: 325–334.

Brewer, Neil and Gary L. Wells 2011, 'Eyewitness Identification', *Current Directions in Psychological Science 20*: 24–27.

Bright, David A. and Jane Goodman-Delahunty 2006, 'Gruesome Evidence and Emotion: Anger, Blame, and Jury Decision-Making', *Law and Human Behavior 30*: 183–202.

Bryan, Amanda C. and Eve M. Ringsmuth 2016, 'Jeremiad or Weapon of Words?: The Power of Emotive Language in Supreme Court Dissents', *Journal of Law and Courts 4*: 159–185.

Budziak, Jeffrey, Matthew P. Hitt and Daniel Lempert 2019, 'Determinants of Writing Style on the United States Circuit Courts of Appeals', *Journal of Law and Courts 7*: 1–28.

Carlen, Pat, 1976, *Magistrates' Justice*. London: Martin Robertson.

Cashman, Peter, 2015, 'Civil Procedure, Politics and the Process of Reform'. In *Ten Years of the Civil Procedure Act 2005 (NSW)*, eds. Miiko Kumar and Michael Legg, 225–263. Sydney: Lawbook.

Chamberlain, Jared and Monica K. Miller 2008, 'Stress in the Courtroom: Call for Research', *Psychiatry, Psychology and Law 15*: 237–250.

Chapple, Alison, Sue Ziebland and Keith Hawton 2012, 'A Proper, Fitting Explanation? Suicide Bereavement and Perceptions of the Coroner's Verdict', *Crisis: The Journal of Crisis Intervention and Suicide Prevention 33*: 230–238.

County Court of Victoria 2019, *Annual Report 2018-19*. Retrieved 9 May 2020, from https://www.countycourt.vic.gov.au/files/documents/2019-10/ccv-annual-report-2018-19.pdf.

Cowan, Dave and Emma Hitchings 2007, '"Pretty Boring Stuff": District Judges and Housing Possession Proceedings', *Social & Legal Studies 16*: 363–382.

Cunneen, Chris, 2014, 'Colonial Processes, Indigenous Peoples, and Criminal Justice Systems'. In *The Oxford Handbook of Ethnicity, Crime and Immigration*, eds. Sandra M Bucerius and Michael Tonry, 386–407. New York: Oxford University Press.

Darbyshire, Penny, 2011, *Sitting in Judgment: The Working Lives of Judges*. Oxford and Portland OR: Hart Publishing.

Davies, Rhiannon, 2017, *Stories of Pervasive Uncertainty: A Victim-Focused Analysis of Victim Impact Statements and Sentencing in Sexual Offence Cases*. PhD Thesis, Faculty of Law, University of Tasmania. Retrieved 9 May 2020, from https://eprints.utas.edu.au/28673/.

Davis, Julia, 2015, 'The Moral and Emotional Landscape of Jury Duty', *University of South Australia*. June. Retrieved 9 May 2020, from http://w3.unisa.edu.au/unisanews/2015/June/story7.asp.

Denne, Emily, Colleen Sullivan, Kyle Ernest and Stacia N. Stolzenberg 2020, 'Assessing Children's Credibility in Courtroom Investigations of Alleged Child Sexual Abuse: Suggestibility, Plausibility, and Consistency', *Child Maltreatment 25*: 224–232.

Douglas, Heather and Kate Chapple 2019, *National Domestic and Family Violence Bench Book*. July. Retrieved 9 May 2020, from http://dfvbenchbook.aija.org.au/contents.

Durkheim, Emile, 1938, *The Rules of Sociological Method*, trans. Sarah A. Solovay and John H. Mueller, ed. George E. G. Catlin. New York: The Free Press.

Durkheim, Emile, 1984, *The Division of Labour in Society*, trans. W.D. Halls. London: Macmillan.

Easteal, Patricia, ed. 1998, *Balancing the Scales: Rape, Law Reform and Australian Culture*. Annandale: Federation Press.

Epstein, Deborah and Lisa A. Goodman 2013, 'Domestic Violence Victims' Experiences in the Legal System'. In *Stress, Trauma, and Wellbeing in the Legal*

System, eds. Monica K. Miller and Brian H. Bornstein, 45–61. New York: Oxford University Press.

Epstein, Lee and Stefanie Lindquist, eds. 2017, *The Oxford Handbook of US Judicial Behavior*. Oxford and New York: Oxford University Press.

Family Court of Australia 2020, *Annual Report 2019-2020*. Retrieved 24 October 2020, from http://www.familycourt.gov.au/wps/wcm/connect/fcoaweb/reports-and-publications/annual-reports/.

Federal Circuit Court of Australia 2020, *Annual Report 2019-2020*. Retrieved 24 October 2020, from http://www.federalcircuitcourt.gov.au/wps/wcm/connect/fccweb/reports-and-publications/annual-reports/.

Federal Court of Australia 2020, *Annual Report 2019-2020*. Retrieved 24 October 2020, from https://www.fedcourt.gov.au/about/corporate-information/annual-reports.

Feigenson, Neal, 2016, 'Jurors' Emotions and Judgments of Legal Responsibility and Blame: What Does the Experimental Research Tell Us?', *Emotion Review 8*: 26–31.

Fielding, Nigel G., 2013, 'Lay People in Court: The Experience of Defendants, Eyewitnesses and Victims', *British Journal of Sociology 64*: 287–307.

Flores, David M., Monica K. Miller, Jared Chamberlain, James T. Richardson and Brian H Bornstein 2009, 'Judges' Perspectives on Stress and Safety in the Courtroom: An Exploratory Study', *Court Review 45*: 76–89.

Flower, Lisa, 2016, 'Dramatic Subtlety: Exploring Anger and Strategic Niceness in the Courtroom', paper presented at the Scandinavian Research Council for Criminology's 58th Research Seminar, Bifröst. Retrieved 9 May 2020, from https://www.nsfk.org/wp-content/uploads/sites/10/2018/11/Report-NSfK-Research-Seminar-2016.pdf.

French, Robert S., 2010, 'Judicial Activisim—the Boundaries of the Judicial Role', *The Judicial Review 10*: 1–10.

Genn, Hazel, 2019, 'When Law Is Good for Your Health: Mitigating the Social Determinants of Health through Access to Justice', *Current Legal Problems 72*: 159–202.

Gibson, James L. and Michael J. Nelson 2014, 'The Legitimacy of the US Supreme Court: Conventional Wisdoms and Recent Challenges Thereto', *Annual Review of Law and Social Science 10*: 201–219.

Gilbert, Michael, 1986, *The Oxford Book of Legal Anecdotes*. Oxford: Oxford University Press.

Gray, Cynthia, 2010, 'Demeanor in Domestic Violence Cases', *Judicial Conduct Reporter 32*: 1, 8–11.

Gray, Ian L., 2002, *The People's Court—into the Future, Twelfth AIJA Oration in Judicial Administration*. Melbourne: Australian Institute of Judicial Administration.

Hall, Maggie, 2016, *The Lived Sentence: Rethinking Sentencing, Risk and Rehabilitation*. Cham: Palgrave Macmillan.

Hans, Valerie P., 2008, 'Jury Systems around the World', *Annual Review of Law and Social Science 4*: 275–297.

Harman, Joe, 2017, 'The Prevalence of Allegations of Family Violence in Proceedings before the Federal Circuit Court of Australia', *Family Law Review 7*: 3–19.

Harris, Lloyd C., 2002, 'The Emotional Labour of Barristers: An Exploration of Emotional Labour by Status Professionals', *Journal of Management Studies 39*: 553–584.

Heimer, Carol A., 2001, 'Cases and Biographies: An Essay on Routinization and the Nature of Comparison', *Annual Review of Sociology 27*: 47–76.

Henderson, Emma and Kirsty Duncanson 2018, 'Design and Ideology: Innovation and the Magistrates' Court', *Griffith Law Review 27*: 207–232.

Herlihy, Jane and Stuart Turner 2016, 'Emotions and the Assessment of Credibility'. In *Emotional Dynamics of Law and Legal Discourse*, eds. Heather Conway and John Stannard, 155–183. Oxford and Portland, OR: Hart Publishing.

High Court of Australia 2019, *Annual Report 2018-2019*. Retrieved 24 October 2020, from http://www.hcourt.gov.au/publications/annual-reports/annual-reports.

Howard, Robert M. and Kirk A. Randazzo, eds. 2017, *Routledge Handbook of Judicial Behavior*. New York and London: Routledge.

Hunter, Jill, Linda Pearson, Mehera San Roque and Zac Steel 2013, 'Asylum Adjudication, Mental Health and Credibility Evaluation', *Federal Law Review 41*: 471–495.

Hunter, Rosemary, 2005, 'Styles of Judging: How Magistrates Deal with Applications for Intervention Orders', *Alternative Law Journal 30*: 231–236, 46.

Hunter, Rosemary, 2008, *Domestic Violence Law Reform and Women's Experience in Court: The Implementation of Feminist Reforms in Civil Proceedings*. Amherst NY: Cambria Press.

Huntington, Clare, 2016, 'Affective Family Law'. In *Emotional Dynamics of Law and Legal Discourse*, eds. Heather Conway and John Stannard, 9–33. Oxford and Portland OR: Hart Publishing.

Jacobson, Jessica, Gillian Hunter and Amy Kirby 2015, *Inside Crown Court: Personal Experiences and Questions of Legitimacy*. Bristol: Policy Press.

Jaffe, Peter G., Claire V. Crooks, Billie Lee Dunford-Jackson and Michael Town 2003, 'Vicarious Trauma in Judges: The Personal Challenge of Dispensing Justice', *Juvenile and Family Court Journal 54*: 1–9.

Johannesson, Livia, 2018, 'Exploring the "Liberal Paradox" from the Inside: Evidence from the Swedish Migration Courts', *International Migration Review 52*: 1162–1185.

Johansen, Louise Victoria, 2019, '"Impressed" by Feelings—How Judges Perceive Defendants' Emotional Expressions in Danish Courtrooms', *Social & Legal Studies 28*: 250–269.

Johnson, Timothy R., Ryan C. Black and Justin Wedeking 2009, 'Pardon the Interruption: An Empirical Analysis of Supreme Court Justices' Behavior During Oral Arguments', *Loyola Law Review 55*: 331–351.

King, Michael, Arie Freiberg, Becky Batagol and Ross Hyams 2014, *Non-Adversarial Justice*. 2nd ed. Annandale: Federation Press.

Kirby, Amy, Jessica Jacobson and Gillian Hunter 2014, *Effective Participation or Passive Acceptance: How Can Defendants Participate More Effectively in the Court Process?* Howard League for Penal Reform Working Paper 9/2014, Retrieved 9 May 2020, from https://howardleague.org/wp-content/uploads/2016/04/HLWP_9_2014_2.pdf.

Kohler-Hausmann, Issa, 2018, *Misdemeanorland: Criminal Courts and Social Control in an Age of Broken Windows Policing*. Princeton, NJ: Princeton University Press.

Kritzer, Herbert M., 2007, 'Toward a Theorization of Craft', *Social & Legal Studies 16*: 321–340.

Lee, H. P. and Enid Campbell 2013, *The Australian Judiciary*. 2nd ed. Port Melbourne: Cambridge University Press.

Lens, Vicki, 2016, 'Against the Grain: Therapeutic Judging in a Traditional Family Court', *Law & Social Inquiry 41*: 701–718.

Lens, Vicki, 2017, 'Engaging Parents in Family Court: Lessons from an Observational Study of Child Protection Cases', *Journal of Social Work 17*: 129–146.

Lind, E. Allan, Jerald Greenberg, Kimberly S. Scott and Thomas D. Welchans 2000, 'The Winding Road from Employee to Complainant: Situational and Psychological Determinants of Wrongful-Termination Claims', *Administrative Science Quarterly 45*: 557–590.

Lustig, Stuart L., Niranjan Karnik, Kevin Delucchi, Lakshika Tennakoon, Brent Kaul, Dana Leigh Marks and Denise Slavin 2008, 'Inside the Judges' Chambers: Narrative Responses from the National Association of Immigration Judges Stress and Burnout Survey', *Georgetown Immigration Law Journal 23*: 57–83.

Mack, Kathy and Sharyn Roach Anleu 2007, '"Getting through the List": Judgecraft and Legitimacy in the Lower Courts', *Social & Legal Studies 16*: 341–361.

Mack, Kathy, Sharyn Roach Anleu and Jordan Tutton 2018, 'The Judiciary and the Public: Judicial Perceptions', *Adelaide Law Review 39*: 1–36.

Mack, Kathy, Anne Wallace and Sharyn Roach Anleu 2012, *Judicial Workload: Time, Tasks and Work Organisation*. Melbourne: Australasian Institute of Judicial Administration.

Mackenzie, Geraldine, 2005, *How Judges Sentence*. Annandale: Federation Press.

Marchetti, Elena, 2019, *Indigenous Courts, Culture and Partner Violence*. London: Palgrave Macmillan.

Marchetti, Elena and Janet Ransley 2014, 'Applying the Critical Lens to Judicial Officers and Legal Practitioners Involved in Sentencing Indigenous Offenders: Will Anyone or Anything Do?', *University of New South Wales Law Journal 37*: 1–33.

Marder, Nancy S. and Valerie P. Hans 2016, 'Introduction to Juries and Mixed Tribunals across the Globe: New Developments, Common Challenges and Future Directions', *Oñati Socio-Legal Series 6*: 163–178.

Maroney, Terry A., 2011, 'The Persistent Cultural Script of Judicial Dispassion', *California Law Review 99*: 629–682.

Mather, Lynn M., Craig A. McEwen and Richard J. Maiman 2001, *Divorce Lawyers at Work: Varieties of Professionalism in Practice*. Oxford: Oxford University Press.

McConville, Michael and Luke Marsh 2016, 'Factory Farming and State-Induced Pleas'. In *The Integrity of Criminal Process: From Theory into Practice*, eds. Jill Hunter, Paul Roberts, Simon N. M. Young and David Dixon, 99–116. Oxford and Portland, OR: Hart Publishing.

McCormack, Nancy and Melanie R. Buekckert 2013, *Introduction to the Law and Legal System of Canada*. Ontario: Carswell.

McKay, Carolyn, 2018, *The Pixelated Prisoner: Prison Video Links, Court 'Appearance' and the Justice Matrix*. Abingdon and New York: Routledge.

Metcalfe, Christi, 2016, 'The Role of Courtroom Workgroups in Felony Case Dispositions: An Analysis of Workgroup Familiarity and Similarity', *Law & Society Review 50*: 637–673.

Mileski, Maureen, 1971, 'Courtroom Encounters: An Observational Study of a Lower Criminal Court', *Law & Society Review 5*: 473–538.

Miller, Monica K. and Brian H. Bornstein 2004, 'Juror Stress: Causes and Interventions', *Thurgood Marshall Law Review 30*: 237–269.

Miller, Monica K. and Brian H. Bornstein 2013, 'The Experience of Jurors: Reducing Stress and Enhancing Satisfaction'. In *Stress, Trauma, and Wellbeing in the Legal System*, eds. Monica K. Miller and Brian H. Bornstein, 247–267. New York: Oxford University Press.

Miller, Monica K., Charles P. Edwards, Jenny Reichert and Brian H. Bornstein 2018, 'An Examination of Outcomes Predicted by the Model of Judicial Stress', *Judicature 102*: 51–61.

Moran, Leslie J., 2009, 'Judging Pictures: A Case Study of Portraits of the Chief Justices, Supreme Court of New South Wales', *International Journal of Law in Context 5*: 295–314.

Mulcahy, Linda, 2007, 'Architects of Justice: The Politics of Courtroom Design', *Social & Legal Studies 16*: 383–403.

Mulcahy, Linda, 2010, *Legal Architecture: Justice, Due Process and the Place of Law*. New York: Routledge.

Mulcahy, Linda and Emma Rowden 2020, *The Democratic Courthouse: A Modern History of Design, Due Process and Dignity*. London: Routledge.

National Center for State Courts 1998, *Through the Eyes of the Juror: A Manual for Addressing Juror Stress*. Retrieved 9 May 2020, from http://www.ncsc-jurystudies.org/What-We-Do/Juror-Stress-Juror-Privacy-and-More.aspx.

National Center for State Courts 2018, *Family Justice Initiative: The Landscape of Domestic Relations Cases in State Courts*. Retrieved 9 May 2020, from https://www.ncsc.org/Services-and-Experts/Areas-of-expertise/Children-and-Families/Family-Justice-Initiative/Report-and-Recommendations.aspx.

New South Wales Law Reform Commission 2014, *Encouraging Appropriate Early Guilty Pleas*. Report 141, available at https://www.lawreform.justice.nsw.gov.au/Documents/Publications/Reports/Report-141.pdf.

O'Brien, Kate, Jane Goodman-Delahunty, Jonathan Clough and Jessica Pratley 2008, 'Factors Affecting Juror Satisfaction and Confidence in New South Wales, Victoria and South Australia'. *Trends & Issues in Crime and Criminal Justice* No 354. Australian Institute of Criminology: Canberra. Available at https://aic.gov.au/publications/tandi/tandi354.

Opeskin, Brian, 2013, 'The State of the Judicature: A Statistical Profile of Australian Courts and Judges', *Sydney Law Review 35*: 489–517.

Paterson, Alan, 2013, *Final Judgment: The Last Law Lords and the Supreme Court*. Oxford and Portland, OR: Hart Publishing.

Pennington, Liana, 2015, 'A Case Study Approach to Procedural Justice: Parents' Views in Two Juvenile Delinquency Courts in the United States', *British Journal of Sociology 55*: 901–920.

Peterie, Michelle and David Neil 2020, 'Xenophobia Towards Asylum Seekers: A Survey of Social Theories', *Journal of Sociology 56*: 23–35.
Pleasence, Pascoe, Nigel J. Balmer, Alexy Buck, Aoife O'Grady and Hazel Genn 2004, 'Multiple Justiciable Problems: Common Clusters and Their Social and Demographic Indicators', *Journal of Empirical Legal Studies 1*: 301–329.
Proeve, Michael and Steven Tudor 2010, *Remorse: Psychological and Jurisprudential Perspectives*. Farnham: Ashgate.
Ptacek, James, 1999, *Battered Women in the Courtroom: The Power of Judicial Responses*. Boston, MA: Northeastern University Press.
Queensland Sentencing Advisory Council 2017, *Classification of Child Exploitation Material for Sentencing Purposes*. Retrieved 9 May 2020, from https://www.sentencingcouncil.qld.gov.au/__data/assets/pdf_file/0017/531503/cem-final-report-july-2017.pdf.
Ray, Laura Krugman, 2002, 'Judicial Personality: Rhetoric and Emotion in Supreme Court Opinions', *Washington and Lee Law Review 59*: 193–234.
Reed, Krystia and Brian H. Bornstein 2013, 'A Stressful Profession: The Experience of Attorneys'. In *Stress, Trauma, and Wellbeing in the Legal System*, eds. Monica K. Miller and Brian H. Bornstein, 217–244. New York: Oxford University Press.
Relis, Tamara, 2009, *Perceptions in Litigation and Mediation: Lawyers, Defendants, Plaintiffs, and Gendered Parties*. Cambridge: Cambridge University Press.
Resnik, Judith and Dennis E. Curtis 2011, *Representing Justice: Invention, Controversy, and Rights in City-States and Democratic Courtrooms*. New Haven, CT and London: Yale University Press.
Richard, Larry, 1993, 'How Your Personality Affects Your Practice: The Lawyer Types', *ABA Journal 79*: 74–78.
Richardson, Liz, Genevieve Grant and Janina Boughey 2018, *The Impacts of Self-Represented Litigants on Civil and Administrative Justice: Environmental Scan of Research, Policy and Practice*. Melbourne: Australasian Institute of Judicial Administration.
Ridgeway, Cecilia L., 2006, 'Linking Social Structure and Interpersonal Behavior: A Theoretical Perspective on Cultural Schemas and Social Relations', *Social Psychology Quarterly 69*: 5–16.
Roach Anleu, Sharyn and Kathy Mack 2005, 'Magistrates' Everyday Work and Emotional Labour', *Journal of Law and Society 32*: 590–614.
Roach Anleu, Sharyn and Kathy Mack 2007, 'Magistrates, Magistrates Courts and Social Change', *Law & Policy 29*: 183–209.
Roach Anleu, Sharyn and Kathy Mack 2017, *Performing Judicial Authority in the Lower Courts*. London: Palgrave.
Roach Anleu, Sharyn and Kathy Mack 2018, 'Judicial Humour and Inter-Professional Relations in the Courtroom'. In *Judges, Judging and Humour*, eds. Jessica Milner Davis and Sharyn Roach Anleu, 141–178. Cham: Palgrave Macmillan.
Roach Anleu, Sharyn and Kathy Mack forthcoming, 'Constructing remorse: Interactional dimensions of finding an emotion'. In *Showing Remorse and Taking Responsibility for Crime: The Ideal Defendant*, eds. Stewart Field and Cyrus Tata. Oxford: Hart Publishing.

Roach Anleu, Sharyn, Russell Brewer and Kathy Mack 2017, 'Locating the Judge within Sentencing Research', *International Journal for Crime, Justice and Social Democracy 6*: 46–63.

Roach Anleu, Sharyn, Kathy Mack and Jordan Tutton 2014, 'Judicial Humour in the Australian Courtroom', *Melbourne University Law Review 38*: 621–665.

Roach Anleu, Sharyn and Jessica Milner Davis 2018, 'Thinking About Judges, Judging and Humour: The Intersection of Opposites'. In *Judges, Judging and Humour*, eds. Jessica Milner Davis and Sharyn Roach Anleu, 1–38. Cham: Palgrave Macmillan.

Roberts, Julian V., 2011, *Mitigation and Aggravation at Sentencing*. Cambridge: Cambridge University Press.

Robertson, Josh, 2018, 'Ex-Wife of Former One Nation Adviser Says Being Grilled over Her Rape "Re-Traumatised" Her', *Australian Broadcasting Corporation*. 17 July. Retrieved 9 May 2020, from https://www.abc.net.au/news/2018-07-17/ex-wife-of-former-one-nation-adviser-shares-rape-trial-trauma/9994238.

Rock, Paul, 1993, *The Social World of an English Crown Court: Witnesses and Professionals in the Crown Court Centre at Wood Green*. Gloucestershire: Clarendon Press.

Roper, Isabel and Vivien Holmes 2016, 'Therapeutic Jurisprudence in the Coronial Jurisdiction', *Journal of Judicial Administration 25*: 134–147.

Rossmanith, Kate, Steven Tudor and Michael Proeve 2018, 'Courtroom Contrition: How Do Judges Know?', *Griffith Law Review 27*: 366–384.

Rossner, Meredith, 2019, 'Storytelling Rituals in Jury Deliberations', *Oñati Socio-Legal Series 9*: 747–770.

Rossner, Meredith, David Tait, Blake McKimmie and Rick Sarre 2017, 'The Dock on Trial: Courtroom Design and the Presumption of Innocence', *Journal of Law and Society 44*: 317–344.

Rossouw, Elna and Sebastiaan Rothmann 2020, 'Well-Being of Judges: A Review of Quantitative and Qualitative Studies', *South African Journal of Industrial Psychology* 46. 29 April. Retrieved 9 May 2020, from https://sajip.co.za/index.php/sajip/article/view/1759/2824.

Rowden, Emma and Anne Wallace 2019, 'Performing Expertise: The Design of Audiovisual Links and the Construction of the Remote Expert Witness in Court', *Social & Legal Studies 28*: 698–718.

Rowden, Emma, Anne Wallace and Jane Goodman-Delahunty 2010, 'Sentencing by Videolink: Up in the Air?', *Criminal Law Journal 34*: 363–384.

Royal Commission into Family Violence (Victoria) 2016, *Royal Commission into Family Violence: Summary and Recommendations*. Parliament Paper No 132 (2014–2016), Retrieved 9 May 2020, from http://rcfv.archive.royalcommission.vic.gov.au/Report-Recommendations.html.

Rush, Elizabeth, Jodi A. Quas and Bradley D. McAuliff 2013, 'Child Witnesses' Experiences of Distress in Criminal Court: Sources, Consequences, and Solutions'. In *Stress, Trauma, and Wellbeing in the Legal System*, eds. Monica K. Miller and Brian H. Bornstein, 89–121. New York: Oxford University Press.

Schrever, Carly, Carol Hulbert and Tania Sourdin 2019, 'The Psychological Impact of Judicial Work: Australia's First Empirical Research Measuring Judicial Stress and Wellbeing', *Journal of Judicial Administration 28*: 141–168.

Scott Bray, Rebecca, 2010, 'Death Scene Jurisprudence', *Griffith Law Review 19*: 567–592.

Sheehan, Rosemary, 2013, 'Introduction: Australia's Children's Courts—the Study and Its Context'. In *Australia's Children's Courts Today and Tomorrow*, eds. Rosemary Sheehan and Allan Borowski, 1–6. Dordrecht: Springer.

Simon, Dan, 2019, 'On Juror Decision Making: An Empathic Inquiry', *Annual Review of Law and Social Science 15*: 415–435.

Smith, Alisa and Sean Maddan 2011, *Three-Minute Justice: Haste and Waste in Florida's Misdemeanor Courts*. Report prepared by the National Association of Criminal Defense Lawyers, Retrieved 9 May 2020, from http://www.nacdl.org/flmisdemeanor/.

Smith, Alisa and Sean Maddan, eds. 2019, *The Lower Criminal Courts*. New York: Routledge.

Smith, Olivia, 2018, 'The Practicalities of English and Welsh Rape Trials: Observations and Avenues for Improvement', *Criminology & Criminal Justice 18*: 332–348.

Smith, Olivia and Olivia Skinner 2017, 'How Rape Myths Are Used and Challenged in Rape and Sexual Assault Trials', *Social & Legal Studies 26*: 441–466.

Solove, Daniel J., 1997, 'Postures of Judging: An Exploration of Judicial Decisionmaking', *Cardozo Studies in Law and Literature 9*: 173–222.

Stewart, Mary White and Steven M. Wood 2013, 'Civil Plaintiffs, Trauma, and Stress in the Legal System'. In *Stress, Trauma, and Wellbeing in the Legal System*, eds. Monica K. Miller and Brian H. Bornstein, 123–147. New York: Oxford University Press.

Supreme Court of New South Wales 2007, 'Court Attire Policy'. Policy issued by J. J. Spigeman, Retrieved 9 May 2020, from https://nswbar.asn.au/docs/webdocs/sc_attire10.pdf.

Tait, David, 2011, 'Glass Cages in the Dock?: Presenting the Defendant to the Jury', *Chicago-Kent Law Review 86*: 467–495.

Tait, David, 2018, 'Rituals and Spaces in Innovative Courts', *Griffith Law Review 27*: 233–253.

Tait, Gordon, Belinda Carpenter, Carol Quadrelli and Michael Barnes 2016, 'Decision-Making in a Death Investigation: Emotion, Families and the Coroner', *Journal of Law and Medicine 23*: 571–581.

Tata, Cyrus, 2007, 'Sentencing as Craftwork and the Binary Epistemologies of the Discretionary Decision Process', *Social & Legal Studies 16*: 425–447.

Tata, Cyrus, 2020, *Sentencing: A Social Process: Re-Thinking Research and Policy*. Cham: Palgrave Macmillan.

Tomkinson, Sue, 2018, 'Who Are You Afraid of and Why? Inside the Black Box of Refugee Tribunals', *Canadian Public Administration 61*: 184–204.

Toy-Cronin, Bridgette, 2015, 'Keeping up Appearances: Accessing New Zealand's Civil Courts as a Litigant in Person'. PhD Thesis, Faculty of Law, University of Otago. Retrieved 9 May 2020, from http://hdl.handle.net/10523/6003.

Toy-Cronin, Bridgette, 2019, 'Leaving Emotion Out: Litigants in Person and Emotion in New Zealand Civil Courts', *Oñati Socio-Legal Series 9*: 684–701.

Tutton, Jordan, Kathy Mack and Sharyn Roach Anleu 2018, 'Judicial Demeanor: Oral Argument in the High Court of Australia', *Justice System Journal 39*: 273–299.

Travers, Max, 2007, 'Sentencing in the Children's Court: An Ethnographic Perspective', *Youth Justice 7*: 21–35

Vaisman, Noa and Leticia Barrera 2020, 'On Judgment: Managing Emotions in Trials of Crimes Against Humanity in Argentina', *Social & Legal Studies 29*: 812-834.

van de Zandt, Pia, 1998, 'Heroines of Fortitude'. In *Balancing the Scales: Rape, Law Reform and Australian Culture*, ed. Patricia Easteal, 124–142. Annandale: Federation Press.

Victorian Law Reform Commission 2016, *The Role of Victims of Crime in the Criminal Trial Process*. 22 November. Report, Retrieved 9 May 2020, from https://www.lawreform.vic.gov.au/sites/default/files/VLRC_Victims%20Of%20Crime-Report-W_0.pdf.

Vincent, C., M. Young and A. Phillips 1994, 'Why Do People Sue Doctors? A Study of Patients and Relatives Taking Legal Action', *Lancet 343*: 1609–1613.

Wallace, Anne, Sharyn Roach Anleu and Kathy Mack 2017, 'Judicial Work and AV Use: Perceptions from Australian Courts', *Oñati Socio-Legal Series 7*: 691–716.

Wallace, Anne, Sharyn Roach Anleu and Kathy Mack 2019, 'Judicial Engagement and AV Links: Judicial Perceptions from Australian Courts', *International Journal of the Legal Profession 26*: 51–67.

Wandall, Rasmus H., 2010, 'Resisting Risk Assessment? Pre-Sentence Reports and Individualized Sentencing in Denmark', *Punishment & Society 12*: 329–347.

Ward, Jennifer, 2017, *Transforming Summary Justice: Modernisation in the Lower Criminal Courts*. Abingdon and New York: Routledge.

Warner, Kate and Julia Davis 2011, 'Using Jurors to Explore Public Attitudes to Sentencing', *British Journal of Criminology 52*: 93–112.

Warner, Kate, Julia Davis, Caroline Spiranovic, Helen Cockburn and Arie Freiberg 2016, 'Measuring Jurors' Views on Sentencing: Results from the Second Australian Jury Sentencing Study', *Punishment & Society 19*: 180–202

Weimann-Saks, Dana, Inbal Peleg-Koriat and Eran Halperin 2019, 'The Effect of Malleability Beliefs and Emotions on Legal Decision Making', *Justice System Journal 40*: 21–38.

Weisman, Richard, 2009, 'Being and Doing: The Judicial Use of Remorse to Construct Character and Community', *Social & Legal Studies 18*: 47–69.

Weisman, Richard, 2014, *Showing Remorse: Law and the Social Control of Emotion*. Farnham: Ashgate.

Weisz, Victoria, Sarah J. Beal and Twila Wingrove 2013, 'The Legal System Experiences of Children, Families, and Professionals Who Work with Them'. In *Stress, Trauma, and Wellbeing in the Legal System*, eds. Monica K. Miller and Brian H. Bornstein, 63–88. New York: Oxford University Press.

Wells, Gary L., Amina Memon and Steven D. Penrod 2006, 'Eyewitness Evidence: Improving Its Probative Value', *Psychological Science in the Public Interest 7*: 45–75.

Westaby, Chalen, 2010, '"Feeling Like a Sponge": The Emotional Labour Produced by Solicitors in Their Interactions with Clients Seeking Asylum', *International Journal of the Legal Profession 17*: 153–174.

Wettergren, Åsa, 2010, 'Managing Unlawful Feelings: The Emotional Regime of the Swedish Migration Board', *International Journal of Work Organisation and Emotion 3*: 400–419.

Wistrich, Andrew J., Jeffrey Rachlinski and Chris Guthrie 2015, 'Heart Versus Head: Do Judges Follow the Law of Follow Their Feelings?', *Texas Law Review 93*: 855–923.

Yazdani, Daniel, 2019, *The Habit of a Judge: A History of Court Dress in England and Wales, and Australia*. Clark, NJ: Lawbook Exchange.

Cases

Barmettler v Greer & Timms [2007] QCA 170. Available from http://www.austlii.edu.au/cgi-bin/viewdoc/au/cases/qld/QCA/2007/170.html.

BJS v R [2013] NSWCCA 123. Available from http://www.austlii.edu.au/cgi-bin/viewdoc/au/cases/nsw/NSWCCA/2013/123.html.

Hinz v Berry [1970] 2 QB 40.

Miller v Jackson [1977] QB 966. Available from https://www.bailii.org/ew/cases/EWCA/Civ/1977/6.html.

R v Dirani (No 6) [2018] NSWSC 891. Available from http://www.austlii.edu.au/cgi-bin/viewdoc/au/cases/nsw/NSWSC/2018/891.html.

R v Oliver [2002] EWCA Crim 2766. Available from https://www.bailii.org/ew/cases/EWCA/Crim/2002/2766.html.

Legislation

Evidence Act 1995 (NSW)

Family Court Act 1997 (WA)

Family Law Act 1975 (Cth)

Magistrates Court Act 1992 (SA)

Chapter 3

Judicial impartiality, emotion and empathy

Introduction

Impartiality is a foundational legal value that shapes the scope for and nature of emotion in judicial work. This chapter[1] addresses how judicial officers[2] frame and perform impartiality in the legal context where emotion experiences and need for emotion work are embedded, but formally disavowed. Impartiality is the touchstone for judicial officers' reflexive monitoring of the myriad emotions they experience. Their commitment to impartiality entails recognising, not denying, a place for emotion, often with attention to empathy. Judicial officers describe several conscious strategies for maintaining impartiality as an internal state and producing an external display which is generally unemotional, impersonal or even stone-faced (Bergman Blix and Wettergren 2018). They sometimes allow the appearance of a human face which can express or evoke some emotion. These strategies entail managing their own felt and displayed emotions as well as the feelings of other participants, most often in the courtroom. Judicial officers understand that, while empathy in judicial work can be considered a challenge to impartiality, it has an important, though carefully circumscribed, place in their work.

Chapters 3, 4 and 5 complement each other. Chapter 3 investigates how impartiality shapes judicial officers' understanding of and approach to emotion and emotion work. Chapter 4 examines the management of judicial

1 This chapter relies on some material previously published in Roach Anleu and Mack (2019).
2 In this book, the terms 'judicial officer' and 'judiciary' are used generically to refer to any member of the judiciary, regardless of court level or type. Within Australia, the term 'magistrate' refers to members of the judiciary who preside in the lower state and territory courts, except in the Northern Territory where magistrates were given the title 'judge' in 2016. Australian magistrates are paid judicial officers, with legal qualifications, and are appointed until a fixed retirement age. The term 'judge' indicates those who preside in the intermediate and higher state and territory courts and all national courts. Jurisdictions outside Australia may use other labels for their judiciary or may use these terms, but the words may not have the same meanings as in Australia.

officers' own emotion experiences and display, while Chapter 5 addresses the ways in which judicial officers manage others' emotions.

Impartiality

In the western legal tradition, being a good judge means being an impartial judge. Judicial impartiality has been vividly documented in the visual iconography of judges and judging and the architecture of courts (Mulcahy 2010; Resnik and Curtis 2011). It is embedded deep in the common law (Noonan 1989; Prest 1991). William Blackstone in his *Commentaries on the Laws of England* (1765) notes that judicial authority depends on a judiciary 'sworn to administer impartial justice' (1979: 361). In a leading High Court of Australia decision, former Justice Gaudron states: 'Impartiality and the appearance of impartiality are so fundamental to the judicial process that they are defining features of judicial power' (*Ebner v Official Trustee in Bankruptcy* (2000) 205 CLR 337 at 345). The institutional importance of impartiality is reflected in judicial attitudes. Overwhelmingly, Australian judicial officers rate impartiality and integrity/high ethical standards as essential to their daily work, according to the *National Survey of Australian Magistrates* and the *National Survey of Australian Judges* (Roach Anleu and Mack 2017).

Impartiality is a concept usually defined by what it is not: the absence of bias, personal preference or favouritism. Impartiality expresses the judicial obligation to be unbiased in relation to any party or issue and to be independent, especially of the government, in rendering a decision (Astor 2007; Council of Chief Justices of Australia and New Zealand 2017; Gleeson 1998). The conventional judicial role casts impartiality as requiring judicial practices to be without emotion. Emotion is assumed to be political, unstable, personal and irrational, the antithesis of the impartial exercise of judicial authority (Bandes and Blumenthal 2012).

'It is easy enough to state the broad indicia of impartiality in court—to be fair and even-handed, to be patient and attentive, and to avoid stepping into the arena or appearing to take sides' (Council of Chief Justices of Australia and New Zealand 2017: 5). However, impartiality, like emotion, is not a reified thing. Impartiality can be understood as a dynamic, relational concept, a goal and a process performed through listening to both sides, an essential practical and normative requirement of judging (Lucy 2005; Resnik and Curtis 2011; Touchie 2001). Impartiality must be displayed and performed, perceived and understood by others.

The centrality of impartiality parallels the dominance of impersonality in Max Weber's ideal type bureaucracy which expects officials to act '"*Sine ira et studio*", without hatred or passion, and hence without affection or enthusiasm' (1978: 225). This again is a negative definition: defining something by what is not present. The dominance of this formal impersonality has led to a 'view of modern organizational culture as rational and impersonal' (Albrow 1992: 317). As emotion and feelings are associated typically with personal and private relationships, they are thought to result in bias (positive and negative), inconsistent with disinterested, detached decision making (Dixon 2012a; McKenzie 2016; Wettergren 2010).

Several other concepts are associated with impartiality, such as neutrality, objectivity, independence, detachment, dispassion and disinterestedness (Jamieson 2019). These concepts also imply excision of emotion and depersonalised decision making. For example: 'objectivity is generally associated with impartiality, neutrality and an emphasis on the factual. It is not associated with emotional or personal accounts' (Jacobsson 2008: 47). While much has been written disentangling these various concepts, this book uses the term impartiality to describe the judicial requirement not to favour any party or claim and to make decisions based only on proven facts using legal reasoning. Rather than having a fixed or natural quality, impartiality can be characterised as a process, constructed and realised in practice. As an abstract category, impartiality must be 'accomplished and manifested in people's everyday practice' (Jacobsson 2008: 47).

Judicial impartiality in practice

Judicial officers must embody, perform and display impartial legal authority, often in circumstances of considerable emotion. Despite the many affirmations of impartiality as central to the judicial role, the meanings and performance of impartiality in everyday judicial work are rarely empirically investigated.

In this chapter, judicial experiences, attitudes and practices are investigated primarily through interviews conducted throughout Australia with judicial officers at all court levels, as well as data from the *National Court Observation Study*, the *National Survey of Australian Judges* and the *National Survey of Australian Magistrates*. Findings identify the ways judicial officers articulate, understand and perform impartiality, especially in the courtroom context where emotion invariably emerges. Three key overlapping themes emerge:

- reliance on the terms of the judicial oath itself;
- the concept of an open mind; and
- the need and capacity to put aside information, attitudes or emotion thought or felt to be inconsistent with achieving impartiality.

The metaphors of 'open mind' and 'put aside' in relation to maintaining impartiality each imply effort required to manage emotions. The 'open mind' suggests a proactive and positive obligation to delay judgment until the full range of legally permitted information has been presented, to avoid partial or premature decisions. In comparison, the metaphor to 'put aside' conveys a more reactive or cleansing process to remove elements deemed extrinsic to or incompatible with impartiality, such as pre-conceptions, personal preferences, political ideology, stereotypes and heuristics or other decision-making shortcuts (Harris and Sen 2019; Klein and Mitchell 2010; Rachlinski and Wistrich 2017). Both of these concepts appear to regard emotion as a thing that can be moved or removed and whose influence can be minimised at least in part through individual, internal processes.

Few judicial officers explicitly use the language of emotion or emotion management when discussing impartiality; nonetheless, insights about emotion are communicated via 'linguistic markers, the construction of sentences, the choice of words, or prosody' (Wettergren 2015: 123; also see Kleres 2011). Impartial judging, as described by the interviewees, aims to resist emotion or exclude it from the judicial process, if impartiality might be or appear to be at risk. This suggests a conception of emotion as volatile and unreliable, yet, as Chapter 4 demonstrates, judicial officers also proactively use emotion to accomplish their everyday work, though they may not frame their practices as emotion work. Perhaps surprisingly, few judicial officers reflect on the practical difficulty of achieving impartiality. At the same time, their recognition of a place for empathy in judging, and the boundaries, suggests the complexities inherent in judging, impartiality and emotion.

The judicial oath

When asked to define impartiality in lay terms, several judicial officers responded by referring to or quoting the judicial oath. One judicial officer states:

> I'm sure I've thought about this from time to time or I've had to give myself a good talking to but I, look, I think we all and I certainly do strive to do it, umm, you know it's what our oath of office is all about … (I 33)[3]

[3] This quote is from a judicial officer interviewed as part of the *Courts, the Judiciary and Social Change* project funded by an Australian Research Council (ARC) Discovery Project grant (DP 1096888). The interviews were conducted in 2012–2013. The data is indicated by the code 'I ##' in which the letter I identifies this as interview data and ## is the number assigned to the individual interviewee. Quotations are used verbatim and have not been edited to correct grammar or reduce infelicities of spoken language, but retain qualities of natural, everyday speech reflecting the narrative quality of the interviews. All identifying, or potentially identifying, details have been deleted. For more information on this phase of the research, see the Appendix.

The judicial oath of office provides for the administration of law: 'without fear or favour, affection or ill-will' (Campbell 1999: 146).[4] Three of the four injunctions—fear, affection and ill-will—suggest emotion or emotional capacities. Fear is typically considered to be an especially powerful emotion and is the topic of large amounts of research in psychology (Gray 1987; LeDoux 1995; Öhman and Mineka 2001; Phelps 2006; Riezler 1944). Because fear of unjustified removal may threaten impartiality, judicial independence, supported by security of tenure, is regarded as essential to legitimate judicial authority (Mack and Roach Anleu 2006). Affection is related to emotions typically involving personal and private relationships, including happiness and joy (Clark and Reis 1988; Dixon 2012a; McKenzie 2016). Such feelings can result in favouritism, or at least perceived favouritism, inconsistent with impartial decision making. Ill-will is associated with feelings of anger, hostility, rage, contempt, dislike, disgust and hatred (Belleau, Johnson and Bouchard 2007; Maroney 2012). Such strong negative emotions are often cast as incompatible with impartiality (Maroney 2012; McIntyre 2019; *Michael v Western Australia* [2007] WASCA 100).

Keeping an open mind

Some judicial officers articulate impartiality by referring to legal method. They stress their essential judicial function of applying law to facts and emphasise keeping an open mind while hearing all the evidence. This approach implicitly supports a characterisation of impartiality as a practice or process, rather than as a static or achieved mental state. One magistrate suggests:

> Umm, you're nobody's friend. You're not there to serve the police or the plaintiff. You're there to apply the law. That sounds simplistic. It's hard to—

[4] A justice of the High Court of Australia is required to take an oath in the following form pursuant to s 11 and sch 1 of the *High Court of Australia Act 1979* (Cth): 'I, [name], do swear that I will bear true allegiance to Her Majesty Queen Elizabeth the Second, Her Heirs and Successors according to law, that I will well and truly serve Her in the Office of Chief Justice [or Justice] of the High Court of Australia and that I will do right to all manner of people according to law without fear or favour, affection or ill-will. So Help me God!' Similarly, s 32 of the *Constitutional Reform Act 2005* (UK) and ss 2 and 4 of the *Promissory Oaths Act 1868* (UK) require a judge of the United Kingdom Supreme Court to take a judicial oath: 'I, _________, do swear by Almighty God that I will well and truly serve our Sovereign Lady Queen Elizabeth the Second in the office of ________, and I will do right to all manner of people after the laws and usages of this realm, without fear or favour, affection or ill will'. Instead of the Judeo-Christian oath, judicial officers of each court may make an affirmation in a slightly different form. We are grateful to Professor Åsa Wettergren for pointing out the oath declares loyalty to the monarchy while stressing impartiality.

INTERVIEWER: Is it difficult at times to do that?

Yes it is. Absolutely. It is very difficult … (I 26)

This magistrate describes impartiality colloquially as being 'nobody's friend', as part of the judicial commitment to serving the values of law and legal process and not any one party or participant. This delineation of the judicial role aligns with the adversarial model of adjudication which casts the judge as detached and passive in the face of arguments put by the opposing sides. However, this magistrate, along with some other interviewees, finds doing this 'very difficult'.

Being impartial and keeping an open mind can require emotion work. One judge refers to 'being self-aware', and practicing 'self-reflection'—a kind of auto-correction—as part of her experience of emotion and her outward display:

> Well, umm, you have to start with an open mind. So to start with an open mind you have to listen, umm, you have to, you know, look at and listen to everything that can properly be put before you and if you're not going to look at something you've got to explain why, umm, and umm, you have to be clear in your reasons for decision as to why you have gone one way or the other particularly, not so much on the law but particularly in factual findings where you're having to rely upon umm, well you're drawing conclusions umm as to whether you should accept the evidence of one person rather than another, that's very challenging to explain that, umm, carefully. Umm, something that I don't think is immediately obvious to, umm, the reader of a decision or somebody watching you do your job is self-awareness … of how you're responding to people in your process and to, if you're finding that the way a particular person is behaving makes you feel a little hostile or prickly about them, you know, what is that, what's that trigger, is it actually them or is it something else about you. So that self-reflection, umm, I think is helpful. … That's the essential aspect of impartiality is that you're focussed on your, your process of decision making and being self-aware in that of your, umm, umm, any inherent bias or emotional response or whatever it is. (I 37)

This comment underscores listening as a key component of an open mind especially as 'factual findings' can be 'very challenging to explain'. Perhaps this judge is implicitly aware that findings of fact entail judgment which can be perceived by others as lacking impartiality. She proposes that 'you have to be clear in your reasons for decision'. Giving reasons can be an important opportunity for the performance of impartiality, including the suppression of some emotions on the part of the judicial officer. Requiring a statement of reasons could avoid '[t]he danger of sentences based on an immediate emotional reaction to some particular feature of the offence' (Thomas 1963: 247). This could be especially important in lower courts, where sentencing decisions are usually given *ex tempore*, and involve interacting directly with the defendant (see Chapter 2). This judge identifies emotion as a trigger: feeling 'a little hostile or prickly', and such an 'emotional response' might be an indicator that a judge is not being impartial. She suggests that locating the source or trigger can facilitate regulating the emotion experience and expression.

Putting aside bias and emotion

Several judicial officers describe their understanding of impartial judicial method as setting aside biases and emotions. A judge, quoted above, elaborates on her approach to impartiality by continuing:

> You know you are to put out of your mind, when dealing with the case before you, any personal prejudices or beliefs or sympathies or hostilities you may have of a preconceived nature but just to decide the case on the factors and on the evidence as presented to you. (I 01)

She expressly operationalises the normative and practical requirements of the judicial oath as requiring a judicial officer to exclude emotion: 'sympathies or hostilities'. These feelings are implicitly characterised as internal, individual, personal and removable. She emphasises the importance of deciding on the evidence, thus invoking the formal judicial role of applying the law to the facts and making a legally valid decision.

In an example from the *National Court Observation Study*, the defendant applies for bail in circumstances where the default position is for the court to refuse bail. She refers to having support available to her if she is granted bail. The following excerpt from the court transcript[5] is an example of a judicial officer frankly acknowledging emotion:

[5] This data comes from the *National Court Observation Study* funded by an Australian Research Council (ARC) Linkage Project grant (LP 021306): *The Changing Role of the Magistrates Court*. Transcript excerpts of the proceedings observed have been given a consistent format rather than retaining the relevant court's local formatting. M indicates magistrate; DR indicates a defence representative; P indicates a prosecutor; D indicates defendant. In the excerpts quoted, names of all participants including judicial officers have been changed, and on occasion other details such as dates or location have been removed if they potentially identify a location or participant. As part of the anonymisation process, each individual magistrate was assigned a code number from 1 to 27, and each matter allocated a discrete number (from 1 to 1287). For more information on this phase of the research, see the Appendix.

M: You may have all of that but that's not working, I don't know why. What makes me so upset about you is that you look as though you're still fairly healthy, you've got a couple of folk who love you and want to try and help, and yet you can't battle this without getting charged again and this is the third time this year, plus you've got a couple of other times you've had. It's very serious stuff. … I understand that fighting these habits and drugs is a terrible nightmare for you and the family but I can't possibly, on what's been given to me today, grant bail. What I can do is remand you to another day. Now if you can speak with Miss Roberts about coming in, you can come in just about any day she chats to you about and put in [a bail] application but I would suggest to get a bit more strength [behind your application] …

(Magistrate 20, matter 723)

The language the magistrate uses conveys the emotion he experiences: 'makes me so upset', which seems to be magnified by the defendant looking 'fairly healthy' thus deviating from the (stereotypical) image of a drug addict and being surrounded by 'people who love you'. This may be an example of the judicial officer using emotion language to elicit in the defendant feelings of shame, embarrassment, guilt or remorse. The judicial officer may also be reminding the defendant of the positive aspects of her life—health, family support—to give her hope while displaying some empathy regarding her situation. However, concern for the defendant cannot prevail over the legal requirements in light of the facts presented—'on what's been given to me today'—including several charges of drug-related offending in a short time (within four months): 'the third time this year, plus … a couple of other times …'. This conclusion demonstrates the boundaries judicial officers draw between the legal decision and their experience of emotion. This magistrate expresses human sentiment, displays emotional engagement, but these do not displace the obligations of the judicial role to apply the law: 'I can't possibly … grant bail'.

A judge pinpoints practical steps to accomplish impartiality in the face of pre-existing attitudes which may be emotionally driven:

> It's the quality of being able to identify and overcome, umm, your biases and prejudices. … we all as judges come to umm a decision making with biases and prejudices but umm so long as you come willing to change your bias to recognise what it is and to change it or to make a decision despite it then you have that quality of impartiality. So far from denying the biases, it's best to identify them to yourself and by identifying them and putting them aside as best you can. I'm not suggesting it's easy or that we do it well always but that's what impartiality is, impartiality is identifying it and putting it aside. (I 23)

This judge enumerates the processes involved in achieving impartiality: first, recognise any bias or prejudice, and, second, 'change your bias' or make the decision 'despite it'. In addition, this judicial officer approaches impartiality as a phenomenon, an object, a thing, that can be moved and removed. Impartiality is also the capacity to 'overcome' biases and prejudices which has to be done 'as best you can', implying that it may not be possible to achieve completely: 'I'm not suggesting it's easy or that we do it well'. The quest for impartiality, for this judge, requires considerable and difficult emotion self-management (also see Bergman Blix and Wettergren 2018). Similarly, the US *Judicial Excellence* report identifies the importance of judicial self-awareness and self-control to neutralise emotion, where necessary to avoid risks of bias or apparent bias (Elek 2019; Elek, Rottman and Spacek Miller et al. 2017).

A slightly different approach is to put aside any emotion assessed as inconsistent with legal method and to focus on the judicial process of finding facts and applying the law:

> I think in terms of impartiality, I think it is picking up that case and looking at, looking at the facts that come before you and deciding it on nothing but the evidence that you have before you and not what the person looks like, is wearing, or whether their lawyer is good or bad, and I think often we would not be human if we didn't pre-judge people and make an assumption … It's about putting all of that to one side as well and no matter how dreadful or unpleasant their lawyer is or they are—it's about looking at the facts that you have before you and making a decision on the facts and as they apply to the law. … maybe it's different in the higher courts because you don't, you do more law than, we're not really doing a lot of law, we're doing really more fact finding and maybe you're doing more law and so you have the longer cases and maybe you don't experience it as much. I would be surprised if any magistrate didn't have to remind themselves because you get some so seriously unpleasant people and doing dreadful things that you've got to go stop. (I 03)

This magistrate views decision making as founded on objective facts and legally determined evidence and so excludes emotion and feeling from the process. If case details evoke or trigger emotions, these can and must be put aside. The magistrate also highlights feelings—negative and positive—that can emerge in interchanges with 'accused persons … and their lawyers'. She distinguishes lower from higher courts which 'do more law … we're [magistrates] doing really more fact finding'. This resonates with Abbott's (1981) concept of professional purification as higher courts deal with disputes that legal professionals have translated into legal argument and so removed emotion and human complexity. The dispute is transformed into one about law (Bourdieu 1987). In contrast, lower courts deal with cases where legal, social and human issues meld and there is less purification (Redden and Scarduzio 2018).

The judicial commitment to impartiality, especially when understood as detachment, is sometimes contrasted with empathy. Some judicial writers and scholars recognise empathy as an important element in judging, though within boundaries which shift.

Empathy and judging

Empathy is a significant theme in the literature on judges, judging and emotions (Bandes 1996, 2009, 2017; Colby 2012; Henderson 1987; West 2012; Wettergren and Bergman Blix 2016). Debates about the role of empathy in judicial work are often couched in relation to the foundational value of impartiality, with disagreement about whether empathy undermines or enables impartial judicial behaviour and decision making (Bergman Blix and Wettergren 2019).

While commentators and researchers recognise the difficulties of attempting a definitive description of empathy, calling it 'not a well defined notion' (Cuff, Brown and Taylor et al. 2016: 144) or 'a moving target' (Bandes 1996: 373), there is broad agreement on several components. Empathy is a capacity or 'emotional process' (Wettergren and Bergman Blix 2016: 23) rather than an emotion *per se*. It contains cognitive and affective components: 'empathy requires both the ability to share the emotional experience of the other person (affective component) and an understanding of the other person's experience (cognitive component)' (Decety and Jackson 2004: 73). Henderson describes empathy as entailing two 'ways of knowing': '(1) feeling the emotion of another; and (2) understanding the experience or situation of another, both affectively and cognitively, often achieved by imagining oneself to be in the position of the other' (1987: 1579). Lee articulates a somewhat wider conception of empathy as the 'capacity to better comprehend through both knowledge and feeling—another's perspective by trying to view the world from that person's position, rather than simply observing another's position from where we stand' (2014: 152). Wettergren and Bergman Blix comment that empathy 'may be partial and instrumental' and the 'inclination to be empathic varies depending on several factors' (2016: 23). Bandes makes a similar point that 'the conceptual utility of empathy varies widely depending on the context in which it is invoked, and the purposes for which it is employed' (1996: 373).

Despite, or perhaps because of, these definitional challenges, there are mixed views about the utility and legitimacy of empathy as part of judging. Claims for the role of empathy in judging range from characterising it as 'a requirement' (Colby 2012: 2015) or 'morally relevant' (Henderson 1987: 1652) to concerns that it compromises impartiality and judicial detachment (Abrams and Keren 2010; Bandes 2009; Lee 2014; Wettergren and Bergman Blix 2016).

One strong theme among proponents of empathy in judging is that being empathic can provide important information, often not retrievable or accessible via conventional, formalistic legal process (Bergman Blix 2019). West points out that empathy 'is a source of information. ... [it] gives the empathizer, including the judicial empathizer, access to a certain kind of knowledge—knowledge of the perspective of others' (2012: 248). Similarly, Henderson argues that empathy 'is a rich source of knowledge and approaches to legal problems—which are, ultimately, human problems' (1987: 1576). To access this additional knowledge or insight, empathy necessarily entails other judicial interactive qualities—patience, listening, communication, courtesy—which themselves entail emotional content and emotion management.

Some scholars go further and argue that empathy is something judges ought to do:

> [A] judge may—and I would argue should—feel empathy for all the litigants before her. It is her job to try to understand what is at stake for the parties. Once she has done so, she must make a legal determination about which side prevails (Bandes 2017: 185).

Here Bandes distinguishes the actual legal decision from a preceding process of empathy to generate understanding.

On the other hand, there are serious criticisms of empathy as part of judging. 'A common concern about the professional use of empathy in court is the [actual and perceived] potential for bias counteracting objectivity and impartiality' (Wettergren and Bergman Blix 2016: 20; also see Abrams and Keren 2010; Bandes 2009, 2016). West (2012) terms this the anti-empathic turn. Lee suggests that this criticism arises because 'the use of empathy has been mischaracterized as something that undermines the impartial and detached ideal of judging' (2014: 146). A major public controversy surrounding empathy in judging followed former US President Barak Obama's suggestion that the capacity for empathy would be a good quality for an appointee to the Supreme Court of the United States (Abrams 2010).

The perceived tension between empathy and impartiality may reflect concerns about selective empathy, where a judge experiences empathy for those who are in some way similar to the judge, and empathy is less available towards those who are different in some way (Bloom 2016).

> Without the use of empathy in judging, it is more likely that judges will gravitate, unconsciously or nearly automatically, toward the claims of parties more familiar to them and more similar to the way they perceive the world. ... In order to truly maintain objectivity in adjudication, the court must use a process of empathizing to fully consider the view of all parties who come before it (Lee 2014: 148).

Here Lee suggests that without empathy, judges may fail to be objective and unbiased (also see Massaro 1989).

Booth's (2012, 2014, 2016) research finds that empathy and neutrality can coexist. She uses the concepts of 'empathic responses' and 'active listening' to describe the ways judges manage victim participation in the courtroom.

> While the sentencing judges maintained the 'affective neutrality' required of their role, most also demonstrated a variety of empathic responses conveying respect, compassion and sensitivity to the family victims' ordeal in reading their [victim impact statements] aloud in the courtroom (Booth 2012: 226).

Empathy is multidimensional and can produce feelings of compassion, sympathy, sadness, upset, distress or concern (Batson 2011; Marsh 2012). Two qualities often related to empathy are sympathy and compassion. Although empathy and sympathy are sometimes used interchangeably, sympathy includes feeling sorry for someone and the situation they are in, usually with expectations of specific action associated with this feeling (Clark 1987). The concepts of compassion and empathy are closely intertwined, though compassion is typically associated with action. Empathy 'is really about perspective-taking' (Bandes 2017: 185) whereas compassion is 'the feeling that arises in witnessing another's suffering and that motivates a subsequent desire to help' (Goetz, Keltner and Simon-Thomas 2010: 351; also see Cuff, Brown and Taylor et al. 2016). Compassion, like sympathy, 'includes a call to action that is not an inherent component of empathy' (Bandes 2017: 185). As with empathy, there is considerable ambivalence about the role of compassion in judicial work: 'it is too capricious a force ever to be capable of steering the judge reliably toward the just' (Acorn 2004: 121).

The main conclusion from this literature is from Bandes who warns:

> against a tendency to uncritically embrace compassion, sympathy and empathy as soft, merciful and therefore a welcome antidote to the hardness of law … whether any particular emotion is beneficial to legal analysis depends on the context (2017: 189).

In the remainder of this chapter, this insight is explored by investigating the attitudes and practices of judicial officers in Australia towards empathy in their everyday work.

Empathy in judicial practice: empirical findings

Over half (56 percent) of judicial officers in Australia evaluate empathy as essential or very important in their everyday work (Roach Anleu and Mack 2017). However, there are some differences among different segments of the judiciary (see Figure 3.1).

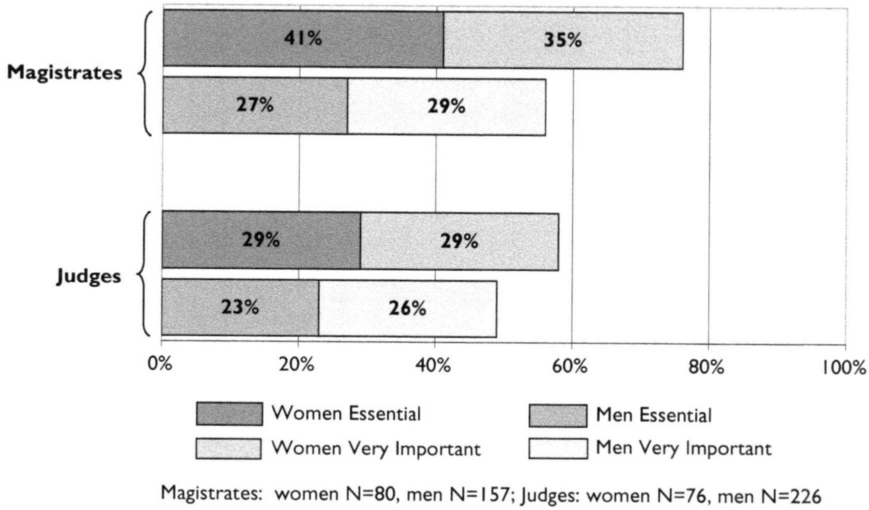

Figure 3.1 Magistrates' and judges' assessment of empathy by gender
Source: *National Survey of Australian Magistrates, National Survey of Australian Judges*

First, judicial officers in lower courts appear to value empathy somewhat more than their higher court counterparts. Nearly two-thirds of magistrates (63 percent) indicate that empathy is either essential or very important to their everyday work, compared with a bare majority of judges of the higher courts (51 percent). Second, women judicial officers rate empathy as more important than their male colleagues. Two-thirds of women regard empathy as essential or very important (67 percent) compared to just over one-half of men (52 percent). Women magistrates are the cohort containing the largest proportion who value empathy as essential (41 percent) or essential and very important (76 percent) (Roach Anleu and Mack 2017).

Compassion is valued slightly more by all segments of the judiciary with seven in ten magistrates and six in ten judges assessing this quality as essential or very important[6] (see Figure 3.2). Gender differences in attitudes toward compassion are similar to attitudes toward empathy.

[6] Note: The numbers of respondents are different in Figures 3.1 and 3.2 because not all respondents answered each question.

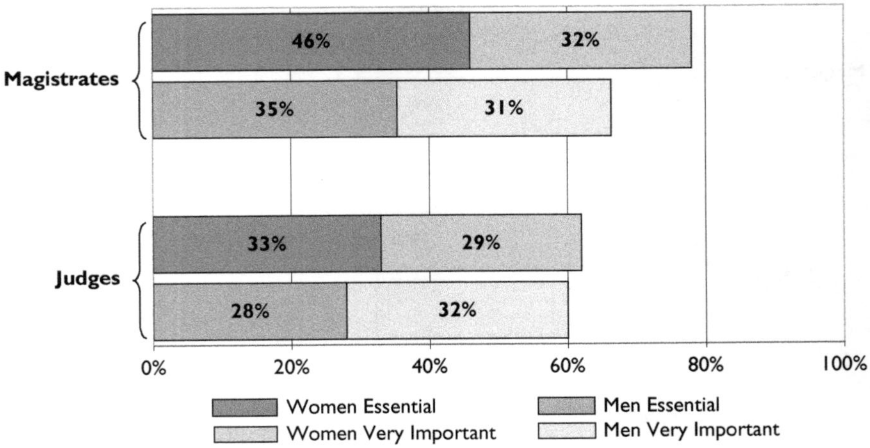

Figure 3.2 Magistrates' and judges' assessment of compassion by gender
Source: *National Survey of Australian Magistrates, National Survey of Australian Judges*

While surveys generate broad data on judicial attitudes, interviews provide deeper insight into the ways in which abstract notions of empathy and compassion shape everyday work in various judicial settings. Interestingly, none of the 38 judicial officers interviewed reject the ideas of compassion and empathy as having a role in their everyday work, and they report a range of experiences and interpretations. In addition, examples from the *National Court Observation Study* depict concrete instances of judicial practice in which empathy or compassion was communicated. Taken together, three main overlapping themes emerge from this data: the nature of empathy and impartiality, judicial tears, and the qualities of empathy and compassion.

Impartiality and empathy

Several interviewees describe their judicial practice as entailing impartiality and empathy, almost as complementary forces requiring careful and persistent monitoring of their boundaries. This magistrate describes empathy in the immediate situation of the courtroom as well as an aspect of the wider circumstances of the case and says:

> I think that anyone who says you've got to rule out compassion and you've got to rule out empathy is probably not being very honest. Umm, it is impossible not to feel distraught and distressed when you are

> sentencing someone for aggravated [driving without] due care, where they have killed their mate and there's no alcohol, no speeding, they've, you know. I did one just before Christmas last year and he'd just come off the road a little bit, any of us could have done it, country road. Just come off, over corrected, killed the brother and the sister, umm. No alcohol, he was the designated driver, he wasn't speeding, he wasn't going over the limit, umm, and a courtroom full of people. The police officer started crying when she read out the victim impact statements. Umm, court staff were crying. Umm, I had to keep signalling to the Sheriff's Officer for tissues because there were so many people crying and, look, I think you have to allow that, those feelings of compassion, emotion. I think you have to allow them to come through you, umm, you know, a little bit like letting the silt settle, I think you have to allow them to come through you because that's very normal, and then when you are, time to write your sentence or decide upon your sentence then you can move them to one side. I don't think you can start by saying I take out of it compassion, empathy. I don't think that's the right process. I think you have to let that all come through you and filter it and then find yourself at the right point where you're ready to deal with it. (I 31)

The magistrate is able to empathise with the defendant's situation as she recognises: 'any of us could have done it'. She also displays empathy for those affected by the deaths who were present in the courtroom by not intervening when 'there were so many people crying'. Her own sense that 'it is impossible not to feel distraught and distressed' is part of an assessment that these displays are 'very normal', and therefore allowable (within limits) and compatible with courtroom feeling rules. She further conveys permission for emotion display by the comment that she 'had to keep signalling to the Sheriff's Officer for tissues'.

This judicial officer articulates the boundaries of emotion, empathy and impartiality through the metaphor of 'letting the silt settle', evoking the notion of a natural, normal process. For this magistrate, the time to exercise impartial judicial authority—'the right point where you're ready to deal with it'—is after the 'silt settle[s]'. She suggests that 'those feelings of compassion, emotion' can be moved 'to one side' in order to make the legal determination that is the central judicial obligation: 'to … decide upon your sentence'. The place for empathy, for this judicial officer, is in the process preceding the decision, so that the judicial decision itself remains impartial (Bandes 2017). After she acknowledges and experiences emotion, these feelings are then 'filter[ed]', but it is not clear whether the empathy she experiences is excluded entirely, or sifted so that some traces remain and become part of the ultimate decision. This magistrate frames the process leading to an impartial decision cognitively—'I think'; 'I don't think'. She does not comment on the effort moving emotion to one side might involve but suggests a kind of natural or inevitable progression following the expression of emotion during the presentation of the victim impact statements.

An intermediate court judge mentions neither empathy nor impartiality, but implies both in the contrast between being 'too sympathetic' and the obligation to 'be detached':

> I mean, in a sense you have to resist the temptation to be overly sympathetic to people. You've got to bear in mind the difficulties that people who come before you have and how they've contributed to their actions or/and how your decision will affect them—in some cases you need to expressly bear that in mind but you've, as I said before, I think—you've got to be detached as well—you can't be too sympathetic because, first of all, it may affect the quality of your decision and secondly it would be likely to affect your capacity to keep doing the job. You just can't get, you've got to be detached. (I 04)

The idea of 'temptation' suggests responses which he must 'resist' because they are not the outcome of considered rational, impartial deliberation or judicial rigour, but derive from personal feelings. Although he rejects being 'overly sympathetic', this judge suggests scope for empathy, and even an obligation: 'you've got to bear in mind the difficulties that people who come before you have … and how your decision will affect them'. The later reference to detachment underscores its importance as an aspect of impartiality, without naming it. Interestingly, he suggests that detachment has two functions. First, it can be a bulwark against a decision influenced by sympathy, thereby supporting impartiality. Second, detachment can be a mechanism or strategy to draw and maintain boundaries between the professional judicial officer and the personal self.

Judicial tears

Interviewees also talk about how they display empathy, but are careful to do it in a way that does not detract from their judicial authority as an impartial decision maker. One particular concern is judicial tears (Dixon 2012b; Feenan 2015). A magistrate quoted above continues:

> I've seen male judges cry. Umm, matters, you know, that are particularly devastating. It's been tough sometimes as a prosecutor not to cry but I am particularly emotional. I cry for everything but, umm, I don't have any great urge to cry in court, and I think that's years of being in court that umm, and I think people have got to remember as a judicial officer you're sitting there, up higher, everybody sees what you do. Everyone sees if you're, you know, slouching or sitting or not taking notes. So you get used to that, umm, and I think really, and I hope I

> don't cry in court one day but I think it's important not to. Not to collapse into the same sort of emotional state and really just try and keep control where you can because everyone's looking to you to keep control, and I think it's really important that if you were to start crying or you were to feel a bit then I think people's confidence in your ability not to break down really would affect people. (I 31)

This excerpt suggests the limits of her display of empathy: 'I hope I don't cry in court one day but I think it's important not to'. She suggests that the display of a controlled, calm demeanour is essential for her judicial credibility and acknowledgement of her 'ability' to embody judicial authority. The display of calm, not collapsing into 'the same sort of emotional state', is also important for public confidence, especially as she is very conscious of her visibility: 'everyone sees what you do'. The magistrate also might be referring to a difference in the evaluation of female behaviour: a display of emotion through crying might corrode a woman's judicial authority and apparent impartiality more than it would her male colleagues. This could damage perceptions of her capacity to 'keep control' of herself and of the courtroom.

Another magistrate focusses on the institutional role and articulates his judicial role to represent the community and not to personally 'empathise and cry' with court users.

> There's often matters which brings tears to your eyes and I think that my role is that, my role isn't to sit there and empathise and cry with them, my role is to be that face of the judiciary, that face of the community, that face that is acknowledging that grief without participating in it as such but I also don't think there's anything too wrong in showing that you've been affected by what's happened. (I 12)

He acknowledges that judicial officers might be emotionally affected by what they see and hear in court, and he asserts that indicating 'that you've been affected by what's happened' does not necessarily detract from being 'the face of the judiciary', detached and distanced. In this way, the magistrate uses his emotions as a strategy to perform judicial authority and reinforce the value of impartiality. Showing some emotion through words or bodily display can enhance legitimacy, and he suggests a willingness to display emotion but does not go as far as 'participating in' the grief in an empathic way.

Compassion

The concept of compassion is often coupled with empathy. One writer suggests that compassion and empathy have similar qualities of shared humanity and sensitivity to the experiences and feelings of another but compassion may have an element of distance or even detachment towards the other who is regarded with compassion (Avgoustinos 2007). The US National Center for State Court's *Judicial Excellence* report finds that:

> [r]espected judges described judicial excellence as adhering to ethical and moral values requiring that people be treated with respect, honesty, and dignity and demonstrating empathy, compassion, and a concern for public welfare (Elek, Rottman and Spacek Miller et al. 2017: 1).

Sometimes judicial officers appear to imply empathy and compassion are entangled and interconnected:

> Umm, look, the everyday work is guided by the law in terms of what things I need to take into account, but in terms of looking at rehabilitation, in terms of looking at protection of the community, you have to bring compassion and empathy into that. It's not something that's seen in isolation—well I don't think it's seen in isolation. I think you do need to umm—we, the most, the people that come before the court are people who are not bad, there are reasons that they are caught up within the judicial system, and I think you have to have some empathy towards them. … it requires you to listen, I think, with an empathetic background and compassionate background. It may well mean that the decision is just the same as you would have been made otherwise. (I 12)

This judicial officer acknowledges the social causes of law-breaking, rather than perceiving 'the people that come before the court' as 'bad'. Her comments invoke the law—what 'I need to take into account'—when formulating the sentencing decision, which includes considerations of rehabilitation and community protection, requiring some degree of compassion and empathy. She describes the importance of displaying empathy through listening. The comment 'the decision is just the same' suggests that emotion—empathy and compassion—may be a legitimate part of the legal determination.

Another interviewee explains that her legal professional experience as a defence practitioner in criminal cases provides a basis for empathy and compassion:

> When you've worked for clients and you've had to hold their hand while they get told that they're going to gaol or go and visit them in the watch house afterwards and commiserate and tell their parents that they're going to gaol and all that sort of thing, you obviously have a much different, umm, attitude to, you know, feeling some sort of sympathy

> for them on a human level. Umm, and you know whilst it doesn't apply to everybody, I think that was probably something a little bit lacking maybe in people who hadn't had that experience. ... But you know you have to balance that with empathy and compassion for the victim as well, so you know you need to sort of keep reminding yourself that there's another side and umm, but yeah I think that plays a fairly major role with me. (I 34)

This judicial officer describes developing the capacity for empathy and sympathy during legal practice before appointment to the bench. These learned emotion skills and the ability to undertake emotion work are transferable to judicial office, yet not all judicial officers may have acquired them. Another judicial officer (I 31) explains that years in court, including as a prosecutor, assisted with learning how to control emotions in the courtroom. The interviewee above distinguishes the two legal contexts—criminal defence and the judiciary—by invoking the central judicial value of impartiality: 'You need to sort of keep reminding yourself that there's another side' (I 34). Other judicial officers describe such 'self-talk' (Goffman 1981: 79) or 'internal conversation' (Archer 2003: 9) between the judge as ordinary person and the judge *qua* judge as an important form of emotion work. Judicial officers imply that maintaining the boundaries between judicial impartiality and empathy is on-going, never complete and requires constant self-reminding. (The role of self-talk as an emotion management strategy is developed in Chapter 4.)

The capacity to empathise or display compassion is constrained by the core judicial obligation of impartiality—to consider all sides—as each may be deserving of empathy and compassion. The courtroom context also shapes the display of these capacities. A judicial officer's feelings of compassion may not be observable by others or may not be able to be displayed in any way. The following male magistrate highlights the difficulties of compassion and the importance of listening in a busy courtroom:

> I try and be compassionate but I don't think people see much evidence of it. I don't think when you're in a busy court and you're, you know, you might end up in a magistrates court and you've got, you know, maybe on a heavy day 115 matters in front of you and then you've got custodies coming in as well as that and on a quiet day you've got 75 matters and you've got to get through them. Umm, it sometimes might look to the observer out there that you're in a rush ... I don't think people can really judge whether you are being compassionate or sensitive or listening, umm, because of the environment that it's in but certainly those are very very important qualities that every judicial officer must have, particularly compassion and the ability to listen and what I mean by that just, umm, hear what's being said, take a note of it

> and be able to repeat it in a sentencing [re]mark, but to be able to listen to a person and umm, not just understand the words that they're saying but understand the meaning and how it's truly affecting them. Umm, and then taking that into consideration and dealing with the matter, umm. So I think listening, umm, so I think obviously compassion is very important, the ability to listen is extremely important because unless you listen and understand a person, you're not really in a position to exercise compassion and if you do exercise compassion, it might be on a wrong basis or a false basis or insufficient or too much or whatever. So I think listening is really important. (I 25)

The magistrate implies that it may not be possible to physically or outwardly display compassion because of the busyness of the courtroom, the volume of cases, and the multiple activities, even 'on a quiet day'. Nonetheless, repeating something in a sentencing remark that was said to the magistrate can convey compassion and demonstrate that the judicial officer has listened. This judicial officer maintains that listening is a pre-requisite to understanding a person, which in turn is necessary 'to exercise compassion'.

In their sentencing remarks, some judicial officers make statements that convey understanding of and concern about the defendant's situation, or display empathy and/or compassion. The language in the following two transcript excerpts from the *National Court Observation Study* suggests empathy when considering the amount of a potential fine. One magistrate states:

M: There's three children there, the wife's having a child in February and I load him up with a fine and it puts a greater impost on the family than he's already, through his own actions, created.

(Magistrate 5, matter 59)

A second magistrate makes a similar point:

M: $200 fine is an enormous amount of money.
D: It is, with four kids.
M: So I accept the explanation and I dismiss the charge under Section 10.
D: Thank you very much, Your Honour, I appreciate it very much. Thank you. Have a nice day.

(Magistrate 13, matter 330)

These magistrates are aware of the financial impact of fines on the defendants' families, especially those with children. To a well-paid judicial officer, the amounts of $200 or $400 may seem relatively small, yet both magistrates were able to display empathy while using legal language to announce the legal decision: 'I dismiss the charge under Section 10'. It appears that this interaction evoked feelings of appreciation and relief for the defendant.

Sentencing remarks are a location where judicial officers can legitimately express compassion as part of making the legal decision. This capacity to act on compassion arises because of the requirement, in law, to consider the defendant's character or background as part of any mitigation of sentence (see, for example, *Sentencing Act2017* (SA) s 11(1)(d); and *Sentencing Act 1991* (Vic) s 5(2)(g)). When applying these principles, courts have stated that compassion can have a place. For example, Spigelman CJ (with whom Wood CJ at Common Law and Kirby J agreed) remarks in *R v Fernando* [2002] NSWCCA 28 at [64] that:

> It is ... often the case that such considerations of deterrence are properly tempered by considerations of compassion which arise when the court is presented with information about the personal circumstances which have led an individual into a life of crime.

It is not only sentencing decisions and penalties that can be affected by judicial officers' empathy and compassion, particularly for a defendant in a criminal case. The following two examples from court transcripts show magistrates (unprompted by a researcher) using emotion language and translating empathy into their everyday work. In the first case, the magistrate's adjournment decision seems to be based on empathy for the defendant in custody rather than concern for the operations of the law firm:

M: I understand that, but I might have to give you a four week adjournment for a mention. How long has your firm been acting in this matter? At least the 28th of June.

DR: Yes.

M: That's a long time, if you have got a person remanded in custody, for your firm to take instructions as to what to do with that matter. In relation to him—I understand that you are an articled clerk, but why have you been told that him being illiterate affects you taking instructions?

DR: I believe that we had arranged for counsel to go out and see him and counsel actually cancelled on the morning of that appointment.

M: But, no, it's nothing to do with your client being able to read. I don't think it's proper to have someone in custody for that long. You can tell your principals that. I will give you a shorter adjournment. I will give you an adjournment of two weeks.

(Magistrate 26, matter 1100)

Here, the magistrate displays empathy via language used: 'I don't think it is proper to have someone in custody for that long'. He reprimands the defence representative and describes the law firm's actions and inaction as inappropriate, citing the situation of the client, rather than accepting the firm's preferences.

In another case, a different magistrate expresses concern about a homeless person and actively seeks a compassionate outcome:

M: Well I am concerned. Two things, (a) that the absence of an on-going capacity to supervise your client. I've read Dr Northeast's report while I've been listening to you. And secondly, the fact that he's homeless, and I mean, that is just terrible.
DR: Yes.
M: It sounds such a trite word, but it is. …
M: All right. Happy to go along with that Mr Evans?
D: I'm happy to do that.
M: OK. Well, we'll do the best we can deal with this matter in a more compassionate and helpful way than the blunt instrument of the criminal justice process.
D: OK.

(Magistrate 23, matter 989)

Interestingly, the magistrate uses the specific language of emotion: 'compassionate', and he suggests that it is a more fine-grained and helpful response than the 'blunt instrument' of the law, which by implication is not compassionate. This interchange suggests the magistrate is adopting a problem-solving approach rather than simply applying the law to the facts.

Conclusion

Accomplishing impartiality is a central goal of judicial officers in their everyday work. However, the commitment to be impartial does not completely determine individual judicial practice. As this chapter demonstrates, judicial officers approach or think about impartiality differently, and the ways they experience, display or suppress emotion when aspiring to be impartial vary.

Several overlapping themes in judicial attitudes and practices are discernible. In order to achieve or maintain impartiality, many judicial officers emphasise the judicial oath itself as part of their practice. Other emotion work goals include keeping an open mind and actively putting aside any basis for bias, including emotion, which they perceive may interfere, or appear to interfere, with impartiality. Emotion work undertaken by judicial officers entails reminding themselves of legal method and their formal judicial role—what they are there for—and its requirements: to decide cases on law and facts.

Empathy and compassion are sometimes bundled together or may be used interchangeably by judicial officers. Each can be regarded as valuable or even essential to judicial work. As one magistrate states:

> I think the day you stop being affected by people's stories then you shouldn't be doing the job basically. (I 34)

These qualities are necessarily relational, requiring awareness of others' situations, concerns and feelings. In the interactive context of a courtroom, these qualities rely on interpersonal skills of communication, especially listening. Empathy can be a way of demonstrating a judicial officer's humanity. By delineating the boundaries of empathy and compassion, whether as internal feelings or judicial display, judicial officers affirm their decisions as impartial, based on rational, reasoned deliberations. This delineation protects their legitimacy.

Despite variations in judicial attitude and practice, and the many kinds of emotion and situations in which they emerge, the conceptualisation of impartiality as dispassionate, detached and impersonal endures. The conventional judicial role that disavows emotion remains the touchstone for judicial officers' reflexive monitoring of the emotions they experience. At the same time, judicial officers themselves must define and refine the space, if any, for emotion as part of judging, including feelings that are accepted as a valid, valuable or even necessary part of judicial work, such as empathy and compassion. The scope or shape of impartiality is thereby constituted by judicial practice.

References

Abbott, Andrew, 1981, 'Status and Status Strain in the Professions', *American Journal of Sociology 86*: 819–835.

Abrams, Kathryn, 2010, 'Empathy and Experience in the Sotomayor Hearings', *Ohio Northern University Law Review 36*: 263–286.

Abrams, Kathryn and Hila Keren 2010, 'Who's Afraid of Law and the Emotions?', *Minnesota Law Review 94*: 1997–2074.

Acorn, Annalise E., 2004, *Compulsory Compassion: A Critique of Restorative Justice*. Vancouver: UBC Press.

Albrow, Martin, 1992, 'Sine Ira Et Studio—or Do Organizations Have Feelings?', *Organization Studies 13*: 313–329.

Archer, Margaret S., 2003, *Structure, Agency and the Internal Conversation*. Cambridge: Cambridge University Press.

Astor, Hilary, 2007, 'Mediator Neutrality: Making Sense of Theory and Practice', *Social & Legal Studies 16*: 221–239.

Avgoustinos, Costa, 2007, 'The Compassionate Judge', *Public Space: The Journal of Law and Social Justice 1*: 1–41.

Bandes, Susan A., 1996, 'Empathy, Narrative, and Victim Impact Statements', *University of Chicago Law Review 63*: 361–412.

Bandes, Susan A., 2009, 'Empathetic Judging and the Rule of Law', *Cardozo Law Review De Novo*: 133–148.

Bandes, Susan A., 2016, 'Remorse and Criminal Justice', *Emotion Review 8*: 14–19.

Bandes, Susan A., 2017, 'Compassion and the Rule of Law', *International Journal of Law in Context 13*: 184–196.

Bandes, Susan A. and Jeremy A. Blumenthal 2012, 'Emotion and the Law', *Annual Review of Law and Social Science 8*: 161–181.

Batson, C. Daniel, 2011, *Altruism in Humans*. Oxford and New York: Oxford University Press.

Belleau, Marie-Claire, Rebecca Johnson and Valérie Bouchard 2007, 'Faces of Judicial Anger: Answering the Call', *European Journal of Legal Studies 1*: 1–41.

Bergman Blix, Stina, 2019, 'Different Roads to Empathy: Stage Actors and Judges as Polar Cases', *Emotions and Society 1*: 163–180.

Bergman Blix, Stina and Åsa Wettergren 2018, *Professional Emotions in Court: A Sociological Perspective*. Abingdon: Routledge.

Bergman Blix, Stina and Åsa Wettergren 2019, 'The Emotional Interaction of Judicial Objectivity', *Oñati Socio-Legal Series 9*: 726–746.

Blackstone, William, 1979, *Commentaries on the Laws of England: A Facsimile of the First Edition of 1765-1769: Volume 3*. Chicago, IL and London: Chicago University Press.

Bloom, Paul, 2016, *Against Empathy: The Case for Rational Compassion*. New York: Ecco.

Booth, Tracey, 2012, '"Cooling out" Victims of Crime: Managing Victim Participation in the Sentencing Process in a Superior Sentencing Court', *Australian & New Zealand Journal of Criminology 45*: 214–230.

Booth, Tracey, 2014, 'The Restorative Capacities of Victim Impact Statements: Analysis of the Victim—Judge Communication Dyad in the Sentencing of Homicide Offenders', *Restorative Justice: An International Journal 2*: 302–326.

Booth, Tracey, 2016, *Accommodating Justice: Victim Impact Statements in the Sentencing Process*. Annandale: Federation Press.

Bourdieu, Pierre, 1987, 'The Force of Law: Toward a Sociology of the Juridical Field', *Hastings Law Journal 38*: 814–853.

Campbell, Enid, 1999, 'Oaths and Affirmations of Public Office', *Monash University Law Review 25*: 132–165.

Clark, Candace, 1987, 'Sympathy Biography and Sympathy Margin', *American Journal of Sociology 93*: 290–321.

Clark, Margaret S. and Harry T. Reis 1988, 'Interpersonal Processes in Close Relationships', *Annual Review of Psychology 39*: 609–672.

Colby, Thomas B., 2012, 'In Defense of Judicial Empathy', *Minnesota Law Review 96*: 1944–2015.

Council of Chief Justices of Australia and New Zealand 2017, *Guide to Judicial Conduct*. 3rd ed. Melbourne: Australasian Institute of Judicial Administration. Available from https://aija.org.au/publications-introduction/guidelines/guide-to-judicial-conduct/.

Cuff, Benjamin M. P., Sarah J. Brown, Laura Taylor and Douglas J. Howat 2016, 'Empathy: A Review of the Concept', *Emotion Review 8*: 144–153.

Decety, Jean and Philip L. Jackson 2004, 'The Functional Architecture of Human Empathy', *Behavioral and Cognitive Neuroscience Reviews 3*: 71–100.

Dixon, Thomas, 2012a, '"Emotion": The History of a Keyword in Crisis', *Emotion Review 4*: 338–344.

Dixon, Thomas, 2012b, 'The Tears of Mr Justice Willes', *Journal of Victorian Culture 17*: 1–23.

Elek, Jennifer K., 2019, 'Judicial Perspectives on Emotion, Emotion Management, and Judicial Excellence in the USA', *Oñati Socio-Legal Series 9*: 865–879.

Elek, Jennifer K., David B. Rottman, Shelley Spacek Miller and Lydia Hamblin 2017, *Elements of Judicial Excellence: A Framework to Support the Professional Development of State Trial Court Judges – Project Final Report*. Williamsburg, VA: National Center for State Courts.

Feenan, Dermot, 2015, 'Emotions at Work', *New Law Journal*. 26 November. Retrieved 9 May 2020, from https://www.newlawjournal.co.uk/content/emotions-work.

Gleeson, Murray, 1998, 'The Role of the Judge and Becoming a Judge', paper presented at the National Judicial Orientation Programme, Sydney, 16 August. Retrieved 9 May 2020, from https://www.hcourt.gov.au/assets/publications/speeches/former-justices/gleesoncj/cj_njop.htm.

Goetz, Jennifer L., Dacher Keltner and Emiliana Simon-Thomas 2010, 'Compassion: An Evolutionary Analysis and Empirical Review', *Psychological Bulletin 136*: 351–374.

Goffman, Erving, 1981, *Forms of Talk*. Philadelphia, PA: University of Philadelphia Press.

Gray, Jeffrey Alan, 1987, *The Psychology of Fear and Stress*. 2nd ed. Cambridge: Cambridge University Press.

Harris, Allison P. and Maya Sen 2019, 'Bias and Judging', *Annual Review of Political Science 22*: 241–259.

Henderson, Lynne N., 1987, 'Legality and Empathy', *Michigan Law Review 85*: 1574–1653.

Jacobsson, Katarina, 2008, '"We Can't Just Do It Any Which Way"—Objectivity Work among Swedish Prosecutors', *Qualitative Sociology Review 4*: 46–68.

Jamieson, Fiona, 2019, 'Judicial Independence: The Master Narrative in Sentencing Practice', *Criminology & Criminal Justice*. Published online 9 April. DOI: 10.1177/1748895819842940.

Klein, David E. and Gregory Mitchell, eds. 2010, *The Psychology of Judicial Decision Making*. Oxford and New York: Oxford University Press.

Kleres, Jochen, 2011, 'Emotions and Narrative Analysis: A Methodological Approach', *Journal for the Theory of Social Behaviour 41*: 182–202.

LeDoux, Joseph E., 1995, 'Emotion: Clues from the Brain', *Annual Review of Psychology 46*: 209–235.

Lee, Rebecca K., 2014, 'Judging Judges: Empathy and the Litmus Test for Impartiality', *University of Cincinnati Law Review 82*: 145–206.

Lucy, William, 2005, 'The Possibility of Impartiality', *Oxford Journal of Legal Studies 25*: 3–31.

Mack, Kathy and Sharyn Roach Anleu 2006, 'The Security of Tenure of Australian Magistrates', *Melbourne University Law Review 30*: 370–398.

Maroney, Terry A., 2012, 'Angry Judges', *Vanderbilt Law Review 65*: 1207–1284.

Marsh, Abigail A., 2012, 'Empathy and Compassion: A Cognitive Neuroscience Perspective'. In *Empathy: From Bench to Bedside*, ed. Jean Decety, 191–206. Cambridge, MA and London: MIT Press.

Massaro, Toni M., 1989, 'Empathy, Legal Storytelling, and the Rule of Law: New Words, Old Wounds?', *Michigan Law Review 87*: 2099–2127.

McIntyre, Joe, 2019, *The Judicial Function*. Singapore: Springer.

McKenzie, Jordan, 2016, *Deconstructing Happiness: Critical Sociology and the Good Life*. New York: Routledge.
Mulcahy, Linda, 2010, *Legal Architecture: Justice, Due Process and the Place of Law*. New York: Routledge.
Noonan, John T., Jr 1989, 'Judicial Impartiality and the Judiciary Act of 1789', *Nova Law Review 14*: 123–142.
Öhman, Arne and Susan Mineka 2001, 'Fears, Phobias, and Preparedness: Toward an Evolved Module of Fear and Fear Learning', *Psychological Review 108*: 483–522.
Phelps, Elizabeth A., 2006, 'Emotion and Cognition: Insights from Studies of the Human Amygdala', *Annual Review of Psychology 57*: 27–53.
Prest, Wilfrid, 1991, 'Judicial Corruption in Early Modern England', *Past and Present 133*: 67–95.
Rachlinski, Jeffrey J. and Andrew J. Wistrich 2017, 'Judging the Judiciary by the Numbers: Empirical Research on Judges', *Annual Review of Law and Social Science 13*: 203–229.
Redden, Shawna Malvini and Jennifer A. Scarduzio 2018, 'A Different Type of Dirty Work: Hidden Taint, Intersectionality, and Emotion Management in Bureaucratic Organizations', *Communication Monographs 85*: 224–244.
Resnik, Judith and Dennis E. Curtis 2011, *Representing Justice: Invention, Controversy, and Rights in City-States and Democratic Courtrooms*. New Haven, CT and London: Yale University Press.
Riezler, Kurt, 1944, 'The Social Psychology of Fear', *American Journal of Sociology 49*: 489–498.
Roach Anleu, Sharyn and Kathy Mack 2017, *Performing Judicial Authority in the Lower Courts*. London: Palgrave.
Roach Anleu, Sharyn and Kathy Mack 2019, 'Impartiality and Emotion in Everyday Judicial Practice'. In *Emotions in Late Modernity,* eds. Roger Patulny, Alberto Bellocchi, Rebecca E. Olson, Sukhmani Khorana, Jordan McKenzie and Michelle Peterie, 253–266. Abingdon and New York: Routledge.
Thomas, David A., 1963, 'Sentencing - the Case for Reasoned Decisions', *Criminal Law Review 10*: 243–253.
Touchie, John, 2001, 'On the Possibility of Impartiality in Decision-Making', *Macquarie Law Journal 1*: 21–61.
Weber, Max, 1978, *Economy and Society: An Outline of Interpretive Sociology*. Berkeley, CA: University of California Press.
West, Robin, 2012, 'The Anti-Empathetic Turn'. In *Passions and Emotions*, ed. James E. Fleming, 289–303. New York: New York University Press.
Wettergren, Åsa, 2010, 'Managing Unlawful Feelings: The Emotional Regime of the Swedish Migration Board', *International Journal of Work Organisation and Emotion 3*: 400–419.
Wettergren, Åsa, 2015, 'How Do We Know What They Feel?'. In *Methods of Exploring Emotions*, eds. Helena Flam and Jochem Kleres, 115–124. London: Routledge.
Wettergren, Åsa and Stina Bergman Blix 2016, 'Empathy and Objectivity in the Legal Procedure: The Case of Swedish Prosecutors', *Journal of Scandinavian Studies in Criminology and Crime Prevention 17*: 19–35.

Cases

Ebner v Official Trustee in Bankruptcy (2000) 205 CLR 337. Available from http://www.austlii.edu.au/cgi-bin/viewdoc/au/cases/cth/HCA/2000/63.html.
Michael v Western Australia [2007] WASCA 100. Available from http://www.austlii.edu.au/cgi-bin/viewdoc/au/cases/wa/WASCA/2007/100.html.
R v Fernando [2002] NSWCCA 28. Available from http://www.austlii.edu.au/cgi-bin/viewdoc/au/cases/nsw/NSWCCA/2002/28.html.

Legislation

Constitutional Reform Act 2005 (UK)
High Court of Australia Act 1979 (Cth)
Promissory Oaths Act 1868 (UK)
Sentencing Act 1991 (Vic)
Sentencing Act 2017 (SA)

Chapter 4

Judicial emotion

Experience, display and management

Introduction

Judicial officers experience, display and manage their own emotion in many facets of their everyday work, in the moment or recalled later. Drawing on interview and court observation data, this chapter examines what judicial officers[1] say and do about their feelings and emotion experiences and shows how emotion and emotion work are integral to the performance of judicial work.

Judicial emotion experience and display are affected by location, the mix of participants—professional or lay—their relations, interactions, values and goals as well as the norms and rituals operating in the locations in which judicial officers work. Strategies available for managing emotion are shaped by the spatial and temporal setting in which the emotion is generated. Locations are not just physical settings; they are also constituted by interpersonal and interprofessional relations which can shift. Management of judicial emotion can rely primarily on the judicial officer's own techniques and strategies, or entail input from others such as colleagues or court staff.

Because interaction is central to emotion, it is somewhat artificial to separate judicial officers' experiences and management of their own emotion from their perception and management of others' emotion, addressed in Chapter 5, and the management of emotion and display to maintain and communicate impartiality, the focus of Chapter 3. Various actions or decisions, for example an adjournment in court, can serve multiple purposes, including managing the judicial officer's own feelings and those of others.

1 In this book, the terms 'judicial officer' and 'judiciary' are used generically to refer to any member of the judiciary, regardless of court level or type. Within Australia, the term 'magistrate' refers to members of the judiciary who preside in the lower state and territory courts, except in the Northern Territory where magistrates were given the title 'judge' in 2016. Australian magistrates are paid judicial officers, with legal qualifications, and are appointed until a fixed retirement age. The term 'judge' indicates those who preside in the intermediate and higher state and territory courts and all national courts. Jurisdictions outside Australia may use other labels for their judiciary or may use these terms, but the words may not have the same meanings as in Australia.

The chapter examines four aspects of emotion: judicial officers' *experience* of emotion, which they may identify or describe as particular emotions; their outward *display* of emotion; the way(s) they *manage*, respond to, deal with or frame the emotion they experience; and the *organisational implications* of judicial emotion, sometimes managed by others within the court.

Judicial emotion experience

Judicial officers describe the physical experiences of emotion as well as the situations or moments in which emotion emerges. These experiences can arise from the facts of a case, the nature of the evidence, interactions with various participants, the challenge of making difficult decisions, particularly sentencing, or concern for the circumstances of others.

One emotion response to these dimensions of work may be stress. Survey research finds that one-third of Australian judicial officers agree that making decisions is very stressful, though one-third are neutral and one-third disagree. Most judicial officers consider their work emotionally draining, at least sometimes, though only one-third of judges do so, compared with almost half of magistrates (Roach Anleu and Mack 2017).

In interviews, judicial officers often follow descriptions of their emotions with immediate discussion of what they do or did to manage their feelings, especially where they interpret them as departing from the requirement to be detached, dispassionate and impartial. One judge (intermediate court) describes emotion in interaction and the physical or bodily signs he experienced and interprets as markers of anger:

> [When] I was first a judge I was determined not to lose my temper, to get short with people, and that's, and very quickly I learnt that patience was part of the job and something that I hadn't expected and so I would, I could feel my jaw setting to keep myself from saying anything and it actually radiated, I would get pains in the neck literally, umm, because of suppressing my need to say something and eventually I just thought 'well I've got to deal with this. I've got to get over this, I've got to stop worrying about it'. (I 23)[2]

[2] This quote is from a judicial officer interviewed as part of the *Courts, the Judiciary and Social Change* project funded by an Australian Research Council (ARC) Discovery Project grant (DP 1096888). The interviews were conducted in 2012–2013. The data is indicated by the code 'I ##' in which the letter I identifies this as interview data and ## is the number assigned to the individual interviewee. Quotations are used verbatim and have not been edited to correct grammar or reduce infelicities of spoken language, but retain qualities of natural, everyday speech reflecting the narrative quality of the interviews. All identifying, or potentially identifying, details have been deleted. For more information on this phase of the research, see the Appendix.

In this comment, the interviewee offers an aspirational image of the judge, requiring patient and calm interaction with others, especially counsel (which he 'hadn't expected'). He reclassifies a situation in which he could experience and display anger—'lose my temper', and 'get short with people'—to one demanding patience. He interprets physical sensations—'my jaw setting' and 'pains in the neck'—as consequences of attempts to manage his emotions and related conduct—'to keep myself from saying anything'. He describes this perceived disjuncture between the judicial ideal—patience as 'part of the job'—and the experience of anger and annoyance needing active suppression as a source of worry. Interestingly, this judicial officer frames his emotion management strategy as an outcome of thinking about it and 'self-talk' (Goffman 1981: 79): 'I just thought well I've got to deal with this'. This aligns with a classical view of emotion, that rational thought, a response, is able to manage emotion which requires control.

Another judicial officer describes her bodily responses to reading files in chambers before going into the courtroom:

> I can remember when I did my first Care List, I had no concept that parents did such atrocious things to their children in this day and age, and I can remember one of the first files I looked at, the house was just appalling, the fridge, I thought I was going to be sick, umm, and my, looking at it in chambers before I went on the bench, my blood pressure, anger, everything was just running rife … and so I had to pull myself back and walk on the bench and think you're not here to judge this person on your own standards, you're here to deal with it on the evidence and only the evidence. (I 19)

Material in the file triggered a mixture of physical reactions associated with emotion: 'blood pressure, anger, everything was just running rife'. The only emotion she explicitly names is anger, though several are implied: surprise, disgust, outrage, sadness, distress, as well as loyalty or feelings of allegiance or commitment to the judicial role and the justice system. Interestingly, this judicial officer reframes the way she assesses the emotion experience, shifting from a personal reaction to a professional, dispassionate stance relying on legal constructs, by tracking a change in physical and socio-legal location. She describes reading the file 'in chambers' (a relatively private, personal setting), highlighting the distressing contents in a fairly narrative manner. As she transitions from chambers to the bench (the public setting of the courtroom), the file material becomes part of 'the evidence' and relevant to the decision of whether a child should be removed. This is an example of the capacity of judges to recast their emotional responses and 'treat vivid stimuli as professionally relevant rather than personally provocative' (Maroney and Gross 2014: 146). This reflection also suggests the idea of a theatre performance: she had to 'walk on the bench' (the stage) and put her feelings into the personal realm (offstage) reminding herself of her judicial role (part) and responsibilities: 'you're not here to judge this person on your own standards'.

Courtroom and chambers evoke Goffman's distinction between 'front and back regions' (Goffman 1959: 123), or, using the theatre metaphor, front stage and back stage. '[F]ront regions where a particular performance is or may be in progress, and back regions where action occurs that is related to the performance but inconsistent with the appearance fostered by the performance' (Goffman 1959: 134). Front stage language and behaviour tend to be formal while back stage is more informal and relaxed, though separation between the two regions is usually not complete: 'activity in a concrete situation is always a compromise between the formal and informal styles' (Goffman 1959: 129). The courtroom setting fits easily into this distinction between front and back stage, and is often compared to a theatre in which the actors perform their pre-defined roles to an audience (Bergman Blix and Wettergren 2018; Carlen 1974, 1976; Mulcahy 2010). There are limits to this analogy. The outcomes of a court determination for defendants, litigants and others such as victims and family members are very different to those of a theatre performance (Carlen 1976; Mulcahy 2007). Carlen further suggests that 'despite the analytic appeal of the imagery of the theatre and the metaphor of the game for the sociological observer and analyst, for defendants, an appearance in the magistrates' courts is only a theatre insofar as it is a theatre of the absurd' (2010: xv).[3]

Two aspects of everyday work identified as particularly generating emotion, and likely to entail emotion work, are interactions with legal practitioners and certain kinds of decisions or types of cases (see Chapter 2).

Interaction with legal representatives

Judicial officers' interactions with legal representatives in court can generate felt emotions which may require management to maintain an emotionless demeanour. As one supreme court judge remarks:

> Like most judges, if I am confronted for several hours on end by a particularly incompetent barrister, I will get annoyed. Well that's an emotion. (I 08)

This judge's annoyance may, in part, reflect the relative rarity with which judges in the higher courts are faced with ill-prepared or less able legal

[3] There is also an in between, neither front nor back stage. Moran identifies judicial swearing in ceremonies as occurring in between, or having a 'liminal nature'. They are held in courtrooms, open to the public, but are outside 'ordinary business' (2018: 220; also see Roberts 2012).

representatives. Other research into interaction between the justices and counsel in the High Court of Australia finds that the rare judicial displays of emotion appear to be linked to frustration arising from the behaviour of counsel (Tutton, Mack and Roach Anleu 2018).

Another judicial officer is more expansive about emotion experiences arising out of interaction with legal representatives in court:

> I've had one exceptionally rude practitioner in … [large city] and I know others have had him be rude to them too but, you know, I mean others said to me you should have said this to him and you should have said that and I bit my tongue and I went home that night and cried my eyes out because he was so incredibly rude to me but I think what happens is you either probably let it out in the courtroom and could regret it or you internalise it but say nothing. (I 03)

This judicial officer describes an interprofessional interaction in court, on stage, that produces emotion experience in the moment, and afterwards at home, far off stage. She describes matching her feelings experienced in court, recalled later, with a congruent display where she 'cried my eyes out'. In contrast, to express her feelings of being upset and offended by the 'rude practitioner' in the moment, in the courtroom, would deviate from the emotionlessness expected of judicial officers. To 'let it out in the courtroom' would possibly result in regret, even professional embarrassment or shame, so she internalises the emotion while in court and 'say[s] nothing'.

Transcripts of matters from the *National Court Observation Study* also illustrate judicial frustration with legal practitioners.[4]

DR: Your Worship, we'd appreciate a six week adjournment. We haven't yet received the brief of evidence from the DPP [Director of Public Prosecutions].

M: How long?

DR: Six weeks.

[4] This data comes from the *National Court Observation Study* funded by an Australian Research Council (ARC) Linkage Project grant (LP 021306): *The Changing Role of the Magistrates Court*. Transcript excerpts of the proceedings observed have been given a consistent format rather than retaining the relevant court's local formatting. M indicates magistrate; DR indicates a defence representative; P indicates a prosecutor; D indicates defendant. In the excerpts quoted, names of all participants including judicial officers have been changed, and on occasion other details such as dates or location have been removed if they potentially identify a location or participant. As part of the anonymisation process, each individual magistrate was assigned a code number from 1 to 27, and each matter allocated a discrete number (from 1 to 1287). For more information on this phase of the research, see the Appendix.

M: We don't normally grant six weeks. Is there any reason why it has to be six weeks?

DR: Well I've been advised by our principal that they haven't yet received the brief of evidence from the DPP or been in contact with you.

M: Well do I take it that you're pleading not guilty?

DR: I certainly believe so, but until we get the brief of evidence.

M: We're not getting the brief of evidence until we know what you're going to do. I'll put it down for case management, Ms McQueen and Ms Brown.

P: Yes, your Worship.

M: And we'll get a bit of control Miss, I'm not having it run by [the law firm], it will be run by the court. All right, the matter is adjourned for case management and Mr Tim Vaughn is to appear, Ms Brown, on that day.

(Magistrate 5, matter 6)

Perhaps the magistrate is displaying further anger or reinforcing his frustration and annoyance by using a diminutive form of address, 'Miss', and not repeating her family name. This gives the interchange the air of reprimand, perhaps paternalism, and likely shapes the emotional environment. A succinct statement of judicial annoyance and frustration directed at a member of the legal profession is the following:

M: Mr Vassiliou [defence representative], I have no idea what you think the process in this court is. I asked you if it was ready to proceed. You want to plead and now you tell me you are not ready to proceed.

(Magistrate 3, matter 688)

These magistrates' emotion, inferred from the language used and the content of the comments, is a response to the difficulties caused by delay resulting from unprepared legal representatives, and perhaps the prosecution failing to supply required information. A wasted court appearance and a lengthy adjournment delays the ultimate resolution of the charges. The matter has to be rescheduled to another already busy day, with repeat handling by the court staff, the prosecution, and inconvenience, at a minimum, to others involved in the case, as well as possible distress to the defendant and any witnesses or victims. In both matters, the magistrates imply experiencing frustration with the apparent unfamiliarity with or deviation from the court's processes: 'We don't normally grant six weeks', 'I have no idea what you think the process in this court is'. There is a suggestion, in the first example, that the magistrate's annoyance arises from the law firm sending an inexperienced lawyer rather than the more senior person responsible for the case. In the second example, it appears that another inexperienced practitioner incorrectly indicated that a plea would be entered, when this was not the case. However, in both instances the lawyers and their clients may have perceived this interchange as judicial bullying and lacking appreciation for the pressures legal representatives face.

An intermediate court judge explains that 'counsel being rude' does not affect him, but counsel 'bullying witnesses' 'does fuss me'. This view may anticipate the anxiety, fear or embarrassment a witness might feel following such bullying or that their evidence may be less clear or persuasive:

> I don't really mind. I don't really mind counsel being rude and inappropriate towards me, I don't, it doesn't fuss me unduly but it does fuss me, increasingly I find, when counsel are bullying witnesses. I mean it's frustrating hearing it, silly and ill-prepared arguments, that's frustrating, leave aside witnesses. It's frustrating people not doing their job properly and people charging, umm, clients. (I 23)

For this judge, lack of preparation by legal practitioners, 'silly and ill-prepared arguments' and 'people not doing their job properly' are additional sources of frustration, perhaps feeling this more intensely as it is less common in the court where this judge sits, compared with the lower courts. Although all courts face lawyers with poor quality legal skills at times, inexperienced or unprepared legal representatives are much more frequent in lower courts, in part due to large caseload pressures on legal practitioners and tight legal aid funding (Flynn and Hodgson 2017; Roach Anleu and Mack 2017).

Kinds of decisions

Judicial officers report experiencing emotion when making particular kinds of decisions, especially sentencing, and most especially imposing sentences of imprisonment (Jamieson 2019). One magistrate describes emotion in the moment of sentencing and identifies physical markers without identifying discrete emotions, perhaps implying a general feeling:

> I used to go through quite a physical response to sending people to gaol. … it really made me feel physically ill. (I 09)[5]

Another judicial officer in an intermediate court specifically mentions emotion and describes the bodily or physical manifestation of emotion:

[5] In 2018–2019 only 12 percent of defendants sentenced by magistrates had custodial sentences imposed (Australian Bureau of Statistics 2020) (also see Chapter 2).

> Like sometimes when I'm going to do a sentence, especially a long sentence of imprisonment, I feel really nervous, really nervous. I feel almost sick. (I 35)

Having to 'impose long prison sentences' can entail a complex emotional state and various feelings that do not sit comfortably together:

> It can be deeply distressing to have to impose long prison sentences on people who you know have had a background which is not always advantageous and, you know, there but for the grace of God go I principle applies, but nonetheless for reasons of public policy which may or may not be arguable, you have to impose often, not often but sometimes, quite long sentences and it's—I always find it stressful to do that, and as soon as I stop finding it stressful, I'll give it away I think because you have to, it forces you to think about it and if you feel angry about behaviour you have to try and set that aside and the process of doing all that is tiring so you can end up at the end of a Friday pretty ready for a drink which many judges do to excess. (I 21)

The stressful nature of sentencing 'forces you [the judge] to think about it', rather than automatically generating a sentence in a routine or entirely detached way. This judge finds the distress engendered by sentencing as a positive reminder of humanity and reinforces a conception of decision making as deliberative, not robotic.[6] Indeed, however 'tiring' this process may be for this judge, experiencing these distressing feelings is essential to proper and legitimate judging. He says he will 'give it away' once it is no longer stressful. This comment suggests that the emotions and feelings he describes as stress also have positive functions—forcing thought and reflexivity—in contrast to the view of such emotion and stress as entirely negative.

Part of the stress of sentencing may reflect tension between two potentially conflicting emotions, as this judge indicates. He acknowledges that he may 'feel angry about behaviour' and he 'must set that aside', and he also implies empathy: 'there but for the grace of God go I principle applies'.

6 There is growing attention to the potential role of artificial intelligence (AI) in decision making, including judicial decision making, especially sentencing (Tata 2020). AI relies on computer systems that use complex algorithms to manipulate a large amount of data, sometimes termed big data, to generate outcomes, traditionally requiring human intelligence and deliberation. Proposals to shift decision making from judicial officers to machine intelligence is controversial. Proponents laud increased accuracy and reduction of bias, while opponents stress the dehumanisation of decision making and point out that increased accuracy and lack of bias are not guaranteed with the shift to AI (Sourdin 2018; Zalnieriute and Bell 2020).

Experiencing and reconciling these two emotions in order to craft a legally appropriate sentence generates further emotion identified as 'deeply distressing'.

A magistrate reflects on the challenges of a difficult sentencing decision:

> But with a particular case where you have done a really difficult sentencing exercise and you are still thinking 'well I did that and did I mention all these things I should have said in my decision that need to be [there] in case there's an appeal' and all that sort of stuff, you are so bound up with it and by the time you get to the end of it you're exhausted. It's really not a question of yeah, you're overwrought emotionally because you've just sent someone to gaol for so long and you've done all sorts of things about probations and paroles and whatever, but it's the, it's the mental and physical exhaustion that you get at the same moment which makes it harder to cope with it. But you know that goes by the next day and you're just doing another case. So you move on. (I 28)

This interviewee frames her reflection on a difficult sentencing decision as cognitive 'thinking', feeling 'overwrought emotionally' and possibly satisfaction and pride, on completing a difficult task: 'well, I did that'. The process is experienced as 'mental and physical exhaustion', perhaps reflecting feeling uncertain or anxious about the possibility of error 'in case there's an appeal'. Nonetheless, a magistrate cannot afford to dwell on anxieties or difficulties in a particular case, or on satisfaction: 'you know that goes by the next day', as there are so many more people and cases and decisions to be dealt with every day.

Occasionally, judicial officers rely on specific emotion language in their descriptions of sentencing. An intermediate court judge uses emotion descriptors—'sad', 'upset', 'emotion', 'anxiety', 'anxious'—to convey his ambivalent feelings about a young man who has apparently made some progress at rehabilitation 'having to go to gaol':

> I feel sad and upset about this young man having to go to gaol where there is a chance that his good work at rehabilitating himself will be reversed and he will be exposed to bad influences. I feel upset about that but there's a limit to which—I recognise that and then there's a question of whether I think, well, that will regulate what I do—it doesn't. I think, yes well, that's interesting, I'm noticing that, well, I, and the emotion also is what I want to do is release him and then another emotion would be anxiety because of the tension involved in this process. So—and I can often tell if I'm tense or anxious, there's some decision that I'm grappling with that, I'm wanting to go one way but for some reason I'm not sure and that tension and anxiety usually surfaces or does

> surface in the early stages when I've come off the bench and before I've done the work. I've just come off the bench now. I've heard a drug case where the fellow's pleaded guilty and he's got 19 kilograms of methamphetamine or something. It carries a maximum of life, it carries a standard non parole period of 15 years so I come off feeling a little anxious about well where do I fit this in. (I 27)

This judge describes feelings of 'tension and anxiety' as a marker of the difficulty of the 'decision that I'm grappling with', expressing fear that if the young man does receive a prison sentence 'there is a chance that his good work at rehabilitating himself will be reversed'. He also recognises the limits of feeling 'sad and upset' in terms of his judicial role and indicates that will not 'regulate what I do'. However, feelings of emotional tension and ambivalence remain—on the one side, the sadness of a gaol sentence, and, on the other, the serious nature of the drug crime (Burkitt 2018).

It is not only imposing sentence that generates strong emotion. In the example below, a magistrate expressly indicates feelings about the difficult circumstances and background of an applicant for bail:

M: I have that feeling that you're a fairly straight forward and honest person and doesn't have a lot of natural cunning in your system.

D: I've never stolen or anything like that or prostituted myself. I realise that I have backed myself into a corner now and that I have to do something about my (indistinct), I don't want to be taken away from my son, he's my whole world. I'd have to send him to a place (indistinct) we lost the house and I just don't know how that would affect me. I don't have any family in Victoria. They all live in Tasmania, which is interstate. Even if I had to come back to the court and see (indistinct) me your (indistinct) or anything like that I wouldn't be fussed.

M: Miss Jones, you're probably one of the saddest cases I've come across for a long time. You are a person who has got a real problem that can't seem to make up your mind, you've got to do something about it.

D: I know now I have.

(Magistrate 20, matter 723)

The circumstances the defendant outlines are difficult, and the magistrate describes the defendant and her situation as 'one of the saddest cases I've come across'. Her apparent candour and emotional pleas about her son and family seem to confirm the magistrate's 'feeling' that she does not have 'a lot of natural cunning'.

Another judicial officer sets out the emotion she experiences when reflecting on the feelings of a 'person who's coming to court', and particularly a defendant waiting for a jury verdict:

—and then I stop and I, and I almost literally say this to myself, not out loud you'll be pleased to know—I say, 'God, if I'm feeling like this, how is that person who's coming to court feeling?' You know, I'm going to stand up and walk off that bench and go and have a coffee and that's how I balance, you know, no matter how I might feel, the sun will come up tomorrow for me so, you know, and I think another example of that, and we all, I think nearly all of us experience this as counsel and as a judge, that the longest time in your life is between the time when you know that there is a jury verdict and the time they deliver that verdict, and as counsel I've always felt sick, not, it doesn't even matter whether I could predict the verdict 99 percent, umm. I have just, that's, I've always felt ill, umm and as a judge I still feel the same way and then I also adopt what I've been doing for a long time, of looking at the dock and thinking, 'oh my God, I don't even know how you can stand up, I feel so sick'. (I 35)

This judicial officer compares her feeling 'ill' and 'so sick' when anticipating a decision she must make, to the emotions of a person awaiting a court decision. These must be greater in magnitude, intensity and more difficult to manage than her own feelings, however intense. She conveys empathy through her awareness that she will be able to return to her daily personal and professional life after the decision, but the person before the court may not be able to do so.

Many of the examples of judicial emotion experience discussed above entail emotion display in various forms, as do some examples in Chapter 3, and all are intertwined with emotion management strategies. The next section highlights the meaning and functions of judicial display of emotion or emotion-related conduct, before discussing judicial emotion self-management strategies.

Judicial emotion display

Judicial work is deeply engaged with emotion, but the emotion norms or feeling rules applicable to the judicial role, especially in the courtroom, demand and prohibit certain emotion displays. Judicial demeanour is an important aspect of communication with different audiences: legal representatives, the prosecution, the defendant, litigants and the public more widely.

Impartiality must be conveyed through the judicial officer's activities, statements, and display or demeanour. The conventional model of judicial conduct assumes a detached judicial demeanour without visible emotion, a display of emotionlessness. For example, the *Commentary on the Bangalore Principles of Judicial Conduct* states: 'A judge's demeanour is crucial to maintaining his or her impartiality because it is what others see' (United

Nations Office on Drugs and Crime 2007: 141; also see American Bar Association 2011: Rule 2.8). This can be understood as requiring a certain display which may include suppression of an inconsistent emotion experience, either the feeling itself or the display.

Judicial understanding and performance of the link between impartiality and a demeanour that does not display feeling is demonstrated in findings from the *National Court Observation Study*. Based on observations of non-trial criminal matters, magistrates displayed a routine, business-like, impersonal demeanour in 74 percent of the 2323 coded interactions in court (Mack and Roach Anleu 2010; Roach Anleu and Mack 2017).

Judicial officers might display emotions such as compassion or even anger strategically or spontaneously. Such displays will shape the emotion and emotion display of other court participants. They may help to perform the judicial role, including 'the cultural work of performing professional authority' (Craciun 2016: 365). Indeed, '[e]mpathy, calm, composure, and control are all part of the affective-relational tools' that judicial officers might rely on 'to identify, understand, and solve problems' (Craciun 2018: 982, 990; also see Bergman Blix 2019). Alternatively, displays of anger or impatience may detract from trust and legitimacy.

Neutral display and dispassion

Several judicial officers describe strong determination to display an emotionally neutral demeanour especially when a situation of intense emotion emerges: 'You've got to check yourself, you've got to try to keep your voice down, try not to get angry. Avoid those sorts of emotions' (I 22). A female magistrate identifies the challenge of:

> not having things show on your face and all that—it's very exhausting to do that. I mean, look, there's been times where I've teared up in court, you know when you're hearing a victim's story or whatever, you know, I think we've all had those moments umm but umm, you know, or I've had to stand down and go, you know, that was full on—umm, yeah, I think it's more, you know, you have the intense ones, I think it's the build-up which I find just talking to my colleagues and, you know, knowing myself, it's the build-up which is the tricky— (I 16)

This magistrate is concerned to maintain a neutral display 'not having things show on your face' and especially to avoid the emotion display of tears in court (see Chapter 3) in response to an 'intense' experience such as 'hearing a victim's story'.

In another example, a judicial officer recounts experiencing intense emotion in the moment, in which she utilises her physical movement to display the calmness and neutral demeanour needed for others in the courtroom:

> Horrible, horrible case. The courtroom was packed full of other victims and family members. This man's behaviour had wrenched this family apart because parents didn't believe children, 'Uncle Charlie wouldn't do that', you know, that kind of thing, umm, anyway. As she [the victim reading out her victim impact statement to the court] was speaking, I was really quite affected by it and, but there was no way I could stop her in her flow and this was so important that people were weeping in the courtroom and it was, you know, just did the, put my hands flat on the bench and just maintained, was just as still and calm as I could be and umm when she finished I then adjourned. I said I think we need a break before we go on. It was very powerful, thank you, but I think we need a break now. And then everyone was able to go 'Oh God'. So they're just strategies I suppose, different people will do different things. (I 37)

Despite feeling 'affected', this judicial officer describes her display as putting her 'hands flat on the bench' which aided her remaining 'as still and calm and I could' in front of people who were 'weeping in the courtroom'. In this instance, the bench became a 'workaday prop' and part of her unemotional or neutral display for a short period of time (Hochschild 1983: 42).

A female magistrate comments on the importance of demeanour to the judicial role:

> You tend to keep a fairly non-emotional façade for yourself and even things that might be churning up inside you, you don't let them get in the way of what you're doing'. (I 28)

This judicial officer describes strong emotion experiences but goes on to invoke the importance of the emotionless demeanour by using the term 'non-emotional façade' recognising the disjuncture between actual feelings and judicial demeanour. She suggests that the display of certain (especially negative) emotions—feelings of distaste, discomfort, annoyance—could be disruptive, even dangerous, as the display of emotion may be perceived by others as compromising judicial impartiality. Accomplishing a non-emotional façade may become more difficult to the extent that the feelings experienced 'that might be churning up inside you' depart from the expected outward display of emotionlessness.

Of course, what judicial officers intend as a calm or dispassionate demeanour may not necessarily be perceived as such by court users. An impassive or impersonal manner may be experienced as cold, aloof, uncaring, or uninterested in the concerns or feelings of those appearing before the court.

Deep and surface acting

Maintaining the required neutral emotion display, and avoiding an inappropriate display, can entail deep acting 'to block or weaken a feeling we wish we did not have' (Hochschild 1983: 43) or surface acting to maintain the desired display, regardless of internal feelings. Deep acting involves 'trying to feel what we sense we ought to feel or want to feel' (Hochschild 1983: 43) in a particular situation. Sometimes this requires generating a feeling we wish to have, other times it entails suppressing a feeling. In contrast, 'in surface acting we deceive others about what we really feel, but we do not deceive ourselves' (Hochschild 1983: 33). A judicial officer's calm and patient demeanour (façade) may not align with internal feelings of frustration, anger, happiness or pride. Some researchers suggest that surface acting is connected to higher levels of stress, unlike deep acting (Grandey 2003; Hoffmann 2016). Occupational status, employees' control over work tasks and autonomy in decision making have been shown to minimise the strain that emotional labour can cause (Grandey and Gabriel 2015; Wharton 2009).

A magistrate mentions that a colleague 'taught me deliberate calm', that is:

> actively thinking of remaining calm and keeping like—you know, your breathing and you know you've got this outer exterior of the Buddha—and you just, but inside there's all the stuff going on so you're just trying to keep it kind of calm. (I 16)

This is a very clear description of deep acting, in which the magistrate attempts to generate within herself the feeling of calmness which she wishes to display. This magistrate controls her breathing, as a way to mimic or achieve the physical components of the desired emotion, a strategy also mentioned by judges in US research (Elek 2019).

Similarly, a male (intermediate court) judge stresses the importance of 'calmness, an ability to be calm in times of emotion in court' (I 20). This comment suggests deep acting; not just the judicial display of calm as an outward demeanour, but the 'ability to be calm' in a situation where there is external 'emotion in court'. This indicates the judicial officer actively seeks to resist the emotional pull of what is happening in court, and to block the formation of such emotion within himself. In contrast, a male magistrate depicts a process more akin to surface acting:

> If you focus on the law then you should be able to manage your emotions but not everybody is like that. You can't remain unaffected by something that's just so distasteful or uncomfortable. Umm, you can only present that poker-faced appearance that perhaps persuades both parties that you're independent. (I 26)

This magistrate suggests reframing a situation in which he is experiencing emotion arising from 'something … distasteful or uncomfortable' to generate a shift to something constructed as emotion-free: 'the law'. However, he finds this is insufficient to actually change internal feelings: 'you can't remain unaffected', so must engage in surface acting to 'present' the desired emotionless display: the 'poker-faced appearance' (also see Bergman Blix and Wettergren 2018).

Judicial emotion and judicial authority

The display of certain judicial behaviour, use of particular words, facial movements and tone of voice, can convey specific emotions and assist judicial officers to perform authority:

> Well I'm not sure that we do have to neuter ourselves not to express emotion. … look I think we do express emotions but in a more restrained way. There are times when I've described child pornography as disgusting and abhorrent, you know, now that's quite emotional stuff and I think about that and I think, am I being, am I being beyond the pale emotional or, I mean I don't like to go too far because I think that does betray an emotion which can overcome the dispassionate imposition of sentence which is important—but we do, we talk about, I mean I've talked about the tragic background of people, of appalling home life, that kind of stuff, so I think we can put emotion in there and we can say, you know, I'm delighted that you've turned the corner and so on. I mean I had some, I had some, a couple who had been quite significant drug dealers … I gave her the opportunity to go to a drug rehab, she passed with flying colours, she, her boyfriend later joined her there, they've done very well, … and I was able to be happy with them for that—now I don't think I laughed and clapped and, you know, it wasn't that kind of emotion but I was, I think in the words that I used I was able to express a degree of restrained emotion I suppose is the way I'd put it. I think, you know, you're not human if you can't express some emotion but it has to be restrained so that it is objectively adequate but not excessive and doesn't, doesn't, or doesn't give a suggestion of interfering with the dispassionate setting of an appropriate sentence. (I 11)

This male judge (supreme court) suggests he intersperses his work with displays of several kinds of felt emotion. He is aware of and perhaps emotionally moved by the 'tragic background' and 'appalling home life' of those appearing in court, which he contrasts with the opportunity to express feelings of pride and satisfaction ('I'm delighted that you've turned a corner'). He describes some crimes using the language of emotion:

'disgusting and abhorrent' in sentencing remarks. He also comments on an occasion of sharing emotion: 'I was able to be happy with them'.

This judge's conduct and understanding of emotion reflects Goodrum's conclusion that 'emotion represents a key mechanism for connecting legal cases to personal biographies' (2013: 259). This display of emotion demonstrates human facets of the judge as more than the embodiment of impersonal, inhuman, dispassionate law: 'you're not human if you can't express some emotion'. Underpinning this comment is a demarcation of the limits of the amount and quality of emotion that can and should be displayed: 'we do express emotions, but in a more restrained way'. He reiterates that the expression of emotion 'has to be restrained'. The measure of 'too far' is when 'an emotion … overcome[s] the dispassionate imposition of sentence'. This demonstrates an awareness of feeling rules that operate in this context, and that he, himself, has to recognise their boundaries, then regulate his emotion display to comply with the norms.

Display of emotion can be didactic, a tool or mode of communication to various participants in court as part of dealing with an issue:

> So I know another colleague of mine was sitting in … [a specialist mental health court] and she got quite upset when this person was suicidal and, you know, openly showed that, was quite embarrassed about that, and I said to her that I think for the first time he actually saw, what he has experienced, impacted upon someone that would be probably more significant than years and years of psychotherapy in terms of seeing that he'd been heard and seen. So although you don't want to be breaking down in a court, I don't think there's anything wrong in showing that you have been affected by what's being said. (I 12)

In the circumstances described, the judicial officer openly showing that she was 'quite upset' in response to a defendant may have had a didactic effect by communicating to the defendant his worth as a person and the distress his experiences or statements cause others, even the judicial officer. Interestingly, the interviewee indicates that the colleague 'was quite embarrassed' about displaying her emotions. It is not clear whether the embarrassment occurred in the moment in court, or later when recounting the incident. The interviewee accepts that a visible emotion display can be an appropriate response to convey being 'affected by what's being said'. Moreover, it is not possible to know how the judicial officer's visible display of being upset affected the person in court. Even so, this magistrate articulates boundaries between appropriate emotion display and 'breaking down in a court', which may jeopardise the judicial obligation of impartiality.

Emotion display can demonstrate concern or empathy in coronial as well as criminal cases:

> Yeah, umm, but I think sometimes it doesn't hurt. Like with the inquests because it's a different type of procedure too, umm, you know the family seeing you obviously a little bit affected by what's happened to them and/or their family member, it's probably a little bit comforting or they, you know, feel like you actually are engaging with what's going on. Umm, and same with defendants, I think you know, if they can see that you actually do have some concern for them, umm, then, then, you know, I hope that has some sort of positive impact on them but umm, but yeah, it's not, I mean I haven't, I haven't sort of found it incredibly difficult. (I 34)

This suggests a moment, a point of intersection, where the judicial officer and family of the deceased in an inquest appear to share an emotion, or where showing concern for a defendant in a criminal case may have a 'positive impact' (Goodrum 2013; Karstedt 2016).

Underpinning these judicial attitudes to their emotion experiences and display, and the need to manage them, is the commitment to impartiality. These situationally required or permitted emotion displays, whether of an emotionless demeanour or a specific emotion, demand a judicial officer engage in considerable emotion work, especially if inward feelings do not align with the expected outward display. The next section discusses the practical strategies judicial officers use to manage their own emotional experiences and display.

Judicial emotion self-management

Maroney and Gross propose that 'good judges should seek not to eliminate emotion entirely, but rather to manage emotion skilfully in light of the diverse professional challenges they face' (2014: 143). This view is evident in the descriptions judicial officers in Australia give of the ways they manage or regulate their own feelings and is similar to the views expressed by some US judicial officers. The *Judicial Excellence* report synthesises the insights generated from respected judges about practical ways to improve judicial practice and court craft including emotional self-awareness and control:

> Good judges, for example, should be aware of the emotions they are experiencing and how those emotions may be expressed in ways that affect public perceptions of the judge (for example, judicial demeanor or temperament) and court. Good judges should be able to anticipate how they may feel or react in certain situations. Doing so allows them to establish a plan to effectively manage anticipated emotions. Judges

> commented extensively on the importance of emotion management skills in maintaining impartiality and the perception of impartiality in the courtroom (Elek, Rottman and Spacek Miller et al. 2017: 19, footnote omitted).

The demand for and availability of emotion management strategies depend on factors such as: the attitudes of the judicial officer regarding appropriate emotion expression and display in a particular situation or moment; events, including actions and behaviours of others, the significance of which depend on the interrelationships; and the situational norms or feeling rules regarding the experience and display of emotion. Location, time and the presence or absence of others all play a role. Emotion management can take place in the moment, on the bench, or can entail temporal and spatial change and involve interaction with others in the courthouse or beyond.

This section takes a close look at the strategies judicial officers adopt as part of their 'emotional *self*-control' (Thoits 1996: 85, emphasis in original). Strategies judicial officers describe include self-talk, adjournment, debriefing with colleagues or family members and friends, and humour. These are similar to strategies for maintaining impartiality described in Chapter 3, and to ways of managing the emotions of others discussed in Chapter 5.

Self-talk

Several judicial officers provide examples of 'self-talk' (Goffman 1981: 79) or 'dialogical reflexivity' (Burkitt 2012: 462) as part of their emotion management strategies or tools. This entails conscious, internal conversations with themselves that serve as reminders about the nature of the situation, their formal role (and that of others), and the appropriate or required feeling rules. One judicial officer states:

> You have to be conscious of guarding against your own emotional reaction, umm, and sometimes things like, you know, the consciously saying to yourself, being aware of your own emotional reaction, umm, and you have to be the calming one in the situation. (I 32)

This comment points to the effort and work involved in managing her own emotion and highlights her role as judicial officer. The emotion work in her self-talk involves being self-aware of the experience and outward display of emotion and practicing reflexivity regarding her role, a kind of auto-correction. This internal self-talk is a conversation between the judge as ordinary person and the judge *qua* judge.

Other examples of this strategy are contained in comments about emotion experience and display quoted above. For example, a judge remarks: 'I almost literally say this to myself, not out loud you'll be pleased to know—I say, "God if I'm feeling like this how is that person who's coming to court feeling?"' (I 35). Her management of her own emotions involves a dialogue with herself that is not visible or audible to others, enabling her to assess and manage her feelings by comparing them to the much more intense feelings she predicts the person appearing before her must be experiencing.

Adjournment

When in court, judicial officers can adjourn the proceedings as a strategy to manage their own emotions (and those of others, as discussed in Chapter 5) and leave the bench for a period of time (that they determine), go into chambers or leave the court building entirely (also see Elek 2019; Leben 2019). As one female magistrate comments:

> I know sometimes you can feel sometimes the anger or something coming up and you just have to go OK this is the time to get off the bench and just walk around for five minutes because of what's been said or the manner in which something's been said and I think most colleagues are aware of those issues. (I 12)

The feeling that she identifies is 'anger', an emotion often associated with loss of self-control and bound by gendered norms about its display and management (Sorial 2019). This female judicial officer does not invoke a gendered portrayal of anger management by saying 'most colleagues are aware of those issues'. As the proportion of women in the magistracy was 38 percent in 2012 (when the interview was undertaken) (Australasian Institute of Judicial Administration 2012), 'most colleagues' includes men and women. Indeed, a male intermediate court judge offers a similar comment about adjournment as a widely used strategy for managing judicial anger:

> Well you have to be very careful. If you ever feel angry on the bench you have to adjourn and come back, that's my rule and a lot of other people have that rule. If you feel angry about something you've just got to let that dissipate and come back and approach it without that feeling affecting you. (I 21)

This is also an approach described by US judges in the *Judicial Excellence* report: 'taking recesses when needed to regain self-composure' (Elek 2019: 874).

Adjournment is an example of situational modification: changing the situation in order to control emotional expression (Maroney and Gross 2014). This also allows physical change and bodily movement to 'just walk around' and time 'to let that dissipate'. Interestingly, both judicial officers explicitly name 'anger' as the emotion requiring management by adjournment, as one explains: 'If you ever feel angry on the bench you have to adjourn' (I 21). This implicitly recognises the force of feeling rules 'you have to', and the comment 'that's my rule and a lot of other people have that rule' suggests it is shared and not idiosyncratic. These interviewees regard it as inappropriate for the judicial officer to express anger in court; letting the feeling of anger 'dissipate' must occur back stage. Given organisational constraints—busy court lists, presence of other participants—adjournment must be used sparingly, and reserved for certain kinds of emotions or situations, and perhaps only when other strategies, for example self-talk, have not been successful.

Another judicial officer reflexively depicts a more general emotional state, or wider array of emotions—'upset or frustrated or angry or … overborne'—that she manages usually by an adjournment:

> Well if I feel that I'm in a position where I'm not handling things well, umm, I will, whether it's because I'm upset or frustrated or angry or whether I feel a bit overborne, umm, then I will usually adjourn—and I mean the wonderful thing is you're in control of the court. Poor counsel and parties and witnesses don't have that, umm, the luxury that judges do so, again, self-awareness, if you think gee I'm beginning to speak really harshly or inappropriately or gee wish I hadn't said that thing I just said, I will, I will say look I think now might be a good time for us to have a morning tea break so I'll adjourn for 15 or 20 minutes and then I'll come out and rant and rave and have my cup of tea and go back in calm. (I 37)

Each of these judicial officers suggests that the adjournment time is relatively short: 'five minutes' (I 12); 'adjourn and come back' (I 21) suggests immediacy. A longer 15 or 20 minutes is embedded in a morning tea break, so will not likely be perceived as an unusually or inappropriately long time out of court.

Vastly different emotion management strategies are available to the judicial officer than to others in court: 'I will usually adjourn … poor counsel and parties and witnesses don't have that' (I 37). This emphasises the value of changing physical space and location as an emotion management strategy. The capacity to transition out of court and into an ordinary setting is not shared by others appearing before the court. Adjournment or leaving the bench during or at the end of a court session can provide more than just a break, or opportunity for an emotional reset; it can create an opportunity to debrief with others in the court work group.

Debrief

The process of debriefing off-stage and in chambers can require emotional labour on the part of others: associates, judicial officers and court staff (Lively 2000, 2002). The judicial officer quoted above (I 37), who comes out of court to 'rant and rave', anticipates a new audience that will observe her display of emotion, perhaps share her emotions and offer a chance to debrief and off-load feelings. The transition to a different setting is a move to a location where a judicial officer might expect to receive emotion work from others, who also might have been present in the emotionally dense courtroom. She continues:

> Yeah, associates and colleagues, yeah. Associates get the immediate brunt, umm, and often I'll talk through a difficult sentence with, with [name of colleague] for example. I'll say 'oh, how did you feel when she said such and such and didn't, wasn't that dreadful or you know I felt so angry when I heard this and I had to put that aside'. So umm, the associates are involved in a fair bit of debriefing which is one of the reasons we, you know, we tend to choose them pretty carefully, umm. Yes we want bright intelligent people but we also want very discreet people with personal qualities of our ability to communicate well with them and to, to trust, because you do, it is a little window into the mind, umm, and my experience on this court has been that my colleagues are very generous with their time and I, and I am generous with my colleagues so that if, umm, a judge comes into me and says 'have you got a couple of minutes, I've just had this horrible sentence'. Well, you know, you sit them down and you close the door and it might be five minutes or it might an hour and a half that you're talking. (I 37)

This judicial officer highlights the importance of trust in relation to debriefing as emotion management. A risk with debriefing is that a communication not meant for a wider audience may be inadvertently shared. The idea of 'discreet people' suggests that they will not share this information and the emotion content with others, especially outside the court work group. The comment 'my colleagues are very generous with their time and I … am generous with my colleagues' suggests '[r]eciprocal emotion management [which] refers to the interpersonal management of others' emotions (for the benefit of that other) done with the experience of or expectation of reciprocity' (Lively 2000: 34). The comment also suggests that the time frame for this emotion work is open-ended and unspecified.

An intermediate court judge suggests reciprocal emotion management and considerable emotion work within the concept of 'camaraderie' and highlights the importance of physical workplace design for enabling emotion work:

> This I think is a fabulous court, there's terrific camaraderie amongst the judges, umm, a real sense that we're all in it together, an amazing sense of, sort of, umm, institutional loyalty, a sense that we're much, the courts are bigger and more important thing than us as individuals and so a real sense of helping people who might be struggling, not only for them but to make sure the court, umm, is doing the best it can for people generally, so the architecture of the building is helpful for that because we congregate and you know we have to, we're forced to come into contact with each other whereas in a more traditional court building, with long corridors and closed doors, people may not see a colleague all day whereas we're sort of physically thrown into contact and people are very supportive, so your judges will walk in and out of each other's rooms and say, 'I hear you're doing a tough trial, how're you going?'. I find that much more supportive than I did at the Bar because here, they're your colleagues all the time, at the Bar, they're your colleagues one day but they're your competitor the next. (I 15)

This comment implies background emotions: 'a real sense that we're all in it together', 'institutional loyalty' and a commitment to 'make sure the court … is doing the best it can' (Barbalet 1998, 2011; Flower 2018). It also suggests sharing emotions: 'I hear you're doing a tough trial, how're you going?'. This sharing can flourish among judicial officers as they are not adversaries as is the case with barristers. Part of this camaraderie can involve the use of joking and humour to manage judicial emotions.

Humour

Several judicial officers describe their use of humour as a way of managing their own emotions. Judicial humour can have a safety valve or relief function (Kuipers 2009). Judicial officers use humour to manage their own feelings of impatience, frustration, anger, especially vis-à-vis the professional participants. (Use of humour for managing others' emotion is discussed in Chapter 5.) This humour, expressed outside the courtroom and away from other court users, who may generate the need for the relief, can also entail reciprocal emotion management as the next two comments illustrate:

> Umm, but I would say most of that, that kind of de-stressing is really an exchange and of, just a, you know sometimes it helps to laugh about things afterwards. I don't want that to sound, well you can't laugh about some things because they're terrible but some of the things that cause the most stress are things that involve counsel being bombastic or over the top and, or misbehaving in some way and those kinds of things. (I 38)

> Well I think having a good sense of humour helps (laugh). Having good colleagues is really good so you know that's the sort of letting off steam. I mean people, I'm pretty gregarious, people will come in here, I will go and talk to other people and you know you can just let off steam—you know I saw—what about this—you know I had this person in front of me today you know, driving me mad, you know, so there's that. Look sometimes there's a group of us who will go out and have a walk. (I 06)

The notions of 'exchange', 'good colleagues' and 'just let off steam' all suggest reciprocity in seeking and providing emotion work.

Another judicial officer outlines emotionally dense areas of work and the use of humour both in court and out of court as a way of coping:

> I've been involved in some fairly stressful areas of law like child sex abuse prosecutions and for extended periods of time and you know coroner's work and you do tend to deal with umm, with that, the content sometimes with black humour so that you know, as a coping mechanism, … Umm, yeah I probably tend more towards the using humour than away from it—but I think it's important and I—it shows that you are human to everybody else and that you've got a bit of a sense of humour and that you're not inflexible and umm, but you know I think it sort of does help you cope a little bit too. (I 34)

Judicial jokes and laughter can take the form of humour sometimes characterised as 'black humour' or 'gallows humour', that is, 'humor which arises in connection with a precarious or dangerous situation' (Obrdlik 1942: 709). Such humour can function as a resource to overcome difficult conditions or emotions and has been observed among barristers (Gunby and Carline 2020), prison staff and inmates (Laursen 2017), fire fighters (Moran and Massam 1997) and hospital medical staff (Coser 1960; Smith and Kleinman 1989). As Goffman notes: 'a "back region" or "back stage"' is a location where things suppressed on the front stage such as emotions and certain kinds of humour may occur (Goffman 1959: 112).

There are limits on what is perceived to be acceptable humour. One judicial officer draws clear boundaries between back stage—a 'safe environment' with colleagues—and front stage—'outside' that environment—in court:

> There are plenty of times when you can have the black humour and say things in a safe environment to your colleagues, that you know, sound grossly insensitive, but it's just a way of off-loading stuff you'd never say outside and you'd be mortified if it was repeated outside because it doesn't reflect your true feelings but it's just a way. (I 15)

These comments demonstrate the use of certain kinds of humour to manage emotions, with a strong recognition of the different feeling rules or emotion regimes operating on stage and off stage, in court and out of court (Reddy 2001, 2009; Wettergren 2010). Black humour is not available as an emotion management strategy in court (Roach Anleu, Mack and Tutton 2014; Roach Anleu and Milner Davis 2018) and should only be deployed out of court among peers—often judicial officers—or others who can be trusted, such as associates. As a judicial officer quoted above said: 'I make jokes around the building about taking pills peculiar to the counsel you're irritated about ...' (I 23). The humour described in this comment is used out of court 'around the building' rather than in court, because its content relates to a particular lawyer who may appear in court, or be familiar to other members of the legal profession. If used in court or outside a private, back stage location, attempted humour might be perceived as expressing bias.

Emotion management can also extend beyond chambers, judicial colleagues and court staff to family and personal lives, sometimes involving debriefing, or managing emotion to maintain a strong demarcation between judicial work and personal life, especially family.

Work-family boundaries

Some judicial officers refer to the transition between work and home and their capacity to switch off, especially regarding thoughts and the emotional dimensions of their job:

> There are always those matters that get to you and no matter how much you'd like to think you can switch off, you do worry about them. There wouldn't be a judge on this court I don't think that's not had a sleepless night over a case or a matter that they've had to deal with. I think we've all had that.[7] Umm, and that inevitably impacts on your home life. (I 36)

Some judicial officers describe debriefing with family, though this is coupled with a strong commitment to protecting family members from the some of the most demanding emotional dimensions of everyday judicial work. One intermediate court judge whose husband had a legal career says:

> We talk legal issues quite a bit, umm, because it's still, it's a passion for him as well as for me, umm, and in a sense it's great to be able to have

[7] Over one-third of judicial officers (37 percent) report that 'difficult decisions keep me awake at night' at least sometimes (11 percent report always/often), but over half (52 percent) report this occurs rarely or never (Roach Anleu and Mack 2017).

> someone who understands and empathises, umm, but we've got to be very careful to make sure we carve time out from that, so that again the time we have together isn't sort of really professional time spilt over, umm, so you know, trying to set the boundaries of making sure that we're not doing it. I talk very little about the detail of the awful cases to him or to anyone—
>
> INTERVIEWER: Right.
>
> because I don't want to take them home so I might say you know there's an interesting legal issue and I'll talk about it in abstract legal terms but last week for the first time in about five years I suddenly found myself blurting out some horrible detail about the case I was just doing, things that normally I wouldn't tell him and wouldn't tell anyone because it's too awful, umm, and ... (I 15)

She acknowledges that her husband retains 'a passion' for the law, suggesting strong emotional attachment, which enables him to empathise with her. However, she recounts attempts to excise emotion from her descriptions of the days' cases or remove vivid details 'of the awful cases' that might evoke unpleasant feelings in another. Focusing on 'an interesting legal issue' or talking about a case in 'abstract legal terms' suggests the process of purification, of removing messy human detail and emotion (Abbott 1981). It also shows actively drawing boundaries, albeit porous, between home and work (Roach Anleu and Mack 2016). Her view that 'I don't want to take them home', and the discussion of legal issues abstracted from 'horrible detail', is a form of emotion work for herself, to reduce the distress of something that was 'too awful' and her practice that 'normally I wouldn't tell him' is care work, directed at protecting her husband's feelings.

In contrast, some family members might seek more detail about judicial work and the emotions that elicits, but this information is not forthcoming from one judicial officer, whose self-management approach is to 'just kind of turn off':

> Look, I'm really awful to my wife because I don't share much at all with her. Occasionally I'll tell her, you know, some of the things I've been doing today and so on but, you know, most of its pretty icky and I just don't feel that's fair on her, which she probably regrets. She would like, I'm sure, to share more but I don't ... I don't talk a lot about the work that I do, I just kind of turn off and that's been my style forever and, you know, sometimes walking helps. I walk every morning with the dog. (I 11)

This judicial officer strives for and may be successful at maintaining work/non-work boundaries. This separation, though framed for the benefit of family, may also help manage the judicial officer's emotion.

Another judicial officer describes not seeking emotion management at home as a way of protecting her children as well as her husband from the emotional content of the cases she decides:

> In my office when they [her two school-age children] came in after school or whatever and they were looking at photos upside down basically, on my desk. Umm, and it was at that moment that I really made a decision that things weren't coming home but I haven't taken home work to do at home and I haven't taken home the experiences of the day. The emotional experiences of the day. So if you went into my house and said to my husband and to the girls, 'oh what's Mum doing in court this week?', they'd probably have to say, 'oh I don't know, she just goes to work'. (I 35)

Emotion work strategies depend on the judicial officer first identifying an experience as containing emotion, and perhaps having an emotion response. Professional socialisation and experience make it less likely that a judicial officer will frame or interpret situations as replete with emotion. One magistrate relates hearing a crime story on the evening news, including details of the murder and body disposal, which would likely evoke strong emotional responses on the part of most viewers and listeners:

> Just, each day, hearing over and over again, tragedy, you know, so it's the, and you get desensitised, like you really, you do, in terms of what you hear then, and I'll hear things on the news and I remember a story once about that—there was a couple who were, who had murdered a man and then dismembered him with a chain saw or something and then burnt him and you know this is all on the news and—but somewhere on the news it had been mentioned that he had gone to … [hardware store] to buy a chainsaw at like nine o'clock at night or something, or whatever, and I kind of thought to myself, like I'd heard all that and then I go, 'oh is … [hardware store] open late?', you know, I'm just not, because you hear all that. (I 16)

This judicial officer is aware that this response to the story of a horrific murder—to notice a relatively trivial fact that the hardware store is open late—might ordinarily be regarded as callous or insensitive. She attributes her desensitisation to 'hearing over and over again, tragedy', which is the experience of many judicial officers (see Chapter 2).

Apart from debriefing and shared humour, judicial colleagues and court staff can themselves support the emotion work of judicial officers in various ways.

Organisational emotion management

Managing judicial emotion is sometimes undertaken by those within courts involved in workload allocation. This emotion work often entails anticipating judicial emotion and adopting strategies to avoid or avert the emergence of emotions such as anger or boredom and the encouragement of other feelings: pleasure, satisfaction or gratitude. One court official describes the goal of work allocation in a lower court as 'keeping them all happy'. (W 18)[8]

The most important work allocation strategies for generating positive judicial emotion are perceived fairness, variety and matching skills and interests to tasks (Mack, Wallace and Roach Anleu 2012; Roach Anleu and Mack 2014). A court administrator highlights the importance to judicial officers of having a variety of cases and tasks, and the anticipation of their emotion reactions if they do not:

> Mix it up a bit. Some are very keen to do certain things, we've got one magistrate here that really likes doing civil matters, so, um, and no-one else is that fussed about it, so I give him the civil matters. ... Um, but all things being equal it's a matter of, um, mixing it up for them so that they're not doing the one thing over and over again. (W 18)

Meeting judicial preferences and matching skills with certain kinds of cases, where possible, is part of work allocation, but this requires awareness of judicial feelings more generally. Although one magistrate 'really likes doing civil matters' it is also important for work allocation to know that others are not 'that fussed', and so the allocation is experienced as fair. This interviewee also emphasises variety 'mixing it up for them', though the reference 'all things being equal' is a reminder that judicial emotion may only be considered at the margins, once other expectations or constraints are met.

Another interviewee specifically names gratitude as an emotion judicial officers might experience:

> If the judges that have been doing [the same] cases for, it might be a number of sittings in a row, they get a break ... and then further down

8 This interview data comes from the *Judicial Officers and Workload Allocation* project supported by an Australian Research Council (ARC) Linkage Project grant (LP 0669168) undertaken in collaboration with Professor Anne Wallace. The quotations used are verbatim based on transcription of the audio-recorded interviews. Any identifying information has been deleted. This data is indicated by the code 'W ##' in which the letter W identifies this interview data from the Workload project and ## is the number assigned to an individual interviewee, whether a judicial officer or court administrator/staff. For more information on this phase of the research, see the Appendix.

> the track they might pick up a few more [different] cases. And for which they might actually be quite grateful to be getting [those different] cases because they probably would perceive it as being slightly less onerous. (W 14)

As well as aiming to engender feelings of satisfaction and gratitude among judicial officers, those undertaking work allocation are mindful of avoiding less pleasant emotion experiences for the judiciary:

> Yes, just to try and give everyone a mix so that everyone gets, doesn't get bored, because if you always did the same thing you'd get bored, you know you could imagine getting five fencing disputes in one lot, and you'd say 'what's going on here?—am I being punished?' (W 06)

This comment suggests that providing variety will avoid judicial officers becoming 'bored' or feeling that they are somehow 'being punished'. Given the long court lists magistrates face, the end of the day is when judicial emotion can become apparent:

> Um, another magistrate who's, who, um, who's not happy, it sort of comes out at the end of the day—they feel the pressure at the end of the day, they might start off OK but then by the time they get to middle afternoon they're wavering a bit and they're not wanting to go on, um, and that is difficult because I might have other cases that I've yet to get in to court and they're letting me know that they've just about had enough. (W 18)

This observation is consistent with Goodman who argues that emotionally linked judicial misbehaviour may derive from 'decision fatigue' generated by the pressure of making many decisions in a short time (2013: 968), as well as judicial officers lacking emotion management skills.

For some judicial officers, even the unpredictability described in Chapter 2 can be source of positive emotion: 'some enjoy the element of surprise' according to a head of jurisdiction (W 01). On the other hand, a preference for variety can lead to different feelings when the necessary work is repetitive or monotonous. Some may feel that there is 'nothing worse than doin' the same old thing again, you know' as a court registrar suggests (W 02). While the criminal list may be a relief after a long civil trial, 'once you've done that three days in a row … you really want to be doing something else'. (W 01)

Ensuring that opportunities for different kinds of work, or 'finishing early' are made available and fairly shared can also help manage judicial emotion, as one court administrator anticipates:

> … trying to organise them to have turn about at finishing early so they can either choose to do their chamber work or go home. They usually choose to go home. Um, just to give them a break from the slog of it. (W 18)

Emotion management through work allocation processes can also manage judicial experience and display of emotion directed at court administrative staff. This interviewee reflects on the difficulty of working with a magistrate, who 'no matter what I did he, sort of, wasn't happy about it':

> Well, like, yeah, a magistrate last year, he's not here anymore and there was pretty much no pleasing this particular magistrate, no matter what I did he, sort of, wasn't happy about it and he'd come storming into my office at the end of the day ranting and raving because he didn't feel the day had gone well at all; of course I couldn't do anything about it at that point, so, um, I discussed it with him time again and before I'd give him a list I'd say to him 'is this list OK?' and he'd say 'yes, it's OK' but by the end of the day he was back to ranting again. I think he must have had other issues besides the workload. That's very, that's very the most extreme example I can come up with, it's never been that bad before or since. (W 18)

The intensity of this judicial officers' emotion and display is indicated by 'ranting and raving' and 'storming into my office'. The interviewee identifies a strategy to manage these feelings by showing him the next day's list and asking him if it is OK, as a way of anticipating and averting the emotional outbursts. Interestingly, she does not attribute the magistrate's emotion display solely to the workload: 'he must have had other issues', outside the workplace, therefore beyond her sphere of emotion work.

On some occasions, or with some judicial officers, managing judicial emotion—'keeping them happy'—may require strategies other than work allocation and demand emotion self-management for the court staff member:

> Um, magistrates are top priority, keeping them happy is the top priority, there's no doubt about it, because if you lose their trust or co-operation it's hard to get it back and it just makes everything more difficult from that point on.
>
> INTERVIEWER: So in terms of keeping the magistrates happy, the sort of things you do is about sharing …
>
> Sharing workload around and, um, mixing up, and talking to them, and 'everything OK? How was that case you did?' And sometimes they want

> to have a little bit of a chat about the funny case that they had, so it's just keeping the relationship rolling along and, um, if they've got a dentist appointment 'yeah, no worries, that's fine you know, we'll work around that'. They tell me the week before they want to cancel their leave: 'That's fine, yeah', and that's all sorts of problems that opens up for me, but, hey, you can't say 'oh no, you can't do that, you can't do that', you've just got to suck it up and go with it. So that's what I mean by keeping them happy. (W 18)

As well as 'sharing workload around' to generate feelings of fairness or equality and providing variety in work, engaging in 'a little bit of a chat' is an important strategy for trust and cooperation. Ultimately, the nature and timing of some specific judicial expectations or requests may require the court official to 'suck it up and go with it', implying frustration, while assuring the judicial officer 'that's fine', in spite of the considerable practical problems and emotion generated for the court staff involved.

Even though there is interaction and engagement between the judicial officer and court staff which entails emotion, the status differences and organisational context determine the nature and limits of emotion work. This emotion work is not reciprocal. Court staff engage in emotion work to manage judicial emotion, but there appears to be little or no expectation or experience of reciprocal emotion work from the judiciary, unlike the debriefing among judicial colleagues. This seems to parallel the experience of paralegals who 'accomplish [emotion work] by engaging in displays of deference in the presence of attorneys but venting to one another behind closed doors in reciprocal acts of emotion management' (Lively 2000: 57).

Conclusion

Judicial experience and display of emotion can be elicited by several dimensions of their everyday work, including the behaviour of lawyers, kinds of cases, the conduct or circumstances of people facing court and the many decisions judicial officers must make. There is considerable judicial recognition of emotion in their work. Some emotion experiences are regarded as inevitable or even valuable, while others must be suppressed, as inconsistent with the central value of impartiality.

Judges' and magistrates' reflections on their emotion work all suggest conscious effort to comply with the norms specifying appropriate judicial emotion experience and display to convey impartiality and avoid bias. Accomplishing this can require deep acting, to elicit the actual experience of a desired emotion, or surface acting, to manage the physical manifestations of an emotion which is inconsistent with feeling rules.

Emotion management is temporal. Many of the examples discussed above relate to emotion management in the moment, in particular the strategies judicial officers adopt to maintain the required neutral or emotionless display in court: 'Actively thinking of remaining calm … not having things show on your face' (I 16); 'put my hands flat on the bench' (I 37); 'try not to get angry' (I 22); 'internalise but say nothing' (I 03); and 'present that poker-faced appearance' (I 26). Certain feelings may not be able to be managed effectively in the moment but rely on management at another time or in another place. A judicial officer describes dealing with a 'rude practitioner' generating emotion managed in the moment: 'I bit my tongue'. Experienced again later, far off stage at home, she 'cried my eyes out' (I 03).

Location is significant. Judicial emotion self-management can take place in and out of court, reflecting a distinction between front stage and back stage (Goffman 1959). It may depend on the presence or absence of others, such as judicial colleagues, court staff or others in the courtroom. Emotion management can involve physical transition, such as leaving the bench or a more metaphorical transition, as a judicial officer implies: 'I had to pull myself back' (I 19). This is a specific example of the 'kinds of transitions involved in emotion work' (Lively and Heise 2004: 1112). Judicial feelings and display can be managed by emotion work from others through debriefing, sharing emotion or humour, often reciprocal, or it can be managed more indirectly and less reciprocally through work allocation processes managed largely by court staff.

As the research findings in this chapter demonstrate, there is a range of approaches for managing the emotions judicial officers experience and for expressing appropriate emotion. Emotion display depends on the context and requires careful management from the judicial officer and perhaps others. Judicial officers may lack some emotion management tools, perhaps a result of the formal disapproval of emotion in judicial work and the associated cognitive frameworks that sort their tasks into legal categories. Nonetheless, emotion experiences and display can themselves be practices or resources to enable judicial officers to accomplish their role. Some visible judicial emotion can indicate or communicate a shared humanity with other court users that enhances rather than detracts from judicial authority.

References

Abbott, Andrew, 1981, 'Status and Status Strain in the Professions', *American Journal of Sociology 86*: 819–835.

American Bar Association 2011, *ABA Model Code of Judicial Conduct*. Retrieved 9 May 2020, from http://www.americanbar.org/groups/professional_responsibility/publications/model_code_of_judicial_conduct.html.

Australasian Institute of Judicial Administration 2012, *Gender Statistics: Judges and Magistrates*. 4 March. On file with the authors, Retrieved 21 March 2012, from http://www.aija.org.au/index.php?option=com_content&task=view&id=32&Itemid=121.

Australian Bureau of Statistics 2020, *4513.0—Criminal Courts, Australia, 2018–19, 'Defendants Finalised – Magistrates' Courts'*. 28 February. Retrieved 9 May 2020, from https://www.abs.gov.au/AUSSTATS/abs@.nsf/DetailsPage/4513.02018-19

Barbalet, J. M., 1998, *Emotion, Social Theory, and Social Structure: A Macrosociological Approach*. Cambridge: Cambridge University Press.

Barbalet, Jack, 2011, 'Emotions Beyond Regulation: Backgrounded Emotions in Science and Trust', *Emotion Review 3*: 36–43.

Bergman Blix, Stina, 2019, 'Different Roads to Empathy: Stage Actors and Judges as Polar Cases', *Emotions and Society 1*: 163–180.

Bergman Blix, Stina and Åsa Wettergren 2018, *Professional Emotions in Court: A Sociological Perspective*. Abingdon: Routledge.

Burkitt, Ian, 2012, 'Emotional Reflexivity: Feeling, Emotion and Imagination in Reflexive Dialogues', *Sociology 48*: 458–472.

Burkitt, Ian, 2018, 'Decentring Emotion Regulation: From Emotion Regulation to Relational Emotion', *Emotion Review 10*: 167–173.

Carlen, Pat, 1974, 'Remedial Routines for the Maintenance of Control in Magistrates' Courts', *British Journal of Law and Society 1*: 101–117.

Carlen, Pat, 1976, *Magistrates' Justice*. London: Martin Robertson.

Carlen, Pat, 2010, 'Introduction'. In *A Criminological Imagination: Essays on Justice, Punishment, Discourse, xiii-xxiv*. London and New York: Routledge.

Coser, Rose Laub, 1960, 'Laughter among Colleagues: A Study of the Social Functions of Humor among the Staff of a Mental Hospital', *Psychiatry 23*: 81–95.

Craciun, Mariana, 2016, 'The Cultural Work of Office Charisma: Maintaining Professional Power in Psychotherapy', *Theory and Society 45*: 361–383.

Craciun, Mariana, 2018, 'Emotions and Knowledge in Expert Work: A Comparison of Two Psychotherapies', *American Journal of Sociology 123*: 959–1003.

Elek, Jennifer K., 2019, 'Judicial Perspectives on Emotion, Emotion Management, and Judicial Excellence in the USA', *Oñati Socio-Legal Series 9*: 865–879.

Elek, Jennifer K., David B. Rottman, Shelley Spacek Miller and Lydia Hamblin 2017, *Elements of Judicial Excellence: A Framework to Support the Professional Development of State Trial Court Judges—Project Final Report*. Williamsburg, VA: National Center for State Courts.

Flower, Lisa, 2018, 'Doing Loyalty: Defense Lawyers' Subtle Dramas in the Courtroom', *Journal of Contemporary Ethnography 47*: 226–254.

Flynn, Asher and Jacqueline Hodgson 2017, 'Access to Justice and Legal Aid Cuts: A Mismatch of Concepts in the Contemporary Australian and British Legal Landscapes'. In *Access to Justice and Legal Aid: Comparative Perspectives on Unmet Legal Need*, eds. Asher Flynn and Jacqueline Hodgson, 1–21. Oxford and Portland, OR: Hart Publishing.

Goffman, Erving, 1959, *The Presentation of Self in Everyday Life*. New York: Doubleday Anchor.

Goffman, Erving, 1981, *Forms of Talk*. Philadelphia, PA: University of Philadelphia Press.

Goodman, Maxine, 2013, 'Three Likely Causes of Judicial Misbehavior and How These Causes Should Inform Judicial Discipline', *Capital University Law Review 41*: 949–997.

Goodrum, Sarah, 2013, 'Bridging the Gap between Prosecutors' Cases and Victims' Biographies in the Criminal Justice System through Shared Emotions', *Law & Social Inquiry 38*: 257–287.
Grandey, Alicia, 2003, 'When "the Show Must Go On": Surface Acting and Deep Acting as Determinants of Emotional Exhaustion and Peer-Rated Service Delivery', *Academy of Management Journal 46*: 86–96.
Grandey, Alicia A. and Allison S. Gabriel 2015, 'Emotional Labor at a Crossroads: Where Do We Go from Here?', *Annual Review of Organizational Psychology and Organizational Behavior 2*: 323–349.
Gunby, Clare and Anna Carline 2020, 'The Emotional Particulars of Working on Rape Cases: Doing Dirty Work, Managing Emotional Dirt and Conceptualizing "Tempered Indifference"', *British Journal of Criminology 60*: 343–362.
Hochschild, Arlie Russell, 1983, *The Managed Heart: Commercialization of Human Feeling*. Berkeley, CA: University of California Press.
Hoffmann, Elizabeth A., 2016, 'Emotions and Emotional Labor at Worker-Owned Businesses: Deep Acting, Surface Acting, and Genuine Emotions', *The Sociological Quarterly 57*: 152–173.
Jamieson, Fiona, 2019, 'Judicial Independence: The Master Narrative in Sentencing Practice', *Criminology & Criminal Justice*. Published online 9 April. DOI: 10.1177/1748895819842940.
Karstedt, Susanne, 2016, 'The Emotion Dynamics of Transitional Justice: An Emotion Sharing Perspective', *Emotion Review 8*: 50–55.
Kuipers, Giselinde, 2009, 'Humor Styles and Symbolic Boundaries', *Journal of Literary Theory 3*: 219–239.
Laursen, Julie, 2017, '(No) Laughing Allowed—Humour and the Limits of Soft Power in Prison', *British Journal of Criminology 57*: 1340–1358.
Leben, Steve, 2019, 'Exploring the Overlap between Procedural-Justice Principles and Emotion Regulation in the Courtroom', *Oñati Socio-Legal Series 9*: 852–864.
Lively, Kathryn J., 2000, 'Reciprocal Emotion Management: Working Together to Maintain Stratification in Private Law Firms', *Work and Occupations 27*: 32–63.
Lively, Kathryn J., 2002, 'Client Contact and Emotional Labor: Upsetting the Balance and Evening the Field', *Work and Occupations 29*: 198–225.
Lively, Kathryn J. and David R. Heise 2004, 'Sociological Realms of Emotional Experience', *American Journal of Sociology 109*: 1109–1136.
Mack, Kathy and Sharyn Roach Anleu 2010, 'Performing Impartiality: Judicial Demeanor and Legitimacy', *Law & Social Inquiry 35*: 137–173.
Mack, Kathy, Anne Wallace and Sharyn Roach Anleu 2012, *Judicial Workload: Time, Tasks and Work Organisation*. Melbourne: Australasian Institute of Judicial Administration.
Maroney, Terry A. and James J. Gross 2014, 'The Ideal of the Dispassionate Judge: An Emotion Regulation Perspective', *Emotion Review 6*: 142–151.
Moran, Carmen C. and Margaret Massam 1997, 'An Evaluation of Humour in Emergency Work', *Australasian Journal of Disaster and Trauma Studies*. Retrieved 9 May 2019, from https://www.massey.ac.nz/~trauma/issues/1997-3/moran1.htm.
Moran, Leslie J., 2018, 'What's a Box of "Bakewell Tarts" Got to Do with It? Performing Gender as a Judicial Virtue in the Theatre of Justice'. In *Judges,*

Judging and Humour, eds. Jessica Milner Davis and Sharyn Roach Anleu, 211–240. Cham: Palgrave Macmillan.

Mulcahy, Linda, 2007, 'Architects of Justice: The Politics of Courtroom Design', *Social & Legal Studies 16*: 383–403.

Mulcahy, Linda, 2010, *Legal Architecture: Justice, Due Process and the Place of Law*. New York: Routledge.

Obrdlik, Antonin J., 1942, '"Gallows Humour"—a Sociological Phenomenon', *American Journal of Sociology 47*: 709–716.

Reddy, William M., 2001, *The Navigation of Feeling: A Framework for the History of Emotions*. Cambridge: Cambridge University Press.

Reddy, William M., 2009, 'Historical Research on the Self and Emotions', *Emotion Review 1*: 302–315.

Roach Anleu, Sharyn and Kathy Mack 2014, 'Job Satisfaction in the Judiciary', *Work, Employment & Society 38*: 683–701.

Roach Anleu, Sharyn and Kathy Mack 2016, 'Managing Work and Family in the Australian Judiciary: Metaphors and Strategies', *Flinders Law Journal 18*: 213–240.

Roach Anleu, Sharyn and Kathy Mack 2017, *Performing Judicial Authority in the Lower Courts*. London: Palgrave.

Roach Anleu, Sharyn, Kathy Mack and Jordan Tutton 2014, 'Judicial Humour in the Australian Courtroom', *Melbourne University Law Review 38*: 621–665.

Roach Anleu, Sharyn and Jessica Milner Davis 2018, 'Thinking About Judges, Judging and Humour: The Intersection of Opposites'. In *Judges, Judging and Humour*, eds. Jessica Milner Davis and Sharyn Roach Anleu, 1–38. Cham: Palgrave Macmillan.

Roberts, Heather, 2012, '"Swearing Mary": The Significance of the Speeches Made at Mary Gaudron's Swearing-in as a Justice of the High Court of Australia', *Sydney Law Review 34*: 493.

Smith, Allen C. and Sherryl Kleinman 1989, 'Managing Emotions in Medical School: Students' Contacts with the Living and the Dead', *Social Psychology Quarterly 52*: 56–69.

Sorial, Sarah, 2019, *Anger and the Defence of Provocation*. Abingdon and New York: Routledge.

Sourdin, Tania, 2018, 'Judge v Robot? Artificial Intelligence and Judicial Decision-Making', *University of New South Wales Law Journal 41*: 1114–1133.

Tata, Cyrus, 2020, *Sentencing: A Social Process: Re-Thinking Research and Policy*. Cham: Palgrave Macmillan.

Thoits, Peggy A., 1996, 'Managing the Emotions of Others', *Symbolic Interaction 19*: 85–109.

Tutton, Jordan, Kathy Mack and Sharyn Roach Anleu 2018, 'Judicial Demeanor: Oral Argument in the High Court of Australia', *Justice System Journal 39*: 273–299.

United Nations Office on Drugs and Crime 2007, *Commentary on The Bangalore Principles of Judicial Conduct*. Retrieved 24 October, from https://www.unodc.org/documents/corruption/publications_unodc_commentary-e.pdf.

Wettergren, Åsa, 2010, 'Managing Unlawful Feelings: The Emotional Regime of the Swedish Migration Board', *International Journal of Work Organisation and Emotion 3*: 400–419.

Wharton, Amy S., 2009, 'The Sociology of Emotional Labor', *Annual Review of Sociology 35*: 147–165.

Zalnieriute, Monika and Felicity Bell 2021, 'Technology and the Judicial Role'. In *The Judge, the Judiciary and the Court: Individual, Collegial and Institutional Judicial Dynamics in Australia*, eds. Gabrielle Appleby and Andrew Lynch, Cambridge University Press.

Chapter 5

Judicial emotion work

Others' emotions

Introduction

This chapter examines the strategies judicial officers[1] adopt to assess, respond to and manage the emotion of other participants, especially in the courtroom. Given the relational nature of emotion and emotion work, these strategies often entail some self-management of their own emotion or display, similar to approaches used to maintain and convey impartiality.

Managing another's emotions typically entails observing their bodily movements, facial expressions, words spoken, tone of voice, as well as absence of expression or silence, then interpreting these as indicators of emotion or particular emotional states, in light of the circumstances or context. Judicial anticipation of situations, moments and participants likely to occasion emotion and emotion display may be the first step in managing emotion.

> Interpreting an emotion 'correctly' is sometimes made more difficult by apparently contradictory bits of information that have to be accommodated and brought into a framework that makes sense. It is also complicated by the practical knowledge that expressions may not correspond with what is felt 'inside' (Scheer 2012: 214).

[1] In this book, the terms 'judicial officer' and 'judiciary' are used generically to refer to any member of the judiciary, regardless of court level or type. Within Australia, the term 'magistrate' refers to members of the judiciary who preside in the lower state and territory courts, except in the Northern Territory where magistrates were given the title 'judge' in 2016. Australian magistrates are paid judicial officers, with legal qualifications, and are appointed until a fixed retirement age. The term 'judge' indicates those who preside in the intermediate and higher state and territory courts and all national courts. Jurisdictions outside Australia may use other labels for their judiciary or may use these terms, but the words may not have the same meanings as in Australia.

As a result, a judicial officer's interpretation of observable external signs may not accurately label a participant's emotion experience, and there may be no opportunity to check or revise this perception (Barrett 2017).

Judicial officers must assess their interpretations of another's emotion experience and/or display against the applicable feeling rules, that is, the norms regarding which emotions should be felt and/or expressed in a situation. This assessment constitutes as well as applies the feeling rules of the courtroom. As one judge states: 'My view is to allow people a reasonable latitude for the expression of relevant emotions' (I 11).[2] This judicial officer aims to assess what is 'reasonable' and 'relevant' in the interaction order of the courtroom and to adopt strategies to manage what he defines as appropriate or inappropriate experience and expression of emotion. Determining the boundaries of 'reasonable' and 'relevant' emotion actively constitutes the feeling rules, against which the conduct of courtroom participants—witnesses, litigants, prosecutors, barristers/legal representatives, members of the public, and others—is assessed.

Judicial strategies have multiple and overlapping goals which can be achieved by generating subjective emotion experiences in others and influencing their outward expression. Some strategies may seek to generate a feeling as an end in itself, such as to relieve anxiety or distress. Other approaches may be more instrumental: to generate feelings of respect or fairness, to increase the legitimacy of judicial authority, to elicit feelings and behaviour that conform with feeling or conduct rules, such as decorum, or to avoid or minimise conduct which breaches such norms.

This emotion work does not occur in a vacuum, but in the complex location of a courtroom setting and wider legal institutional values and norms, in which the boundaries of the judicial role in an adversarial system enable and constrain the judicial officer's capacity to undertake this emotion work. The complex nature of judicial emotion work is displayed vividly in the following description of an emotionally dense situation in court. This judicial officer seeks to:

> engender in the courtroom a sense that everybody will get their hearing and their say in their time and people will have a sense they'll

2 This quote is from a judicial officer interviewed as part of the *Courts, the Judiciary and Social Change* project funded by an Australian Research Council (ARC) Discovery Project grant (DP 1096888). The interviews were conducted in 2012–2013. The data is indicated by the code 'I ##' in which the letter I identifies this as interview data and ## is the number assigned to the individual interviewee. Quotations are used verbatim and have not been edited to correct grammar or reduce infelicities of spoken language, but retain qualities of natural, everyday speech reflecting the narrative quality of the interviews. All identifying, or potentially identifying, details have been deleted. For more information on this phase of the research, see the Appendix.

> all get an open hearing, umm, trying to defuse things when tempers get high or feelings run high, umm, trying to recognise the strains that people are under and so take that into account and so make allowance for that, umm, dealing with the difficult people often, you know, with a firmness, umm, that will try and have them understand there're rules that everybody has to adhere to so that umm, everybody does get their time and their opportunity and people will feel ultimately as comfortable as they can about having their say, umm, so often I use time out as a strategy, tempers getting high, I'll call a break because it's a pressure cooker in there. (I 15)

This judicial officer begins with a goal: that 'everybody will get their hearing', implementing the central value of impartiality through notions of fairness and everyone having 'their say' (see Chapter 3). Treating people fairly from the start may elicit appropriate feelings in court users, avert display of inappropriate emotion, and maintain the desired emotional environment. She recognises the importance of the courtroom context in generating emotion ('it's a pressure cooker') and identifies the kinds of emotions she perceives as threatening the emotion regime ('tempers get high or feelings run high'). She first deploys interpersonal strategies: empathy for those who are experiencing and displaying strong emotion, 'trying to recognise the strains people are under' and compassion in wanting to 'take that into account' as well as patience, enabling her to 'make allowance for that'. Nonetheless, at some point these qualities of empathy and compassion give way, once she determines she is 'dealing with difficult people'. She then acts with 'firmness'. This marks a shift from reliance on interpersonal skills to reliance on impersonal legal 'rules that everyone has to adhere to'. In some circumstances, neither interpersonal strategies nor invocation of legal rules may be sufficient to defuse heightened emotions, so she then uses 'time out' and 'call[s] a break', recalling the use of adjournments as a strategy for self-management, now deployed as a strategy to manage others' emotions. This description suggests an implicit sequence or hierarchy of strategies from generic, giving people a say, followed by more specific use of interactional resources, then explicit invocation of norms, and finally, 'time out'. It also suggests that feeling rules in this context are flexible and can apply differently to different court participants. Those whose emotions are interpreted as being 'under strain' are managed differently than those defined as 'difficult people'.

This chapter expands on three main strategies judicial officers adopt when managing the emotions of others:

1 anticipate, predict, avert emotion(s);
2 allow expression of emotion, albeit within limits; and

3 respond, control, regulate after an observed or perceived emotional expression.

While these strategies are analytically separate, they can overlap and emerge in a single interaction. Each involves regulation or control and, in so doing, expresses the implicit feeling rules of the moment, as well as drawing boundaries around the judicial role in relation to emotion management.

Anticipate, predict, avert emotion

A first step in managing emotion in the courtroom may be a judicial officer's anticipation of emotion in others and the deployment of strategies to avert any emotion or display assessed as likely to be unhelpful or inappropriate. Such anticipation will be informed by the judicial officer's experience—on the bench or as a legal practitioner—and professional socialisation, ranging from formal professional development activities to informal conversations with colleagues. Judicial officers are aware of particular kinds of participants, settings, contexts or moments that are likely to present demands for emotion work, for example, litigants or criminal defendants without legal representation or when communicating a decision, especially a sentence. Judicial officers also identify several interactive and interrelational approaches to their goals of anticipating, predicting and averting emotion. They highlight the value of communication, empathy, patience and humour as examples of 'affective-relational tools' to facilitate smooth proceedings (Craciun 2018: 966). They also rely on courtroom formality as a resource to proactively manage the anticipated or expected emotions of others.

Awareness of participants or circumstances

Unrepresented participants and certain kinds of decisions are regarded as likely to require judicial management of others' emotions. Unrepresented parties may be 'frustrating' for the judicial officer:

> I've just finished a case with an unrepresented party, the case went for four days, the other side was represented by a barrister, umm, and it's, that wasn't at all an unusual case for an unrepresented party, but judges generally find it very frustrating dealing with unrepresented parties. So it's very important with them to make them feel as though they're listened to and their cases are important and that they get a fair hearing and so you really have—so patience is a very important virtue for a judge. (I 20)

By anticipating the emotional needs of an unrepresented litigant, especially using patience, this judge expects that the unrepresented party will 'feel' as though they are listened to, as part of a 'fair hearing', and so will not experience or display emotions that would breach courtroom norms and feeling rules.

In an example from the *National Court Observation Study* of the non-trial criminal list, a magistrate allows an unrepresented defendant, charged with driving whilst disqualified, to speak at length. The magistrate displays patience, giving the defendant plenty of opportunities to speak and to respond to several questions from the magistrate about his financial and family circumstances. When the magistrate says, 'All right, well, I've heard what you've had to say so far. Is there anything else you wish to say concerning this matter?' The defendant has nothing further, and the magistrate imposes sentence. The defendant then says, 'Thank you very much, your Honour, for being fair today' (Magistrate 14, matter 409).[3]

When legal representatives are not present, the judicial officer may be less able to resist strong emotion and must engage in exceptional emotion work. It may be more difficult to draw boundaries between judicial and lawyers' tasks, and the boundaries themselves may have become more porous with decreases in legal representation and increasing numbers of litigants in person:

> The number of self-represented litigants are on the increase, they have been for years. To an extent, the emotions of parties were managed by their own lawyers. Lawyers are very successful as an intermediary, umm, where you don't have lawyers and we're facing that more and more in areas where this is emotion, family domestic violence, family violence, personal safety stuff, where both parties are not, or are representing themselves, it becomes, it becomes a difficult task I think, you've got to treat the parties as humanely as you can. You've got to treat them, you've got to genuinely, you've got to genuinely see them as fellow human beings, you've got to try to treat them as though you would want them to treat you. Sounds biblical doesn't it? (I 17)

[3] This data comes from the *National Court Observation Study* funded by an Australian Research Council (ARC) Linkage Project grant (LP 021306): *The Changing Role of the Magistrates Court*. Transcript excerpts of the proceedings observed have been given a consistent format rather than retaining the relevant court's local formatting. M indicates magistrate; DR indicates a defence representative; P indicates a prosecutor; D indicates defendant. In the excerpts quoted, names of all participants including judicial officers have been changed, and on occasion other details such as dates or location have been removed, if they potentially identify a location or participant. As part of the anonymisation process, each individual magistrate was assigned a code number from 1 to 27, and each matter allocated a discrete number (from 1 to 1287). For more information on this phase of the research, see the Appendix.

This magistrate identifies the increase in the numbers of unrepresented parties as leading to greater demands on judicial officers to undertake emotion work; such demands are affected by type and level of court. Magistrates are far more likely than higher court judges to have to take time to explain things to unrepresented litigants and less likely, for whatever reason, to have well-prepared legal representatives in their court (Roach Anleu and Mack 2017; Toy-Cronin 2019). According to this magistrate, these obligations of emotion work are magnified in circumstances that typically entail strong, negative emotions such as in cases of family violence. He suggests that 'You've got to treat the parties as humanely as you can … to genuinely see them as fellow human beings'. This judicial officer emphasises the similarities—as human beings—between him and the parties, suggesting the importance of empathy. However, empathy is problematic; it may not be possible or appropriate to be equally empathic with all parties. By seeing parties as 'fellow human beings' he may be anticipating reciprocity: treating the parties 'humanely' may cause them also to be patient, communicate effectively and be courteous. He goes on to say: 'You've got to try to treat them as though you would want them to treat you', articulating a feeling rule which this judicial officer seeks to apply.

Emotion work is required for communicating decisions in a way that generates the expected emotion response. Judicial officers identify certain kinds of decisions that entail more emotion and emotion work than others. Delivering a sentence might lead to potentially disruptive emotion display from others in the courtroom (Maynard 2003). The following comment illustrates one judicial officer's reflexivity regarding the difficulty of delivering a decision in light of the emotional reaction she predicts the decision will elicit:

> The actual assessment of the evidence would often be clear but it's what I have to brace myself for is facing the family to be able to deliver the bad news to them knowing that this was going to be very traumatic for them or umm, and it's also difficult to be able to explain without, without, to explain what is for most people an emotional thing in, in terms of just evidence and law. It's hard, it's hard to make it palatable. (I 38)

This judicial officer anticipates the meaning of the decision for some recipients—it is 'bad news'—in this case for family members, though it is not clear whether it is the family of the accused person, or of the victim(s). She displays empathy in anticipating their likely reaction and shows compassion by expressing concern for those who will experience those feelings. This judicial officer uses legal skills to make the decision in terms of 'evidence and law' and engages in emotion work to frame the communication of the decision in light of the perceived emotion implications. Distinguishing 'an emotional thing' from 'evidence and law' reinforces the notion of the judicial role as bounded by the facts and the law, with a limited role in relation to emotion. Yet there is realisation that the decision must be communicated to lay participants through talk and in social interaction which will entail emotion (Maynard 2003).

Effectively anticipating and averting undesired emotion can require some empathy for those accused of crime:

> The people that come before the court are people who are not bad, there are reasons that they are caught up within the judicial system and I think you have to have some empathy towards them. Umm, I think the way—even just in terms of a represented—an unrepresented bail application, to make people feel they have been heard and listened [to] I think's important and that just requires you to listen—it doesn't—but it requires you to listen I think with an empathetic background and compassionate background. ... So even they might disagree with the decision, they actually come away from court at least feeling they were heard. (I 12)

A bail application is a relatively minor or routine matter in a lower court, but this judicial officer implicitly recognises the emotion such a decision may engender in the applicant. The judicial officer anticipates the needs of the defendant to 'feel ... heard' and so engages in emotion work to 'listen ... with an empathetic and compassionate background'. Even if the decision goes against the defendant, judicial emotion work may assist in maintaining the emotional regime of the courtroom and the feelings generated may enhance the legitimacy of judicial authority and acceptance of the decision (Burke and Leben 2007–2008; Tyler 1990, 2006). Further, the judge suggests that being empathetic 'just requires you to listen', an interpersonal skill, not a specialised legal or judicial ability.

Another judicial officer describes a very concrete example of averting anticipated and possibly disruptive emotion expression in advance of communicating a sentencing decision. She proposes giving the accused person an opportunity to read any victim impact statements before they are heard in court:

> So that serves two purposes. One is when these are read out in court, if they are, umm that he's not hearing it for the first time. That he's had an opportunity to read it beforehand so he knows what's in it, he knows what's coming and he can better process it. I think a lot of the time if those things were just read to you cold, you'd switch off. You simply couldn't deal with, with the emotion associated with it so it serves that purpose and it also serves a purpose of their authors knowing that he has read them, umm, and at whatever level he's taken them in, who knows but, umm. (I 35)

This emotion work is designed to engage the feelings of victims and the person convicted of the offence. Victims have some basis for believing that their concerns have been presented to the perpetrator in writing as well as in court, and the defendant may be able to 'take in' the often emotional message of the victim impact statement; only hearing it in court might cause the defendant to 'switch off', as a way of apparently resisting or avoiding the intense emotion, and lead to further distress for the victims. This strategy underscores the intensely interactive and interpersonal nature of judicial emotion work (Booth 2016; Schuster and Propen 2010).

Interpersonal approaches and resources

A large proportion of judicial officers interviewed (30 out of 38) mention the importance of communication, for example, to explain the court process to participants, especially when they are not legally represented. Judicial officers anticipate that unrepresented litigants will feel distress, confusion or anxiety, perhaps resulting from (reasonable) frustration or anger at the court and the legal system. Giving an explanation may address these feelings and avoid court participants acting out in ways that disrupt the court process or breach feeling rules regarding courtroom decorum (Rock 1993):

> I think by giving, being given information, such and such is very anxious and very concerned to get out of court quickly by actually acknowledging that in court initially, I know you're really anxious and want to get out but we've just got a few things we need to do before we get there, just to set those boundaries again I think helps kind of calm things down. (I 12)

This comment suggests that anticipating and expressly acknowledging the emotion a court user is experiencing, as well as giving information about court process, can 'calm things down'. By framing the cause of the emotion as a lack of knowledge or information, it becomes emotion the judicial officer can manage by providing information. This comment shows that the goal of the explanation is to generate different feelings—calm instead of anxiety—and, perhaps, to reduce emotion-related behaviour or display. This magistrate suggests that modifying the emotion experiences and display of other participants will enable her to perform judicial authority, making it collaborative 'at least' in appearance She frames the tasks as 'we' not 'I' or even more impersonal 'the court': 'We've just got a few things we need to do'.

Empathy, as shown above by identifying a concern 'to get out of court quickly', is apparent in this exchange from a matter in the *National Court Observation Study*:

M: 13th July it is. You're anxious to have the matter determined to finality rather than later, Mr Blythe, aren't you?
D: Yes sir.
M: All right, well I'm anxious to help you. 13th July at 9.30. Thank you. We'll see you here on that occasion and, hopefully, for the last time.
(Magistrate 23, matter 982)

This magistrate used the word 'anxious' to describe the defendant's feelings, and the defendant agrees. The magistrate perhaps reached this conclusion following something the defendant said or by interpreting the defendant's body language or demeanour. The magistrate then uses the same word—'anxious'—to describe the goal of assisting in resolving the case. By articulating and naming the defendant's feeling, the magistrate communicates understanding; by using the same word again in relation to his actions, the magistrate creates a sense of shared purpose in relation to the new date.

For most litigants and defendants, the courtroom setting is unfamiliar, even alien, yet it is a place where personal details, which ordinarily would be private or remain confidential, become public. This situation can produce anxiety. Anticipating this 'challenging environment' enables a judicial officer to undertake appropriate emotion work to limit the distressing emotions which might be experienced. An intermediate court judge observes:

> It's just a very challenging environment because you're trying to, you know, you're having quite intense conversations with people about very difficult stuff, umm, and there's all this distraction between you and them and around them and it's such a false setting, you know, it's not like a therapist's room, not that you're doing therapy but you are talking about things that are challenging, you know, and personal, and private and you know, it's very difficult ... (I 21)

This judicial officer draws an interesting contrast between 'a therapist's room' and the courtroom though suggesting some similarity: 'you are talking about things that are challenging' but 'not that you're doing therapy'. While there are significant differences between judicial authority and providing therapy, both occupations entail emotion work and use emotion as strategies to identify, understand and solve problems and accomplish professional goals (Craciun 2018).

The next interviewee, who presides in a higher court, anticipates potentially disruptive circumstances such as 'mobile phones going off' or other 'discourtesies' from court participants, but has chosen, in advance, to be patient rather than expressing other emotion:

> I am patient with mobile phones going off—some judges make a big deal about it and threaten to put it in a glass of water—but that is more a distraction than the phone going off. I am businesslike, I

don't worry about little discourtesies from lay people—but I would not tolerate it in barristers. (I 13)

This judge displays patience in a situation that could produce emotion felt and displayed by the judge or others, including embarrassment, humiliation, frustration and anger. He suggests that patience is appropriate as lay participants in court may be unaware of, rather than deliberately flouting, courtroom norms, or may have simply forgotten them in stressful circumstances. This approach can generate a positive emotion atmosphere in the court and help manage the judge's own emotions, in circumstances that might otherwise involve disruptive emotional displays. However, this interviewee strongly condemns similar conduct from legal professionals, suggesting different feeling rules govern judicial conduct vis-à-vis different court participants. This interviewee emphasises the importance of being 'businesslike', suggesting an emotionless demeanour, performing impartiality as detachment (Mack and Roach Anleu 2010). This approach may anticipate and avoid the loss of emotion control which a less formal court might experience. The contrast with judicial officers who 'make a big deal' of such conduct and thereby generate more 'distraction' implies judicial emotion this interviewee regards as inappropriate, and as a departure from feeling rules specifying emotionless judicial demeanour. Judicial behaviour such as 'threaten[ing] to put it [a phone] in a glass of water' can be experienced as bullying by others in the courtroom.

Judicial officers do not always tolerate what they might interpret as incivility or discourtesy. In the following example, the magistrate expresses annoyance that the defendant has not undertaken required community service hours and speaks abruptly about the defendant's conduct in court:

M: Well what's the latest—do you want to spend the balance of the time in custody? Or do you want to do these hours and pay them out?
D: I want to complete the hours.
M: Pardon?
D: I want to finish the hours.
M: Take your hands out of your pockets when I'm speaking to you. Well look, I've got no great confidence that you're going to do that. The court has directed you to do this as an alternative to any other form of punishment. And the alternative form of punishment is periodic detention or full-time custody. …
M: It's not a matter of you deciding whether you turn up. Maybe you turn up—it's an obligation that is imposed upon you by the court. What's your situation?

(Magistrate 9, matter 258)

Hands in pockets may convey the defendant's feelings of shame, nervousness or defiance, or may be a habit of which the defendant is unaware, but the judicial officer seems to have interpreted this as lack of respect for judicial authority, rudeness and deviation from courtroom or broader social norms. Rather than giving a courteous or neutral reminder, the magistrate abruptly interrupts the flow of the proceeding to give an order, perhaps reminding the defendant of the power of the judicial officer, then returns to criticising the defendant's more serious (mis)conduct in failing to complete community service hours.

Humour can be effective to manage felt and displayed emotion, to clarify norms and to manage norm-breaking, including deviation from feeling rules (Coser 1960; Holmes 2000; Holmes and Marra 2002; Roach Anleu and Milner Davis 2018). In the courtroom context, use of humour is risky as it can violate the feeling rules and depart too much from the ideal of the detached, impersonal judicial officer (Gleeson 1998; Roach Anleu, Mack and Tutton 2014). Nonetheless, humour can contribute to anticipating and averting emotion. Juror or witness anxiety for example is understandable but is something to be reduced if possible. A judicial officer recounts making a joke about lunch time and the jury's hot lunch getting cold:

> Umm, everybody relaxes and smiles and realises that you know, and you get a smile out of the jury and I'll ask them, umm, just things like that where I try to help them, to encourage them, to relax a bit and to tell them what their job is and make sure they're comfortable and there's a place for judicial humour or appropriate levity, not inappropriate levity. (I 27)

To this judge, the 'smiles' are interpreted as conveying positive emotion, indicating that potential juror anxiety or confusion has been reduced or averted. Observing the jurors 'relax a bit' appears to be regarded as an appropriate absence of emotion, which might otherwise have interfered with their capacity to understand and perform their task.

Another interviewee indicates that humour can be used more broadly to make a wider range of court participants feel at ease, but also cautions about the risks of humour:

> You try to bring a bit of light heartedness into the matter or, you know, make, try to make some comment that makes people feel at ease.
>
> INTERVIEWER: And when you say people you mean the defendants, the barristers, the litigants—

> The lawyers, the litigants, the witnesses. … but humour's a dangerous thing in court. I mean some cases there's no place for humour, deadly serious, there's a lot at stake. (I 22)

Humour in the courtroom conflicts with the importance of courtroom formality, which can be a part of proactive judicial emotion management.

Court formality and civility

Courtroom formality has multiple dimensions, ranging from formal terms of address to the demarcation of professional roles within the legal process. Emphasising use of titles, and other markers of civility and courtesy (van Krieken 2019), can have an important practical function of avoiding overt expressions of anger or other emotion displays which may transgress courtroom feeling rules:

> So that civility and politeness is a very important part of actually keeping control of proceedings and even when people are, you know, potentially dangerous people, if, my experience is and I think a lot of other people's experience is also that, if you treat people politely and respectfully, you call them Mr or Madam or Miss or Mrs or whatever and you don't speak disrespectfully to them, then not only you're more likely to get the truth but you get a more viable court, a court where you're able to conclude it without people throwing things. (I 21)

This interviewee identifies formality as valuable for the substance of the case—'you're more likely to get the truth'—as well as for emotion management and respect functions. On the other side, emphasising courtroom formality, such as removing hands in pockets, as in the example above, can be used to intimidate court participants.

A legal practitioner's failure to conform to courtroom roles, or to meet expected standards of conduct, can create a situation that generates emotion and requires the judicial officer to act to avert emotion:

> We all have experiences with new lawyers and lawyers who say silly things and you know walk, walking that line between being able to pick someone up for something that is just blatant, plainly a silly thing to say, umm, and not, but not humiliating them. It's a case of, 'yes I've heard that and I don't agree with that, let's move on to something else' but doing that in a courteous and tactful way so I think courtesy and tact—but at the same time not putting up with rubbish. (I 32)

This judicial officer anticipates that some lawyers may 'say silly things' and recognises that a judicial officer's response could lead to embarrassment or humiliation. However, she attempts to 'walk ... that line' between pointing out the 'silly things' and 'rubbish' but 'not humiliating them'. Her reliance on courtesy and tact is a strategy to remove emotion from the interaction between judge and lawyer and to avert potential feelings of humiliation perhaps even embarrassment and anger.

Other judicial officers might seek to evoke these kinds of emotion states in legal practitioners to accomplish judicial work goals and delineate interprofessional boundaries:

> One would hope that it's embarrassing for them [counsel] that I point out the deficiencies, but I don't point it out in an aggressive loud way that used to be the, used to be the way, and therefore I don't know that it stings as much that—because I don't see any great improvement over the months that followed, but yes the, I think the approach from the bench these days is far less venomous, with a few exceptions on certain courts as you may expect but I think we are very, very tolerant and of course you know it's difficult to get the right balance. (I 10)

This judge seeks to elicit embarrassment among barristers as a way of conveying their 'deficiencies'. The implication is that embarrassment is an emotion most people seek to avoid so that generating these feelings will motivate them to improve the quality of submissions (Goffman 1956). Yet the judge suggests that embarrassment may not 'lead to any great improvement' and that in the past judicial officers were 'venomous', perhaps evoking stronger emotions of shame, feelings of incompetence, anger and outrage at judicial behaviour which these days might be labelled judicial bullying (Kirby 2013; also see Quality of Working Life Research Group 2018).

Allow expression of emotion

Many of the interviewees describe situations in which they would allow expression of emotion, even when such display might appear to violate courtroom feeling rules and norms of decorum and respect. Some judicial officers find it more efficient to allow some overt emotion expression, rather than intervene and try to stop it. Others emphasise that these situations involve particular participants, such as family members, or are inevitable in the adversarial legal system that relies on cross-examination or occur in significant proceedings such as sentencing.

Allowing emotion expression may be less disruptive than attempting to avert or limit the emotion and can result in a better response to the decision itself:

> I've actually discovered umm, that it's better if you can let people say their piece. Feel that they've fully ventilated what their issue is and then

> have them and then they've usually got a better, umm, regard for what your decision is at the end of the day. (I 36)

Even in a busy, time-pressured courtroom, deliberately allowing a person to 'say their piece' can be an effective emotion and court management strategy:

> I had to change strategies because the way I was trying to deal with them obviously wasn't working and so I actually, which I've never done before, I actually just sort of thought OK right I'm just going to be quiet and let them talk it out and it was a woman in particular and so I just let her say her piece which took three times as long as the matter needed to but I thought that's really the only way to deal with her is just let her exhaust herself and umm, when she finished, I made my ruling on that particular issue and then we moved on. But trying to actually control her or keep her to any sort of time frame or on relevance or anything else was just not working. (I 34)

This magistrate consciously decides to give the court participant scope to continue talking and taking up more time, complemented by a judicial display of calm and patience: 'I'm just going to be quiet and let them talk'. In contrast, the court list and work schedule, especially in lower courts, can militate against this emotion management approach of allowing participants to keep going:

> You don't often have problems with people going on and on and on which is the fear that you have because you're under pressure to deal with so many matters efficiently, umm. (I 16)

It is interesting that this judicial officer uses the language of emotion—fear—to describe an important aspect of her work: dealing with large volumes of matters and the tension that may arise when 'people [are] going on and on'.

Types of participants

Judicial tolerance of a family member who displays distress can sometimes extend to allowing fairly extreme conduct (though perhaps quite reasonable from point of view of the family member). In a case involving a child sexually abused by a family member, the judicial officer (male) in an intermediate court recounts the reaction of the mother sitting at the back of the court:

> I was reading out the facts and I don't think the mother had ever heard them before, or the full details, and she started throwing things at the accused in the witness—the accused was in the dock and she started throwing things at him and it was—it became a very tense time. The

> court—the sheriff's officers started to press panic buttons and I was advised to get extra people in and all that sort of thing but I, I could see that it was something that was going to be short lived and it was her brother-in-law in the dock and it was just—there was a limit to how much she had to throw at him. I just sat everybody, told everybody to just settle down and get on with it and I just went on—it interrupted what I was reading for a few minutes and I went on with it but, umm, it could have gone the other way, I could have had it dealt with for contempt and you know, interrupted the proceedings and everything else, it could have gone on multiple other days while she was dealt with but that's ridiculous that sort of thing. (I 20)

This judge describes behaviour from the victim's mother—'throwing things' at the defendant—suggesting anger and hostility, though he does not name particular emotions. His interpretation of the emotional display—'I could see'—identified it as a limited though intense outburst: 'it was something that was going to be short lived', but that it was 'a very tense time'. His interpretation of this emotion was of a sudden outburst which would soon dissipate. Rather than delegating the emotion work to others, this judicial officer describes modifying the actions and emotions of other court staff: I 'told everybody to just settle down'. In his view the sheriff's officers overreacted, potentially escalating anger and hostility and generating further breaches of courtroom protocol. The judicial officer also reflects on other available resources to manage this emotion-filled moment. One option would be to assess the situation as violating contempt rules, but he rejected this, as to do so would unreasonably delay and extend the proceedings. The comment also suggests the judicial officer displayed a calm demeanour—'I just went on' and continued performing the judicial role. This also demonstrates that feeling rules are flexible and can be applied differently to different court participants and in different moments.

A victim's emotions at sentencing can also require direct emotion work from judicial officers. In their US research, Schuster and Propen comment: 'the judges we talked with expressed the need to maintain authority in the courtroom balanced with their sensitivity to the victim's feelings' (2010: 88). In Australian research, Booth (2012, 2016) deploys Goffman's concept of 'cooling the mark out' (1952: 452), a form of emotion work, to describe the ways judicial officers in sentencing hearings defuse or reduce victims' feelings, especially anger and/or resentment. Express judicial acknowledgement of a victim's emotions at sentencing can have a significant therapeutic effect, especially in sexual assault cases. Research identifies the emotional power for victims and others, of judicial acknowledgement of victim credibility and strength and the wrongfulness of what was done to her (Davies 2017; van de Zandt 1998).

Under certain conditions, judges also allow civil litigants to express emotion, especially when the court's ruling will go against them. One judge reflects:

> And I thought, you know, he needs to get it all out, it's never going to solve his problems, he's never going to be satisfied, he's always, because I'm going to refuse his application, you know, so he's never going to like me and in fact he's made several applications for me to disqualify myself but that's fine, and all the rest of it, but the fact is I think, I mean this is really deep stuff for him and he's entitled to have his emotions validated, if not determinative of the legal outcome, which it wasn't, and to allow him to express himself in this way, I think, was important for him and for the court to recognise that he will be taken seriously and we will listen to him and what he says. (I 11)

Here, the judge recognises that the emotion of the defendant will linger, or remain almost as a permanent residue, rather than take the form of a short-lived outburst as his application will be refused: 'he's never going to be satisfied'. In line with classical conceptions of emotion, the judge characterises the litigant's emotion as internal which needs to be externalised and so 'get it all out'. The judge allowed the litigant 'to express himself in this way' and 'have his emotions validated', significant for legitimacy by acknowledging that it 'was important for him and for the court to recognise that he will be taken seriously'. This is akin to the idea of a 'letter to the loser' (Des Rosiers 2000: 56), that is a judgment, or passage in a court's judgment, which explicitly indicates that the court has heard a party's case and validates the litigant's experience, including emotion, to some extent. This judge clearly distinguishes between emotion management and procedural fairness on the one hand and the substance of the decision, which he affirms is not influenced by either the litigant's or the judge's feelings. This description again confirms that some emotion in the courtroom is reasonable or at least understandable in certain circumstances, and so is not regarded as breaching feeling rules.

In other instances, judicial officers allow emotion expression they interpret as part of the inevitable (and appropriate) working of the adversarial legal system. Felt and displayed emotion on the part of witnesses can convey credibility and evidentiary strength. In trials, for example, barristers routinely seek to elicit emotions in cross-examination to challenge credibility (Ask 2018; Bandes and Blumenthal 2012). One judicial officer comments: 'just because people [witnesses] are getting emotional does not mean you necessarily have to stop it' and explains:

> With witnesses who get upset because they're being asked questions about things that they say they didn't do, you've got to be careful as to whether you're judging that they're upset because people are getting too close to the truth or whether they're getting upset because they are totally affronted and it's just something so different from what actually happened that they think they're being badgered by someone. So you just have to observe that sort of thing. … Sometimes you have to say to a person, if the barrister or prosecutor doesn't already, because of the job he has to do in these proceedings, he is required to ask you some of these questions, you should not be totally affronted by them. It's his job to put them to you even if he, you know, whatever happens because you say you didn't do it, he's got to put these things systematically to you, just answer the questions. Umm, sometimes you have to make a decision about whether to suggest to cross-examiners that maybe the line of questioning which they're pursuing may not help the court very much to determine what I have to decide and so do they really need to do it and sometimes they get the message. Other times you've just got to let them do it and get the people as upset as they like … (I 28)

The judicial officer's interpretation of where the emotion is coming from, the nature of the interaction between the barrister and the witness, and knowledge that during cross-examination the experience and expression of emotion is expected and reasonable are all aspects of judicial emotion work. The emotion generated may be interpreted as simply the result of the barrister doing the job, part of the function of the adversarial system; the resulting emotion, or at least certain types or amount of emotion, is not out of place in this moment. Some judicial officers might explicitly normalise the expression and experience of emotion in the situation of witnesses 'getting agitated giving evidence … you might say something like "you know other people in this situation do break down, it is not unusual for this to happen in the courts"' (I 27). Nonetheless, judicial officers place limits on the nature of the cross-examination: 'there will necessarily be occasions when there will be aggressive cross-examinations but I think that it's important to keep that within boundaries' (I 10) (also see Booth, Kaye and Wangmann 2019; Ellison and Munro 2017; Royal Commission into Family Violence (Victoria) 2016).

Sentencing and remorse

Sentencing can be an occasion for dense felt emotions and overt emotion display on the part of many present in the courtroom (Tata 2007, 2020). Judicial officers are aware of this and engage in various forms of emotion work. They also experience several and diverse emotions themselves when formulating a sentence (see Chapter 4). Sentencing is also an occasion where there is more sustained interaction between the judicial officer and the defendant, regardless of legal representation.

In spite of the time demands, numbers of cases, multitasking, and the routine nature of many cases, magistrates look directly at and speak directly to the defendant during sentencing in more than 80 percent of matters, whether defendants have legal representation present or not, despite a legal convention that the judicial officer speaks to the legal representative. When looking, the magistrate will likely see and interpret any emotion displayed by the person being sentenced. Court observation research shows those being sentenced display fear or anxiety more frequently than during other procedures, while defiant, aggressive or impassive demeanours are less common (Roach Anleu and Mack 2017). These findings reinforce sentencing as emotionally demanding, most obviously for the person being sentenced, but also for the judicial officer who anticipates, perceives and must interpret and perhaps manage these apparent emotional states.

Some judicial officers indicate that emotion at sentencing is often understandable and should be allowed, not penalised. While conduct expressing emotion might appear inconsistent with formal norms of courtroom decorum, it may not violate the feeling rules operating in the moment. As one judicial officer notes:

> You also, you do get emotional outbursts in court and people, if you've given them five years gaol, they may stand up and abuse you. It doesn't happen very often, I must say, but you just have to ignore it because people, you know, that's fair enough, it's just emotion. (I 21)

This comment frames the reaction of a convicted offender as an 'emotional outburst', a characterisation of emotion as internal and volatile, indicated by bodily movement—'stand[ing] up'—and language—'abuse'—but short-lived. As the emotional outburst will not last long, it may not be difficult for a judicial officer to ignore it. The idea that the outburst is 'just emotion' suggests that it is something ephemeral and will dissipate; it is something that does not matter, is not significant in this context. There is no acknowledgement of more enduring felt emotions, less readily discernible from outward bodily display.

Assessment of remorse is an aspect of sentencing which explicitly requires the judicial officer to interpret emotion against legal expectations for sentencing and associated feeling rules. Remorse is typically taken to be a 'painful and intense emotion' (Proeve and Tudor 2010: 33), which signals contrition and deep regret or guilt for causing harm, a desire to atone for the wrongdoing and commitment to change future behaviour. In law, remorse is often characterised as an internal feeling, something a judge can discern in a defendant by interpreting external demeanour (Bandes 2016a, 2016b; Johansen 2019; Rossmanith 2015; van Oorschot, Mascini and Weenink

2017). This judicial perception appears to operate 'as a feeling' experienced by the judge (Rossmanith 2015: 171), who may not recognise the extent to which 'legal decision-makers evaluating remorse do so through their own cultural and emotional lens' (Bandes 2016b: 15). The legal focus on 'true' remorse—as a discoverable thing—diverts attention from the social, relational and interactive nature of emotion experience and display.

One judge emphasises the importance of directly observing a defendant's emotion display and demeanour:

> In sentencing I like to hear and see the accused. I know that I'm no better at judging whether they're little liars than anyone else and sometimes they are and sometimes they're smart but you do get a bit of a sense of what people are like and, you know, whether they're genuine often or not and to see them express their emotions can be quite, you know, if they do break down in the witness box, that's a good sign that this is really, you know, a matter of great emotion for them and therefore you're, you're meeting them at a vulnerable place where you've got an opportunity to actually do something that will build on that opportunity. (I 11)

This judge describes the ability to directly perceive emotion by interpreting demeanour as a 'bit of a sense' based on a display in court which is 'a good sign that this is really … a matter of great emotion … for' the person being sentenced. While the judge acknowledges the limits of his capacity—'I know I'm no better at judging whether they're little liars than anyone else'—he believes that, by observing and listening to an offender's testimony, he can determine whether or not an offender is 'genuine'. In the courtroom, where feeling rules generally require emotional restraint, 'to see them express their emotion' and 'break down in the witness box' may enhance the judge's assessment that claims of remorse are genuine (Weisman 2004). This interviewee's comments track the view expressed in case law that the 'assessment of the genuineness and value of remorse is likely to be better informed in circumstances where it is expressed directly by an offender to the Court, as remorse is an intrinsically subjective matter, the evaluation of which depends on the subtleties of human interaction' (*Nguyen v The Queen* [2019] NSWCCA 209 at [81], citing *Alvares v The Queen* [2011] NSWCCA 33 at [44]). This places a high premium on the sentencing judge's ability to correctly interpret emotion displays as felt remorse.

A judicial officer's assessment of remorse demonstrates the interdependence between law, emotion and judicial work. Remorse is infused with emotion and feeling on the part of the defendant and perhaps for the judicial officer. Thought, behaviour and feeling become difficult, perhaps impossible, to disentangle.

> What makes remorse assessment so curious is that when someone climbs into the witness box and testifies to their remorse, and when they're cross-examined about it, the court is not simply finding out whether or not that person is telling to truth; it is testing for the presence of a *feeling*. (Rossmanith 2013: 18, emphasis in original)

However, elements courts have identified as evidence of remorse include reports of behaviour, action or use of specific language, rather than direct observation of a defendant's display or demeanour. Such elements include the guilty plea, a letter to victims, confessions to significant others, statements to police acknowledging wrongdoing, cooperation with police, restitution to a victim and/or assisting a victim in various ways (Judicial College of Victoria 2019; Maslen and Roberts 2013; Rossmanith, Tudor and Proeve 2018).

In the lower courts, the defendant's direct performance of remorse is limited. The judicial officer often does little more than agree that remorse has been shown or state that there is remorse, perhaps referring to the early guilty plea as the main indicator (Roach Anleu and Mack forthcoming). More elaborate assertions of remorse usually come from statements of the defence lawyer rather than from the defendant personally. These representations often include descriptions of emotion display that could be read as remorse, as well as other actions identified as evidence of remorse. For example, a defence representative submits:

> Ultimately, Your Worship—and it's to her credit—her own innate sense of honesty and responsibility came to the surface and she could not continue with the lying … As your Worship will appreciate from the statement provided by her, she broke down in tears, called her mum and admitted that she indeed was the person who was driving the car …
>
> (Magistrate 5, matter 54)

The use of feeling words ('innate sense') and descriptions of behaviour recognised as a physiological manifestation of emotion ('broke down in tears') convey the defendant's strong emotion. Although the word 'remorse' is not used, her initiative in calling her mother and admitting that she was the driver accords with the kind of conduct associated in law with remorse. The claim that 'she could not continue with the lying' also suggests the defendant was feeling a range of emotions including remorse, guilt, regret, shame and embarrassment.

The transcript example below is atypical, as the defendant personally and explicitly expresses her remorse, though the magistrate does not expressly acknowledge this:

M: Thank you. What do you want to say about the matter, Ms Brown?
D: I understand I was wrong to drive while I was under the influence of alcohol and I'm very sorry.
M: Are you working?
D: Yes, I am.
M: Thank you. You are convicted and fined the sum of $250 in default 12 days in gaol. You are disqualified from holding a license for one month from today. How long do you need to pay the fine, Ms Brown?
D: One month, your Honour.
M: One month is allowed. Thank you. You are free to go.
D: Thank you.

(Magistrate 27, matter 1232)

While the language used does not suggest emotion on the part of the magistrate or the person being sentenced, there is a statement suggesting remorse: 'I was wrong ... I'm very sorry'. There is a sense that both participants are working from a routine script.

Judicial assessment of remorse does not usually require conscious or explicit management of or attempts to shape the defendant's emotion experience or display, though the feelings and actions of others in the courtroom during sentencing may generate an occasion for emotion work.

Judicial management after a participant's emotion display

Judicial officers employ several strategies to manage emotion expression when it occurs, apart from allowing the expression. Many of these approaches are illustrated in the judge's (I 15) description discussed at the beginning of this chapter, and some are similar to strategies for maintaining judicial impartiality and judicial management of the judicial officer's own emotion discussed in Chapters 3 and 4. These may include invoking formal procedures or articulating feeling rules, taking a break, relying on the judicial officer's own demeanour, calling on other resources or combining or sequentially using all these approaches.

Articulating formal procedures and feeling rules

When court participants, especially unrepresented litigants, appear to become frustrated or upset if they are not able to speak when they wish to do so, judicial officers may attempt to reduce this frustration by explaining the required conduct and sequence of speaking opportunities:

> So I often, umm, will say when everyone's getting angry and the defendant's calling out and prosecutor's getting antsy, I'll say, 'look could everyone just stop, there are rules about how we behave in court.

> The first rule is that I'll give the prosecutor an opportunity to speak, you will get an opportunity to speak'—because that's usually what they're angry about. 'I guarantee you will get an opportunity to speak but you cannot interrupt, there are rules about how we umm, all behave in court, some respect, courtesy'. I talk to them like my 12 year old, umm, but it generally works. People are anxious they are not going to get heard so if you reassure them, 'you will get an opportunity to say something', even if it's completely irrelevant. You let them have, I mean obviously we won't let them go on for half an hour but let them have their couple of minutes. (I 31)

In this example the judicial officer invokes rules as a way to manage visible emotion: courtroom participants 'getting angry', 'getting antsy', and 'anxious'. Invoking rules of courtroom behaviour depersonalises the interaction and request to stop. She interprets the cause of the anger and distress as arising from people not feeling they have had 'an opportunity to speak'. Nonetheless, the judicial officer—a magistrate—makes it clear that this opportunity is narrow: a 'couple of minutes'. Another magistrate emphasises the notion of turn-taking in conversation:

> 'Yes I've heard you, Mr so and so, I'd now like you to sit down and I'm now going to hear from so on'. They will continue talking, [and I] say, 'I just said to you I would like you now to sit down, you've had your turn'. Oh yeah, and then it's, 'you will have another turn later but now it's someone else's turn'. (I 32)

A magistrate observed in the *National Court Observation Study* adopts a similar approach:

> M: Just one moment. I'll hear from you in a moment. Just remain quiet and then I'll give you a chance to speak. ...
> D: I want to plead guilty.
> M: A plea of guilty is entered. Be seated now and listen carefully to what the prosecutor is about to say and once she has finished speaking, then I'll give you an opportunity to address me. Just be seated for the moment.
> D: OK.
>
> (Magistrate 14, matter 464)

These judicial officers invoke the central judicial value of impartiality through the notion of turn-taking, that each side will get an opportunity to speak, though the concept of impartiality is not explicitly referenced. (See Chapter 3 for a fuller discussion of judicial understandings of and practices to maintain impartiality.) The interaction between the magistrate and the participant makes explicit the procedural rules about appropriate behaviour: 'the first rule is that I will give the prosecutor an opportunity to speak'; then 'you will have another turn later but now it's someone else's turn'. It is expected that this explanation will reduce frustration, distress or anxiety, which may be the source of conduct such as 'continue talking', 'calling out', becoming 'antsy' or 'angry'. Because letting one participant continue without limit may be perceived by others as unfair or indicating bias, the judicial officer invokes the powerful norm of impartiality to legitimately and temporarily silence a participant. Explicit invocation of overriding legal institutional norms in terms of everyday, ordinary social practices—to hear both sides—becomes a resource to manage the emotions of others in the courtroom. This strategy may be especially valuable as there may be no shared definition of the situation and its feeling rules between lay and professional participants.

Explaining courtroom norms can be coupled with another emotion management approach—to let the participant speak, perhaps in a way that includes emotional expression, but within limits 'let them have their couple of minutes' (I 32). In the example below, the defendant became somewhat agitated or frustrated at not receiving an expected opportunity to speak:

> D: Well, Your Worship, I haven't had—I haven't heard the matter [inaudible] there. I haven't had a say in what's happened. I'd just like to have a say how I've actually breached it, how they've alleged that I breached it.
>
> M: Well yeah—you'll be given that opportunity—aahh—aahh …
>
> D: Well I haven't had a say on the evidence, Your Honour—umm—that umm—well I've got a lot of evidence here stating that—it's not even her phone—she stole it. I've been asking from day one—I'd like her to be charged for stealing the company's phone, and I've got evidence here stating a lot of what—what she's did.
>
> [The magistrate ascertains that the defendant is before the court for breach of an apprehended violence order (AVO), arranges for a prosecutor with the brief of evidence to appear later in the day, and communicates to the defendant who is in custody.]
>
> M: Yes, thank you. Well we'll get that brief of evidence and you'll be able to air the matter further at two o'clock …
>
> D: Oh thank you, Your Worship.
>
> M: Will you see that the file [inaudible].
>
> (Magistrate 9, matter 273)

In this matter, the magistrate takes concrete action to obtain the information the defendant and the court need, assures the defendant of an opportunity to speak and indicates when that would take place. The defendant appears to accept this calmly, perhaps even with gratitude.

Lay people are not the only court participants who can become disruptive.

Some interviewees describe reminding legal practitioners of the feeling and associated conduct rules in the courtroom:

> I don't tolerate any sniping at the bar table between the practitioners and, you know, I expect them to behave better than that and I think that that helps to take the sting out of it and if there's going to be a problem I'll send the jury out and I'll speak to them. I might add, having said all this, that's not something that I was very good at at the Bar. I was quite aggressive and, but I don't think that's the way to go and I tend not to tolerate it now which is terribly hypocritical. (I 10)

This comment suggests the importance of situational modification—'sending the jury out'—that is separating the audience so the judge can speak directly to counsel. Judicial officers might also reframe the behaviour of counsel:

> There's one lovely story about a judge of this court who umm, was a woman, is a woman and a mother and, I wasn't there but I heard the story, umm, and counsel were sledging one another and umm, and just making, making life difficult and she, she just said, 'look I have to go home and deal with my children by telling them off, I am not going to start doing this now here in court, you two are adults, grow up and behave yourselves'. Now I certainly wouldn't have said something like that. Perhaps that's the sort of thing that a mother says because, I don't know why because, perhaps they're more engaged or closer to the children or more exposed but why is that these days, no? Umm, that's really an anecdote that just appealed to me, not something that I do. (I 27)

This story suggests a similarity between the behaviour of counsel 'sledging one another' and that of children. (Sledging is a term used mostly in sports to describe personally insulting remarks.) Another judge also suggests similarity between emotion management strategies in court and dealing with children 'I talk to them like my 12 year old' (I 31).

Taking breaks

Judicial officers use shorter and longer breaks in different ways and combine these with other strategies to manage emotion in the courtroom including their own feelings. This strategy can be used even when the emotion may be understandable, and some expression allowed, but control is needed. When a witness is becoming distressed 'crying' or 'emotional', offering a 'glass of water' or a 'break' are seen as useful methods for calming the witness:

> Well I mean, look, if people are emotional, let's say somebody's in the witness box and crying, well you can't say 'stop crying' because it is emotional for them, you have to just accommodate them as best you can. You know sometimes it's pretty pathetic, you know, here's a glass of water, have a break, something like that. (I 06)

This judicial officer demonstrates some empathy and compassion for the witness and acknowledges the need 'to just accommodate as best you can', which may include allowing some emotion expression, reinforcing the flexibility of feeling rules in the courtroom. It also suggests the judge's recognition of the limits of his emotion management skills and capacity. The belief that the emotion which the judicial officer interprets from the crying cannot be managed by the witness implicitly reflects a concept of emotion as spontaneous and uncontrollable.

The limited acceptance of (uncontrollable) emotion is coupled with attempts to assist the witness to regain composure. The efficacy of offering a glass of water as 'pretty pathetic' is also recognised by another interviewee who comments: 'Well, I don't know how water helps, except that having a drink sometimes makes you take a deep breath' (I 28). Taking a break or an adjournment can also be a strategy for managing the (understandable) emotions of a defendant, emotions which must remain within boundaries:

> You don't know, you don't know why they're crying, it might be just they're feeling incredibly sorry for themselves that they've got themselves into this, this position or they might be terrified of going to gaol or whatever so I think the only way I'd deal with that sort of emotion is to, to perhaps stop, hesitate, and let them collect themselves. (I 18)

This judicial officer recognises the challenge in interpreting external signs of emotion: 'you don't know why they're crying' and displays empathy in considering the likely sources. With no specific indicators, a pause in the proceedings 'stop, hesitate, and let them collect themselves' may be an effective emotion management strategy.

Use own emotion or demeanour

Judicial officers use their own emotions—both felt and displayed—as resources to manage the emotions of others and to contribute to the emotional climate and maintain the emotion regime in the courtroom. Calmness is an important quality for judicial officers to generate and to display as part of managing their own emotions. It is also a key quality for managing the emotions of others. An intermediate court judge describes the emotion work of helping court participants to become calm, to shape their understanding of their experience in the legal context:

> Well you've got to try to keep people as calm and productive as you can. …
>
> INTERVIEWER: How would you do that? Can you give an example?
>
> Umm, an accused might be getting angry with the way the prosecutor is putting an argument and so you might just say something to indicate that it's, it's an argument and, you know, it might not be necessarily have the effect that the Crown's aiming for. In other words you've still got to decide the question according to the merits but you might try to temper the presentation by a counsel who's getting someone angry or just interpose, just interpose your own quiet manner so as to calm the situation. You can do that with witnesses who you see them getting upset, you see them being bullied and even if you can't in the long term, stop some of the questioning, you can calm the situation by simply saying something even if it's not in the end going to stop the behaviour, it will temper it and a distressed witness can see that even though you might not be able to stop what's going on, the witness knows that you're sympathetic to his or her position. (I 23)

This judge uses his own bodily display of a 'quiet manner' to counter what he perceives as 'inflammatory behaviour' from counsel. Using his demeanour and making comments, he might 'temper' the way counsel is asking questions or change the participant's interpretation of the questions to remedy a situation where (lay) participants are 'getting angry' or 'getting upset'. He explains that he might indicate to an accused person that the prosecution 'is putting an argument' rather than stating proven or accepted facts. He also emphasises the outward display of judicial empathy or sympathy: 'a distressed witness can see … that you're sympathetic'.

These strategies serve as boundary work between the judge and the legal representatives. The judicial officer's concern to 'calm the situation' is counterpoised against a counsel's presentation that results in witnesses 'being bullied'. This judge tries to balance maintaining an emotionally appropriate climate in the courtroom with the obligation to be impartial. Ultimately, the judicial role limits his authority to 'stop some of the questioning' and protect courtroom participants, especially witnesses.

The following comment emphasises the importance of a detached judicial demeanour to the emotions of others in court, especially given the relentless visibility of the judicial officer. It also demonstrates the intricacy and interconnectedness of judicial emotion work:

> I think people have got to remember as a judicial officer you're sitting there, up higher, everybody sees what you do. Everyone sees if you're, you know, slouching or sitting or not taking notes. So you get

> used to that, umm, and I think really, and I hope I don't cry in court one day but I think it's important not to. Not to collapse in to the same sort of emotional state and really just try and keep control where you can because everyone's looking to you to keep control and I think it's really important that if you were to start crying or you were to feel a bit then I think people's confidence in your ability not to break down really would affect people. (I 31)

The judicial officer equates crying with an 'emotional state', 'collapse' and 'break down' which potentially jeopardises courtroom control: others' emotions may become more frequent, visible and disruptive. Crying indicates weakness and inability rather than empathy and compassion; sharing emotion is not appropriate in this context (Karstedt 2019; Rimé 2009). This judicial officer underscores the importance of judicial emotion display in managing the emotions and expectations of others in court who 'are looking to you to keep control'. Not crying entails managing the judicial officer's own emotions and the associated display that 'everybody sees' to shape the emotions of others: 'your ability not to break down really would affect people'.

In contrast, there are some situations in which judicial officers might be more willing to share or at least participate in an emotion-infused moment. An example is judicial use of humour or judicial laughter as a response or reaction to other participants' felt or displayed emotion (Roach Anleu, Mack and Tutton 2014). One judicial officer remarks:

> Even in the courtroom, like I'd, I would use humour reasonably often, umm, sometimes to just, as a bit of a circuit breaker but other times just to be human. (I 34)

The idea of humour as a 'circuit breaker' suggests its capacity to manage emotions of others and to reduce the social distance of the judicial officer 'just to be human'. Such loss of distance can also jeopardise judicial authority to the extent that authority depends on impersonality.

Other resources

In some circumstances, judicial management of another's felt emotion or display may require input or effort from other professionals in the immediate situation. One judicial officer describes a sequence of strategies she adopts, including first, self-talk and reflexivity regarding her feelings in the moment and the judicial role, allowing some emotion expression, then reminding court users of the importance of turn-taking, all the while 'staying calm'. When she assesses that the strategies available to her as a judicial officer are not successful, she delegates emotion work by:

> Calling in some of the other resources that you might have in the courtroom … you might say or say to the lawyer, 'I'd like you now to speak to your client, it's really important that you speak to your client and you tell your client the position you're in'. (I 32)

A request to a lawyer to explain court procedures, behavioural norms or other aspects of the client's situation, is also implicitly a request to manage the client's emotions or conduct in a way which a judicial officer cannot do directly. Although the judicial officer does not explicitly invoke impartiality or the judicial role as the justification for the request, it is clear that the lawyer has a responsibility for and obligation to the client that the judicial officer does not.

In the comment below, a judicial officer expresses empathy for and understanding of the difficulty a victim of crime experiences when describing the emotional impact and trauma to the court:

> … with the people reading the victim impact statements are always very, you know, appropriate towards them and it's a very difficult thing to do. Have them stand at the bar table, make sure that they have some support for them when they're doing that, umm. You know if it becomes too difficult for them to carry on I make sure I've got a backup plan with ensuring the prosecutor will take over from them or someone will. (I 35)

This judicial officer reinforces the importance of the statement by having the victim 'stand at the bar table' so it is central to the court's activities during the reading of the statement. She also describes managing the anticipated emotion and distress by enabling the victim to stop reading the statement and have the prosecutor take on that task.

In the two examples above, judicial officers describe specific requests to other participants in the courtroom to do something directly to manage displayed emotions they assess as beyond the judicial role to manage directly. In another situation, a judicial officer describes the importance of the physical presence of others and symbolism—'police in uniform'—as a strategy for managing actual or anticipated emotion:

> … or to have police in uniform in the Family Violence list so when the parties are in court there's some presence there of an authority figure, so, yeah, it's things like that, it's a challenging … (I 16)

It is interesting to note that the presence of the judicial officer as an authority figure is not deemed sufficient; police presence brings a different form of authority.

Judicial officers can invoke more daunting courtroom formality, to avert unwelcome or inappropriate emotions of court users:

> I think the thing I learnt very—because I'm quite an informal magistrate—but I learnt very quickly that you need to keep the formality of the courtroom so I found like if you started to lose the formality then you can lose control of the courtroom very quickly so that if you then do have some conflict you suddenly can't regain that authority ... there is a role in managing the emotions of the place by the sheer formality of it and just even the things like using the protective services officers to come in and just sit at the back of the courtroom, be a presence. (I 16)

This suggests the delegation of some emotion work to 'the protective service officers'. By virtue of their uniforms, they are highly visible symbols of authority and can move about within the courtroom, unlike the judicial officer, whose only choice of movement is to remain on the bench or leave the courtroom. Through this delegation of emotion work, the judicial officer defines the affective boundaries of the judicial role.

These comments describe examples of a judicial officer sharing or delegating emotion management work to other professional personnel in the courtroom: the lawyer, the prosecutor, or the police. This delegation reminds others of the scope of their duties and identifies the parameters of the judicial role, a form of boundary work (Lamont and Molnár 2002). They further illustrate the way managing others' emotions is relational, not only individual or behavioural.

Conclusion

Judicial officers adopt a range of strategies to defuse or limit emotions before and after they emerge. They are especially mindful of the needs of unrepresented participants which require careful anticipation and deployment of qualities such as courtesy or patience and associated demeanours to avert or allow expression of a participant's emotion. Articulation of requirements such as turn-taking may be helpful to avert or respond to a participant's emotion when it appears likely to or does breach feeling rules. Some kinds of decision, such as sentencing, require particular care in delivery and in managing an emotional response from others, and may include tolerating even extreme behaviour. A judicial officer's display of calmness can itself elicit desired emotion or conduct in others.

Even though there is interaction and engagement between the judicial officer and other court users which entail emotion management, the status differences and organisational context constrain the nature of emotion work and the capacity for sharing emotion. Some tasks are within and others are outside the judicial role. An important dimension of judicial emotion work is boundary maintenance, ensuring that others meet their responsibilities of emotion management to comply with the feeling rules and institutional norms. This may include expecting legal representatives to manage their own emotion and display or to manage their client's feelings and conduct.

This chapter illustrates the interdependence among strategies, practices, formal procedures and feeling rules to manage the judicial officer's own emotion and display and the quest to achieve impartiality. Judicial officers allow some emotion display, indicating the flexibility of feeling rules. They also maintain strong institutional limits on emotion in court. The location, nature and extent of these limits can depend on the participants, the circumstances and the context which shape the felt and expressed emotions, as interpreted by the judicial officer. It is the judicial officer who determines those boundaries, constituting and enforcing formal legal requirements and feeling rules.

References

Ask, Karl, 2018, 'Complainant Emotional Expressions and Perceived Credibility: Exploring the Role of Perceivers' Facial Mimicry and Empathy', *Legal and Criminological Psychology 23*: 252–264.

Bandes, Susan, 2016a, 'Remorse and Demeanour in the Courtroom: Cognitive Science and the Evaluation of Contrition'. In *The Integrity of Criminal Process: From Theory into Practice*, eds. Jill Hunter, Paul Roberts, Simon N. M. Young and David Dixon, 309–326. Oxford and Portland, OR: Hart Publishing.

Bandes, Susan, 2016b, 'Remorse and Criminal Justice', *Emotion Review 8*: 14–19.

Bandes, Susan A. and Jeremy A. Blumenthal 2012, 'Emotion and the Law', *Annual Review of Law and Social Science 8*: 161–181.

Barrett, Lisa Feldman, 2017, *How Emotions Are Made: The Secret Life of the Brain*. Boston, MA: Houghton Mifflin Harcourt.

Booth, Tracey, 2012, '"Cooling out" Victims of Crime: Managing Victim Participation in the Sentencing Process in a Superior Sentencing Court', *Australian & New Zealand Journal of Criminology 45*: 214–230.

Booth, Tracey, 2016, *Accommodating Justice: Victim Impact Statements in the Sentencing Process*. Annandale: Federation Press.

Booth, Tracey, Miranda Kaye and Jane Wangmann 2019, 'Family Violence, Cross-Examination and Self-Represented Parties in the Courtroom: The Differences, Gaps and Deficiencies', *University of New South Wales Law Journal 42*: 1106–1142.

Burke, Kevin and Steve Leben 2007–2008, 'Procedural Fairness: A Key Ingredient in Public Satisfaction', *Court Review 44*: 4–15.

Coser, Rose Laub, 1960, 'Laughter among Colleagues: A Study of the Social Functions of Humor among the Staff of a Mental Hospital', *Psychiatry 23*: 81–95.

Craciun, Mariana, 2018, 'Emotions and Knowledge in Expert Work: A Comparison of Two Psychotherapies', *American Journal of Sociology 123*: 959–1003.

Davies, Rhiannon, 2017, *Stories of Pervasive Uncertainty: A Victim-Focused Analysis of Victim Impact Statements and Sentencing in Sexual Offence Cases*. PhD Thesis, Faculty of Law, University of Tasmania. Retrieved 9 May 2020, from https://eprints.utas.edu.au/28673/.

Des Rosiers, Nathalie, 2000, 'From Telling to Listening: A Therapeutic Analysis of the Role of Courts in Minority-Majority Conflicts', *Court Review 37*: 54–62.

Ellison, Louise and Vanessa E. Munro 2017, 'Taking Trauma Seriously: Critical Reflections on the Criminal Justice Process', *The International Journal of Evidence & Proof 21*: 183–208.

Gleeson, Murray, 1998, 'The Role of the Judge and Becoming a Judge', paper presented at the National Judicial Orientation Programme, Sydney, 16 August. Retrieved 9 May 2020, from https://www.hcourt.gov.au/assets/publications/speeches/former-justices/gleesoncj/cj_njop.htm.

Goffman, Erving, 1952, 'On Cooling the Mark Out: Some Aspects of Adaptation to Failure', *Psychiatry: Journal of Interpersonal Relations 15*: 451–463.

Goffman, Erving, 1956, 'Embarrassment and Social Organization', *American Journal of Sociology 62*: 264–271.

Holmes, Janet, 2000, 'Politeness, Power and Provocation: How Humour Functions in the Workplace', *Discourse Studies 2*: 159–185.

Holmes, Janet and Meredith Marra 2002, 'Having a Laugh at Work: How Humour Contributes to Workplace Culture', *Journal of Pragmatics 34*: 1683–1710.

Johansen, Louise Victoria, 2019, '"Impressed" by Feelings—How Judges Perceive Defendants' Emotional Expressions in Danish Courtrooms', *Social & Legal Studies 28*: 250–269.

Judicial College of Victoria 2019, *Victorian Sentencing Manual*. Retrieved 9 May 2020, from https://resources.judicialcollege.vic.edu.au/article/669236.

Karstedt, Susanne, 2019, 'Emotions and Criminal Law: New Perspectives on an Enduring Presence'. In *Emotions in Late Modernity*, eds. Roger Patulny, Alberto Bellocchi, Rebecca E. Olson, Sukhmani Khorana, Jordan McKenzie and Michelle Peterie, 101–113. Abingdon and New York: Routledge.

Kirby, Michael, 2013, 'Judicial Stress and Judicial Bullying', *Australian Law Journal 87*: 516–527.

Lamont, Michèle and Virág Molnár 2002, 'The Study of Boundaries in the Social Sciences', *Annual Review of Sociology 28*: 167–195.

Mack, Kathy and Sharyn Roach Anleu 2010, 'Performing Impartiality: Judicial Demeanor and Legitimacy', *Law & Social Inquiry 35*: 137–173.

Maslen, Hannah and Julian V. Roberts 2013, 'Remorse and Sentencing: An Analysis of Sentencing Guidelines and Sentencing Practice'. In *Sentencing Guidelines: Exploring the English Model*, eds. Andrew Ashworth and Julian V. Roberts, 122–139. Oxford: Oxford University Press.

Maynard, Douglas W., 2003, *Bad News, Good News: Conversational Order in Everyday Talk and Clinical Settings*. Chicago, IL: University of Chicago Press.

Proeve, Michael and Steven Tudor 2010, *Remorse: Psychological and Jurisprudential Perspectives*. Farnham: Ashgate.

Quality of Working Life Research Group 2018, *The Victorian Bar: Quality of Working Life Survey*. Final report and analysis, Retrieved 9 May 2020, from https://www.vicbar.com.au/sites/default/files/Wellbeing%20of%20the%20Victorian%20Bar%20report%20final%20Oct%202018.pdf.

Rimé, Bernard, 2009, 'Emotion Elicits the Social Sharing of Emotion: Theory and Empirical Review', *Emotion Review 1*: 60–85.

Roach Anleu, Sharyn and Kathy Mack 2017, *Performing Judicial Authority in the Lower Courts*. London: Palgrave.

Roach Anleu, Sharyn and Kathy Mack forthcoming, 'Constructing Remorse: Interactional Dimensions of Finding an Emotion'. In *Showing Remorse and Taking Responsibility for Crime: The Ideal Defendant*, eds. Stewart Field and Cyrus Tata. Oxford: Hart Publishing.

Roach Anleu, Sharyn, Kathy Mack and Jordan Tutton 2014, 'Judicial Humour in the Australian Courtroom', *Melbourne University Law Review 38*: 621–665.

Roach Anleu, Sharyn and Jessica Milner Davis 2018, 'Thinking About Judges, Judging and Humour: The Intersection of Opposites'. In *Judges, Judging and Humour*, eds. Jessica Milner Davis and Sharyn Roach Anleu, 1–38. Cham: Palgrave Macmillan.

Rock, Paul, 1993, *The Social World of an English Crown Court: Witnesses and Professionals in the Crown Court Centre at Wood Green*. Gloucestershire: Clarendon Press.

Rossmanith, Kate, 2013, 'Getting into the Box: Risky Enactments of Remorse in the Courtroom', *About Performance* (*12*): 7–26.

Rossmanith, Kate, 2015, 'Affect and the Judicial Assessment of Offenders: Feeling and Judging Remorse', *Body & Society 21*: 167–193.

Rossmanith, Kate, Steven Tudor and Michael Proeve 2018, 'Courtroom Contrition: How Do Judges Know?', *Griffith Law Review 27*: 366–384.

Royal Commission into Family Violence (Victoria) 2016, *Royal Commission into Family Violence: Summary and Recommendations*. Parliament Paper No 132 (2014–2016), Retrieved 9 May 2020, from http://rcfv.archive.royalcommission.vic.gov.au/Report-Recommendations.html.

Scheer, Monique, 2012, 'Are Emotions a Kind of Practice (and Is That What Makes Them Have a History)? A Bourdieuan Approach to Understanding Emotion', *History and Theory 51*: 193–220.

Schuster, Mary Lay and Amy Propen 2010, 'Degrees of Emotion: Judicial Responses to Victim Impact Statements', *Law, Culture and the Humanities 6*: 75–104.

Tata, Cyrus, 2007, 'Sentencing as Craftwork and the Binary Epistemologies of the Discretionary Decision Process', *Social & Legal Studies 16*: 425–447.

Tata, Cyrus, 2020, *Sentencing: A Social Process: Re-Thinking Research and Policy*. Cham: Palgrave Macmillan.

Toy-Cronin, Bridgette, 2019, 'Leaving Emotion Out: Litigants in Person and Emotion in New Zealand Civil Courts', *Oñati Socio-Legal Series 9*: 684–701.

Tyler, Tom R., 1990, *Why People Obey the Law*. New Haven, CT: Yale University Press.

Tyler, Tom R., 2006, 'Psychological Perspectives on Legitimacy and Legitimation', *Annual Review of Psychology 57*: 375–400.

van de Zandt, Pia, 1998, 'Heroines of Fortitude'. In *Balancing the Scales: Rape, Law Reform and Australian Culture*, ed. Patricia Easteal, 124–142. Annandale: Federation Press.

van Krieken, Robert, 2019, 'Law and Civilization: Norbert Elias as a Regulation Theorist', *Annual Review of Law and Social Science 15*: 267–288.

van Oorschot, Irene, Peter Mascini and Don Weenink 2017, 'Remorse in Context(s): A Qualitative Exploration of the Negotiation of Remorse and Its Consequences', *Social & Legal Studies 26*: 359–377.

Weisman, Richard, 2004, 'Showing Remorse: Reflections on the Gap between Expression and Attribution in Cases of Wrongful Conviction', *Canadian Journal of Criminology and Criminal Justice 46*: 121–138.

Chapter 6

Professional regulation of judicial emotion

Introduction

Professions are regulated through a complex mix of formal and informal processes governed by explicit and implicit norms (Haller 2010). Because emotion experience and display are generally regarded as inconsistent with, or even antithetical to, judicial impartiality and legitimacy, they are subject to regulation in a range of ways. This chapter[1] considers the general regulation of judicial conduct as it relates to judging and emotion. This regulation is located within the framework of an independent judiciary[2] structured as a self-regulating profession. The norms and processes described here inform the emotion management judicial officers undertake in their everyday work, and the implicit feeling rules governing judicial conduct discussed in Chapters 3, 4 and 5.

A starting point is judicial ethical guidelines or codes of conduct and other systematic, authoritative statements of appropriate judicial behaviour, which may communicate requirements of emotion management, display and performance. These guides or codes are sometimes linked to discipline procedures or formal judicial performance evaluation (JPE), though public disciplinary processes and JPE are not part of the Anglo-Australian regulatory landscape. Other processes which may delineate acceptable from unacceptable judicial emotion or its display are appeals (or other forms of legal review) on the basis

1 This chapter relies on some material previously published in Roach Anleu, Mack and Elek et al. (2020) and Roach Anleu, Elek and Mack (2021).

2 In this book, the terms 'judicial officer' and 'judiciary' are used generically to refer to any member of the judiciary, regardless of court level or type. Within Australia, the term 'magistrate' refers to members of the judiciary who preside in the lower state and territory courts, except in the Northern Territory where magistrates were given the title 'judge' in 2016. Australian magistrates are paid judicial officers, with legal qualifications, and are appointed until a fixed retirement age. The term 'judge' indicates those who preside in the intermediate and higher state and territory courts and all national courts. Jurisdictions outside Australia may use other labels for their judiciary or may use these terms, but the words may not have the same meanings as in Australia.

of judicial conduct claimed to lead to an apprehension of bias or denial of a fair hearing. Mentoring and judicial education or professional development programmes can be key elements constituting and transmitting formal or informal norms regulating judging and emotion. Judicial writings outside court, presentations and personal accounts also inform regulation of judicial emotion and emotion work (Roach Anleu, Elek and Mack 2021).

These sources all contain normative statements about how judicial officers ought to conduct themselves. Although the precepts are rarely framed in the explicit language of emotion or emotion work, they anticipate emotion from the judicial officer or others in court and communicate standards which regulate judging and emotion. They articulate what is required, allowed or prohibited, or may provide aspirational guidance, education, feedback or discipline to assist judicial officers to achieve acceptable or improved emotional performance in their everyday work. They indicate the emotion management expected of a good judge and good judging, while recognising the judiciary as a self-regulating profession. Taken together, they contribute to an ethical infrastructure[3] which governs the emotion experiences, display and work undertaken by judicial officers.

Guidelines and codes

Codes of conduct or ethics guides are often associated with professionalisation, the maintenance of professional status and detached professional service which may require emotion management (Abbott 1983, 1988; Wilensky 1964). For the judiciary, written ethics codes or guides for judicial conduct are visible, well-documented and readily accessible, though their official standing, and their link to judicial disciplinary processes, if any, varies widely (Devlin and Dodek 2016; Parker 2004; Parker, Evans and Haller et al. 2008; Tenbrunsel and Smith-Crowe 2008; Treviño, den Nieuwenboer and Kish-Gephart 2014).[4]

[3] It appears that the term 'ethical infrastructure' was first proposed by Schneyer (1991, 1998) in an analysis of law firms and professional discipline: 'a law firm's organization, policies, and operating procedures constitute an "ethical infrastructure"' (Schneyer 1991: 10; also see Schneyer 1998). Since then, it has been used in parallel bodies of literature: legal ethics, especially in relation to large law firms (Chambliss 2012; Chambliss and Wilkins 2002) and organisational psychology (Tenbrunsel, Smith-Crowe and Umphress 2003; Victor and Cullen 1988) with some cross-reference (Robbennolt 2015). We are using the term 'ethical infrastructure' to signify the diverse material or artefacts—statements of ethics, codes of conduct, institutional and organisational procedures, appeal cases, extra-curial judicial statements—which constitute the ethical values and norms of the judiciary and seek to promote good judging (Appleby and Le Mire 2019; Elek, Rottman and Spacek Miller et al. 2017).

[4] An important aspect of such ethics codes and conduct guides is to specify conflicts of interest which is not the focus of this chapter.

In Australia, the Australasian Institute of Judicial Administration (AIJA) *Guide to Judicial Conduct* (Council of Chief Justices of Australia and New Zealand 2017) (AIJA *Guide*) is endorsed by the Council of Chief Justices of Australia and New Zealand, confirming its status as the most authoritative and widely accepted resource for judicial conduct guidance in those jurisdictions. Another significant resource is the *Bangalore Principles of Judicial Conduct* (United Nations Office on Drugs and Crime 2002) (*Bangalore Principles*). The *Bangalore Principles* have been especially influential in Britain and the British Commonwealth. The *Guide to Judicial Conduct* for England and Wales (*Guide* (E & W)) specifically references the *Bangalore Principles* (Courts and Tribunals Judiciary 2020). Other jurisdictions which expressly reference these principles include Ghana, Scotland and Northern Ireland (Devlin and Dodek 2016; McIntyre 2019). These two resources are framed in general aspirational terms and have no formal role in judicial discipline.

In contrast, the American Bar Association (ABA) *Model Code of Judicial Conduct* (2011) (ABA *Code*) contains more concrete detail and is directly linked to judicial discipline. The *Code* consists of four canons, which state overarching principles of judicial conduct. Each canon is followed by the black-letter rules. 'Commentary then adds explanation, interpretation, and aspirational goals' (Arkfeld 2007: 318). Versions of the ABA *Code* have been adopted (or adapted with modification) by most US states (see, for example, the *Arizona Code of Judicial Conduct* (2009) discussed below). Most US states have established commissions to investigate complaints against judicial officers and, where appropriate, impose disciplinary sanctions (Gray 2007). In those proceedings, judicial conduct is assessed against provisions of the ABA *Code* as adopted or adapted by the jurisdiction. This *Code* also has significant international influence, reflecting its long history, extensive commentary, and frequent updating. An example is Canada's *Ethical Principles for Judges*, which acknowledges the influence of the ABA *Code* (Canadian Judicial Council 2004).

While there is rarely language in any of these sources directly addressing emotion, several provisions relate implicitly to judicial emotion and emotion management. The AIJA *Guide* articulates three objectives: public confidence, respect and reputation, based on basic principles: 'impartiality, judicial independence, and integrity and personal behaviour' (p. 5). The *Bangalore Principles* are similar: Value 1 is independence, Value 2 is impartiality and Value 3 is integrity (also see Devlin and Dodek 2016). The ABA *Code* emphasises the importance of 'public confidence in the independence, impartiality and integrity of the judiciary' (Canon 1, Rule 1.2).

To achieve these goals, a judicial officer must maintain decorum in court proceedings while being patient, courteous and dignified and displaying a demeanour of emotionless detachment (ABA *Code*; AIJA *Guide*; *Bangalore Principles*; *Guide* (E & W); also see Shetreet 2014). The AIJA *Guide* states that it is 'desirable [for a judge] to display such personal attributes as punctuality, courtesy, patience, tolerance and good humour' and '[a] judge must be firm but fair in the maintenance of decorum' (p. 19). Similarly, Rule 2.8 of the ABA *Code* provides:

A. A judge shall require order and decorum in proceedings before the court.
B. A judge shall be patient, dignified, and courteous to litigants, jurors, witnesses, lawyers, court staff, court officials, and others with whom the judge deals in an official capacity ...

These normative statements reinforce the ideal of professional detachment or distance as a marker of impartiality. They stress the importance of well-managed emotion and emotional expression to reinforce core judicial values of independence, impartiality and integrity and so advance public confidence in the judiciary (ABA *Code*; AIJA *Guide*; *Guide* (E & W); see Devlin and Dodek 2016; Green and Roiphe 2008). The converse implication is that the presence of emotion and its display, and inappropriately managed judicial emotional conduct, indicates partiality leading to a loss of public confidence (Appleby and Le Mire 2014; Green and Roiphe 2008; Richmond 2012).[5]

The relationship among the desired qualities is complex and reflects contradictory views of the place of emotion in judicial work. The emphasis on maintaining decorum reinforces the formality of judicial authority: 'The ideal judge, as described by codes of judicial conduct, is unreadable, detached, and impersonal' (Lens 2016: 714). However, qualities such as courtesy and patience and recognising the dignity of others implicitly acknowledge the interactional nature of judicial work, especially in court. These guidelines assume that others may be acting in ways that demand judicial patience, courtesy, tolerance or the maintenance of decorum, but do not adequately recognise the considerable judicial emotion management necessary to achieve the required qualities. While the ABA *Code* stresses that efficient case processing and the obligation to behave with courtesy and patience need not be in conflict (see Rule 2.3), it does not provide concrete assistance on how to reconcile these duties. There is no similar claim in the AIJA *Guide* or *Bangalore Principles.*

Judicial conduct complaints and discipline

Some displays of judicial emotion may lead to complaints from litigants, lawyers or others, claiming that such conduct violates applicable codes or rules

[5] These qualities are sometimes included in the general term 'judicial temperament' a quality often identified in relation to judicial appointment (Australasian Institute of Judicial Administration 2015; Maroney 2020).

of judicial conduct. Neither the AIJA *Guide* nor the *Guide* (E & W) provide a formal or official basis for judicial discipline (also see Canadian Judicial Council 2004).[6] The AIJA *Guide* itself states that '[t]his publication does not purport to be a code in any sense of that word, or to lay down rules' (p. 2). Similarly, the *Guide* (E & W) states that those responsible for judicial discipline processes 'may choose to have regard to this Guide, [but] they are not obliged to follow it' (p. 5). In most US states, the ABA *Code*, or its state-specific adaptations, is enforceable through disciplinary mechanisms.

Processes for considering complaints about judicial conduct, the standards applied and the information available to other judicial officers or the public at large vary widely across jurisdictions, making it difficult to generalise about judicial emotion or emotion (mis)management in judicial misconduct complaints (Appleby, Le Mire and Lynch et al. 2019; Devlin and Dodek 2016; Gray 2007; Geyh, Alfini and Lubet et al. 2013; Roach Anleu, Rottman and Mack 2016). The US Center for Judicial Ethics specifically identifies displays of impatience and anger as a frequent basis for complaints: '[c]harges of impatient, angry, and impolite behavior on the bench generate a large proportion of complaints filed with judicial conduct commissions' (Gray 2009: 4). This suggests that a judicial officer's failure to manage his/her own emotions elicits responses from others that lead to complaints. Forms of judicial misconduct leading to disciplinary action that may entail or imply lack of emotion regulation include 'rude and abusive behavior', biased comments and 'misuse of the contempt power' (Gray 2009: 4). Some judicial conduct generating complaints leading to discipline may reflect the considerable stress judicial officers experience in light of the emotional demands of their work, which may not be adequately recognised or supported, an issue raised in some of the discipline cases discussed below.

Matters where judicial behaviour is the subject of complaint raising questions of emotion or emotion management are a small subset of all complaints, and complaints resulting in a public record of discipline are an even smaller subset. According to the US Center for Judicial Ethics in 2018, complaints against US state court judges resulted in:

- seven judges being removed from office;
- 25 judges or former judges resigning or retiring 'in lieu of discipline pursuant to public agreements with conduct commissions';
- one judge resigning and being publicly admonished;
- 11 judges being suspended without pay (no further sanction);
- one judge being indefinitely suspended with public censure; and

[6] There has been a suggestion that Canada's *Ethical Principles* should be a 'binding ethics code' rather than 'advisory ethics guidance' (Salyzyn and Devlin 2020).

- other outcomes including public censure, reprimand, admonishments or warnings being given to 84 judges or former judges (Gray 2019: 2).

In New South Wales in Australia from 2011 to 2019, only 14 complaints were referred for a conduct inquiry and only four resulted in publicly available reports. (See Table 6.1 and text below.)

While the extreme rarity of any judicial discipline limits what can be directly discerned about emotion or emotion display in judicial work, examining available information can help clarify the scope of the formal and informal norms that regulate emotion and judicial behaviour. However, accessing and systematically analysing disciplinary records in the USA and in Australia is challenging. As a result, such materials only provide limited guidance for how good judging can incorporate judicial emotion management as part of everyday practice or when poor emotion management breaches disciplinary standards.

Australia

Four Australian states and territories have standing judicial commissions or similar agencies to receive and handle complaints (*Judicial Commissions Act 1994* (ACT) s 14(1); *Judicial Officers Act 1986* (NSW); *Judicial Conduct Commissioner Act* 2015 (SA) s 12(1); *Judicial Commission of Victoria Act* 2016 (Vic) s 5). The Northern Territory expects to create one in 2020 (Breen 2019). For example, the *Judicial Officers Act 1986* (NSW) provides: 'Any person may complain to the Commission about a matter that concerns or may concern the ability or behaviour of a judicial officer' (s 15(1)). Information about these processes is publicly available on various websites. If the misconduct is so serious as to possibly warrant removal, the complaint, along with any supporting information, is referred to the Parliament of the jurisdiction, which has the sole constitutional authority to remove a judicial officer (Appleby and Le Mire 2016; Mack and Roach Anleu 2006; see, for example, *Constitution Act 1902* (NSW) s 53(1)-(2)).

In those Australian jurisdictions without such commissions, complaints about judicial conduct can be made directly to the court, to be handled internally, informally and confidentially by the head of jurisdiction. This may be inherent or implicit in the authority and duty to manage the court (Mack and Roach Anleu 2004) or authorised by specific legislation (see, for example, *Federal Court of Australia Act 1976* (Cth) s 15(1)(c), (1AAA)). In addition, some courts have developed published protocols for processing complaints against judicial officers (see, for example, Local Court of the Northern Territory 2019; Supreme Court of Western Australia 2019). These protocols do not necessarily require publicly available information about the substance or outcome of any complaints, or the identity of the judicial officer involved to be made public (Law Reform Commission of Western Australia 2012).

Table 6.1 Resolution of complaints* about judicial officers: New South Wales, July 2011 to June 2019

Category	2011–12	2012–13	2013–14	2014–15	2015–16	2016–17	2017–18	2018–19	Total
Number of complaints	**136**	**110**	**69**	**67**	**55**	**89**	**91**	**89**	**706**
Complaints examined and dismissed	79	79	58	49	40	69	55	66	**495**
Complaints referred to head of jurisdiction	7	4	1	4	0	2	5	1	**24**
Complaints referred to Conduct Division	4	2	2	2	0	1	2	1	**14**
Complaints withdrawn	7	4	0	1	1	0	3	1	**17**
Number of matters finalised	**97**	**89**	**61**	**56**	**41**	**72**	**65**	**69**	**550**

* Not all complaints are finalised within the year they are made, some are still pending, so the total number of matters finalised may be different than the total number of complaints.
Source: Judicial Commission of New South Wales (Judicial Commission of New South Wales n.d., 2017, 2018, 2019).

Data from New South Wales, the largest Australian jurisdiction with the longest standing process for responding to complaints about judicial conduct, illustrates the judicial commission process in Australia. As indicated in Table 6.1, there are several possible outcomes of a complaint to the New South Wales Judicial Commission (JCNSW) under Part 6 of the *Judicial Officers Act 1986*: dismiss, either because it is unsubstantiated or not within the Commission's authority, or refer it to the head of jurisdiction or to the Conduct Division. The Conduct Division examines the complaint and then may dismiss it, report on the complaint to the head of jurisdiction or provide a publicly available report to Parliament where dismissal may be warranted. The Commission itself does not have power to discipline judicial officers.

Complaints referred back to the head of jurisdiction are less serious, but not so trivial as to justify summary dismissal (JCNSW 2019). Appleby and Le Mire describe this process as providing 'little more than a triage service' (2016: 43). These matters are handled confidentially. No information is required to be made available to enable judicial officers or the public to discern what types of emotion-related conduct generate complaints or to identify the boundary between those complaints deemed not serious enough to warrant formal processing and those regarded as more serious.

Of the 14 complaints referred to the Conduct Division since 2011, only four reports have been issued (as of May 2020). Three matters involving multiple complaints against magistrates contain extensive written submissions and oral evidence at hearings (In re Betts 2011; In re Burns 2018; In re Maloney 2011).[7] Although judicial emotion and lack of effective emotion management are implicated in the nature of the complaint, the judicial conduct is rarely described in explicitly emotion language nor is there direct discussion of emotion (mis)management in the responses of the judicial officer to the complaint and the Conduct Division's findings.

One magistrate was found to have used 'intemperate' language as shown by the 'tone of voice as well as the language used' (In re Betts 2011: at [105]–[106]), suggesting an inappropriate display of emotion. A second magistrate made demeaning, racialised comments in court, with the effect of making a court participant 'an object of jest' (In re Maloney 2011: at [84]), in contrast to appropriate and inclusive humour used to generate positive feelings in court. A third magistrate's experiences of anxiety, depression and stress could have been characterised as feelings or emotion, but were medicalised. In their submissions and in the Conduct Division's analysis, each magistrate's conduct and attitude was explained on grounds of mental health issues, rather than characterised as emotion and lack of emotion management.

7 The fourth matter which was the subject of a report involved extreme delay by a judge in producing judgments: 15 delayed more than 12 months, including five delayed more than 20 months, and others more than 24, 34 and 35 months (In re Maiden 2019).

These reports also consider the distinctive demands and resulting stress of work in an overburdened, time-pressured lower court (In re Betts 2011; In re Burns 2018). One magistrate described the workload as 'crushing' and 'unrelenting' (In re Burns 2018: [102], [106]) and emphasised the demands of the list days, often entailing very long sitting days, exceptionally long work days in addition to court hours, and the complexity of sentencing matters (at [105], [130]–[131]). These are stressful and emotionally difficult aspects of work for all courts, especially lower courts. In its findings, the Conduct Division normalised these working conditions, stating that the sitting times and work hours were 'not excessive or unreasonable' (at [133]). However 'normal' such conditions might be, in the sense of frequently occurring, that does not relieve a judicial officer working in those circumstances of the emotion demands presented and the need for considerable emotion work to manage them.

In these three cases, the Conduct Division was unpersuaded by the claims of work pressures or currently controlled mental illness as justifications. The reports comment on the extent to which the magistrates appear to lack insight into their conduct. In each matter, the Conduct Division concluded that the magistrate did not demonstrate sufficient judicial capacity and that parliamentary removal could be warranted. In two cases, Parliament declined to act, and the magistrates continued as judicial officers. In the third, the magistrate resigned before parliamentary consideration (JCNSW 2019).

Two of the reports rely in part on the AIJA *Guide* in their analysis of whether the judicial conduct complained of amounted to misbehaviour. This suggests there may be a greater role in the future for the AIJA *Guide* in formal disciplinary processes (In re Burns 2018; In re Betts 2011; also see Sackville 2015).

In addition to these detailed reports, the Commission website provides case studies as examples of complaints regarded as serious enough to be considered and responded to (see, for example, JCNSW 2019). Unfortunately, the information is expressed as conclusions, rather than giving factual details of the judicial conduct in a way that would assist judicial officers or others to understand the limits of proper judicial conduct, including the emotional aspects of judging. One recent example in which the magistrate participated in a 'heated exchange' with the respondent to an application for an apprehended violence order, suggests that conduct implying emotion was involved (JCNSW 2019). While the Commission described the conduct as inappropriate, no further details are given. Similarly, in another matter, the Commission found that a 17 year old was not bullied or belittled, as asserted by the complainant. However, it did consider that 'the comments made … were inappropriate, insensitive and discourteous' (2017: 50). 'The Commission was further of the view that the judicial officer's attempt at humour was out of place in a courtroom' (2017: 50). While each of these examples indicates that conduct which might imply improperly managed emotion is of concern, sufficient information is not available to understand the nature or place of emotion.

This lack of emotion language in the Commission materials is not surprising, as these are legal processes which translate emotion into legal categories such as 'capacity'. To the extent that emotion is recognised, it is equated with stress or is medicalised, or a reflection only on an individual's capacity. This provides a very limited view of emotion and judging and does not consider the relational context in which emotion emerges. Even detailed reports do not consider judicial emotion and emotion work in a broad or systematic way. As a result, complaint and discipline processes in Australia provide little insight into judicial emotion and emotion work and have minimal value in supporting good judging practice in relation to emotion and emotion management.

England and Wales

In England and Wales, complaints about judicial conduct of magistrates and justices of the peace may be made to the local Advisory Committee for the relevant court (Judicial Conduct Investigations Office n.d.). Complaints about any other judicial office holders are made to the independent, statutory Judicial Conduct Investigations Office (JCIO). Disciplinary action includes formal advice, warning, reprimand and removal. The way the JCIO handles complaints may be reviewed by the Judicial Appointments and Conduct Ombudsman (JACO).

Most complaints relate to judicial decisions and case management, not within the JCIO's authority; 498 complaints were about inappropriate behaviour and comments which could be investigated. Of those investigated, 39 were upheld, of which 17 resulted in removal from office (JCIO 2019a).

Disciplinary statements are published on the JCIO website, though only for one year, unless the judicial officer is removed, in which case the statement remains for five years. These statements are usually only one or two sentences. Many of the complaints for 2019 involved judicial officers not showing up for scheduled sitting. A typical example:[8]

> The Lord Chancellor and the Lord Chief Justice have removed Mr Abraham Hussein, from his position as Member of the … Tribunal for failing to meet the minimum sitting requirements of his appointment (JCIO 2018).

One statement suggests anger 'in the heat of the moment' that was 'intended to be threatening', but outside of any court process or location:

> The Lord Chancellor and Mrs Justice Sonja Blake have issued William Turner JP, a magistrate … with a formal warning after he referred to his

[8] All names given in the following excerpts from JCIO statements have been changed.

> judicial status in a way that was intended to be threatening—'Just wait until you are in front of me'—during a telephone conversation with a former friend. While finding that Mr Turner made the remark in the heat of the moment, the Lord Chancellor and Mrs Justice Sonja Blake DBE concluded that he had misused his judicial status (JCIO 2019b).

A review of all 150 disciplinary statements available from May 2012 to June 2017 finds very few complaints raising any kind of in-court behaviour and only two complaints that arguably could implicate judicial emotion. In both examples, the descriptions are so brief it is not possible to discern whether emotion was involved.[9] For example:

> An investigation into a complaint against Mr Phillip Jones JP, a magistrate ... found that he demonstrated an inability to take a dispassionate view of a case. The Lord Chancellor and Lord Chief Justice concluded that his actions fell below the standard expected of a magistrate and have removed him from the Magistracy (Office for Judicial Complaints 2013).

Discipline on the basis of inability to be dispassionate reinforces the importance of this quality, but without more, it is impossible to tell if this entailed emotion or a substantive view of certain kinds of cases or issues or participants. In another matter:

> Judge James Black was subject to a conduct investigation following a complaint about his behaviour during court proceedings. The Lord Chancellor and the Senior President of the Tribunals considered that Judge Black used both an inappropriate tone and inappropriate language with a party during the hearing over which he presided. They found that Judge Black's behaviour failed to demonstrate the standards expected of a judicial office holder and have issued him with formal advice (JCIO 2016).

The inappropriate tone and language may have entailed judicial emotion and display, as in examples discussed earlier, but it is not possible to discern more from these very brief statements.

[9] A research assistant read all 150 statements, categorising the conduct complained of within each as (1) in-court behaviour ($n = 6$); (2) appearing to be to in-court behaviour, but insufficient detail to be more certain ($n = 2$); or (3) conduct occurring outside of the courtroom ($n = 142$). Each of the eight statements appearing to relate to in-court behaviour was read carefully to discern whether the statement related to judicial emotion display or regulation.

United States of America

In most US states, judicial conduct commissions or similar bodies investigate complaints against judicial officers and can impose disciplinary sanctions including private or public reprimands, censure or removal from office (Geyh, Alfini and Lubet et al. 2010; Gray 2007, 2019; Green and Roiphe 2008). In many states, some information about the nature of complaints and the outcomes is publicly available, potentially giving concrete elaboration of unacceptable judicial emotion and display. The Center for Judicial Ethics provides an important national clearinghouse including a regular newsletter which summarises ethics violations from across the USA (see National Center for State Courts 2020). As with the JCNSW case studies and the disciplinary statements for England and Wales, it is not always possible, from the descriptions provided, to identify sufficient concrete detail to discern the boundaries between acceptable judicial emotion and display and that which merits discipline (Gray 2019).

Rather than a national overview, focusing on a single state may provide a better understanding of disciplinary processes regulating judicial emotion. Arizona's Commission on Judicial Conduct has an archive of complaints against judicial officers publicly available via its website, typically including the complaint, the judge's response (perhaps via a lawyer) and the Commission's order disposing of the complaint. Some cases may include the judicial officer's motion for reconsideration and the Commission's response. Matters involving a public reprimand, or recommending a more severe sanction, provide some information outlining the ways the behaviour and demeanour of the judge breached the Arizona *Code of Judicial Conduct* and so enable investigating the apparent role of emotion in judicial discipline.[10]

Rule 2.8 of the *Arizona Code of Judicial Conduct*, tracking Rule 2.8 of the ABA *Code*, requires that the judge maintain 'order and decorum' and 'shall be patient, dignified, and courteous'. Reprimands identifying breaches of this rule are likely to be the most strongly indicative of judicial emotion and lack of emotion management. In 2015, for example, Rule 2.8 was cited in four of the six reprimands issued by the Commission. In these matters, the judicial conduct complained of took place in court and appears to implicate emotion and emotional conduct as part of courtroom interaction.

One of these four cases was an eviction proceeding involving a plaintiff without legal representation seeking rent from an elderly defendant, also

[10] This discussion draws on a study of all judicial disciplinary matters reported publicly on the Arizona Judicial Commission website between 2010 and 2015. This research, undertaken with Dr Jennifer Elek and Dr David Rottman of the US National Center for State Courts. began by identifying all complaints and supporting information including dispositions. Cases where sanctions were imposed were analysed to identify those in which unmanaged or inappropriate judicial emotion appeared to be an aspect of the conduct giving rise to the complaint.

without legal representation (Commission on Judicial Conduct (AZ), Case 15–125).[11] According to the Disciplinary Counsel's Response to Motion for Reconsideration (filed on 27 August 2015):

> When [the judge] commenced the trial, he was either oblivious to or deliberately ignored the fact that the elderly defendant [using a walker] was having a difficult time in finding a chair that would accommodate her. She likely did not hear him request her opening statement, and instead of patiently waiting for her to get situated at the table, he forfeited her right to an opening statement.

The Commission noted in its first order (made on 14 August 2015) that the judge then:

> told the plaintiff to call her first witness. After the plaintiff made a brief statement of the relief she was requesting [her house and rent] he asked 'You're done. Really?' in a sarcastic tone ...

and proceeded to dismiss the case. The Disciplinary Counsel characterised this conduct as the judge being 'very curt and abrupt with the plaintiff, who was clearly a struggling self-represented litigant'. The Commission's analysis of the interaction and the judicial conduct reinforces the importance of patience and the need for empathy in relation to the litigant's circumstances.

The Commission's first order points out that the judge 'did not provide the litigants any guidance as to how the trial would proceed'. In his motion for reconsideration, the judge claims that 'As a practical matter, even 5 minutes of procedural guidance per case would swamp the lower courts. Courts can have over 100 such cases on the daily calendar'. This comment echoes the concerns in a JCNSW matter, as well as the findings of other research into the work of lower courts reviewed in Chapter 2, that judicial capacity to meet the practical and emotional needs of the litigants in such a context is necessarily limited. Nonetheless, as in the JCNSW matters discussed above, this claim was not regarded as persuasive, and the Commission denied the motion for reconsideration.

In making the determinations in this case, the Commission had to interpret and apply the very general, abstract and aspirational words of Rule 2.8, clarifying its scope and meaning. There is a recognition of the special needs, including likely emotions, of an elderly unrepresented litigant distracted by finding a chair and perhaps confused by the unfamiliarity of the court and so deserving of special patience. The case emphasises the importance of

[11] Documents published by, and filed with, the Commission in respect of this case are available online: https://www.azcourts.gov/portals/137/reports/2015/15-125.pdf.

dynamic interaction between the judicial officer and parties in a busy court with a heavy workload, time pressure and the emotional as well as practical burden these create. The Commission recognises that, though this judge's emotion and conduct may have been reactive and appeared spontaneous, it is something that can be anticipated and managed.

Fair hearing: Judicial emotion and conduct

A display of judicial emotion in court might indicate an attitude which is interpreted as bias or otherwise impact upon a party's right to a fair hearing and so could provide the basis for an appeal against a judicial decision. Appeals or other forms of review are important regulatory mechanisms as they detail the emotion-related judicial conduct complained of, and whether or not the challenge is successful. They also have the potential to provide clearer demarcation of the regulatory distinction between acceptable and unacceptable judicial emotion and practice (Kirby 2003; Roach Anleu, Mack and Tutton 2014). While the legal criteria applied are not the same as the aspirational principles articulated by the AIJA *Guide* or other guidelines, the qualities of judicial (mis)conduct identified are similar: lack of courtesy, patience, dignity and respect for others in the courtroom.

A review[12] of Australian cases claiming denial of a fair hearing or actual

[12] The case review was conducted in stages, using electronic sources including Austlii, Firstpoint and Casebase, and index categories including 'conduct of trial judge' and 'conduct of magistrate'. While the search included cases from 1907 to 2016, only more recent cases available online from 1980 were read. Cases selected for further review involved claims about judicial demeanour, attitude or language, in particular displays of judicial anger, hostility, irritation or rudeness or the use of specific emotion words. This resulted in 32 cases. These cases were then read more carefully along a range of dimensions including:

- the type of proceeding (for example, criminal or civil; pre-trial, trial or sentencing);
- nature of the judicial conduct at issue such as the words spoken and the quality that attracted attention (for example, tone, frequency or language used), the judicial demeanour or behaviour (for example, hands shaking or the appearance of anger) or any accompanying legal decision (for example, use of contempt power);
- the nature of the behaviour of other participants in court such as the legal representatives or parties (for example, if legal representatives were perceived to be wasting time or rude);
- the legal issue presented and the outcome of the case (for example, appeal or judicial review; whether the reviewing body was considering that the judicial conduct created an apprehension of bias, led to a miscarriage of justice, denied a party a fair trial, denied a party procedural fairness); and
- the materials relied upon by the reviewing court (for example, transcript of proceedings in the lower court, audio recording of the proceedings in the lower court, evidence from a legal representative who was present in the lower court, a report from the judicial officer herself or himself).

or apparent bias identified 32 cases where the nature of the judicial behaviour at issue implies the presence and impact of judicial emotion or lack of effective emotion work. While judicial emotion or feelings are sometimes expressly stated, or judicial conduct is described in a way that implies an emotional state (for example, the trial judge 'displayed frustration and irritation'), most cases have no express indication of judicial emotion or use of emotion words, and few are framed specifically about judicial emotion or emotion (mis)management. Even when an emotion or feeling may be named or implied, it is rarely the emotion itself which is considered; rather it is the impact of the judicial conduct on the fairness of the proceedings which is of concern. This is similar to the other disciplinary processes discussed above, where emotion is reframed into a legal category. It is rare for challenges to be successful explicitly or solely on the basis of such judicial behaviour and the associated feelings, though judicial emotion conduct is sometimes criticised as inappropriate or unacceptable. Alternatively, the conduct may be regarded sympathetically or as understandable in the particular context in the course of the judgment.

A recurring theme across many of these cases is that judges are human and will therefore experience and display emotion. For example, in *Michael v Western Australia* [2007] WASCA 100 at [71], Steytler P remarks that 'judges are human, and can be expected to react with impatience or irritation from time to time' (also see *Galea v Galea* (1990) 19 NSWLR 263). In some cases, the appeal court may describe the difficulties the judicial officer faced, suggesting some justification. For example, in *Percival v The Queen* [2015] VSCA 200 at [15], the Court of Appeal criticised the 'lack of care' in the preparation of the case and the way one barrister conducted cross-examination. The Court comments at [14] that '[t]here is no doubt that the [trial] judge exhibited signs of impatience ... His Honour was justified in doing so'.

The Judicial Conference of Australia also points out that 'judicial officers are human' and therefore 'imperfect' and so may 'fail to conduct ourselves as judicial officers should' (2010: 2). This view equates judicial humanity with inappropriate judicial conduct. In *Long v Mayger* [2004] WASCA 41, the Court stated at [42]:

> Judicial officers are not mindless automatons. They have emotions and may, on occasions, be affected by them. It can be normally assumed that an experienced judicial officer will recognise when judgment may be being swayed by emotion and take steps to avoid injustice by postponing proceedings or even standing aside.

Note the similarity to the strategies outlined in Chapters 3 and 4, expecting that judicial officers 'will recognise' and 'take steps' to avoid the impact of emotion on judgment, including postponement.

In *Ford v The Queen* [2016] NSWCCA 69, the trial judge sentenced the defendant for multiple counts of sexual offending against several children, part of a wider network of child pornography and paedophilia, including offences committed by the parents of two of the children. On appeal, the Court maintained at [28]:

> Although … a sentencing judge must maintain a degree of detachment in order to judge the moral culpability of an offender whose liberty is at stake, that does not mean that the judge is to be drained of any legitimate emotional response. … [S]uch impersonal and absolute detachment is not required.

In this comment, the Court directly addresses the tension between the legal requirement of impersonal judicial detachment and the practical reality of judicial emotion experience. Sexual offences involving children and sentencing are two of the most emotionally demanding aspects of judicial work. In this case, the entire judgment reflects intense judicial emotion reaction to offences involving 'an unfathomable degree of cruelty and depravity' (at [66]). The paragraph quoted above confirms that the obligation of judicial detachment is not 'absolute', and that 'legitimate emotional response' is acceptable.

Even extreme facts may not justify insufficiently managed judicial emotion. *Piccolotto v The Queen* [2015] VSCA 143 was an appeal against conviction on charges of threatening to kill and false imprisonment of the defendant's then partner, including holding a gun to her head and throwing her against a wall. Reviewing the transcript of a six-day jury trial, the Court commented that there were 'numerous … occasions where the [trial] judge was impatient, demeaning and ridiculed counsel [for the defendant] … in the presence of the jury', including accusing counsel of 'wasting time and engaging in repetitive or pointless cross examination' (at [21]). The Court recognised that 'the trial judge was entitled to feel exasperated' and to 'reprove counsel to ensure that witnesses were treated fairly and that the [trial] court's time was not wasted'. Further, the Court recognised at [44] that the judge 'was … faced with a difficult task' (at [36], [42] and [44]). In this case, the context in which the judicial emotion arose was specifically identified and at least some judicial emotion, such as 'exasperated', is acknowledged as justified. Nonetheless, the Court found that the extensive manifestation of judicial impatience breached the boundaries of the judicial role, especially before a jury, and held 'that the atmosphere of the trial was tainted in a manner so adverse to the [defendant] that … [i]t could not be asserted that there had been a fair trial' and upheld the appeal and granted a new trial (at [53]).

In appeal cases, judicial conduct is described in some detail, in its context, and characterised or criticised in light of the core principle of impartiality.

A court has the opportunity to define boundaries between appropriate and inappropriate emotion display or expression and related conduct. Ultimately though, no clear line between acceptable and unacceptable judicial conduct can be discerned across the cases reviewed. Comparing cases where the impugned conduct was upheld with those where it was not is confounded by the multiplicity of issues affecting the actual appeal judgment.

Judicial performance evaluation

JPE can encompass a range of purposes, processes and assumptions about the nature of judicial work and appropriate judicial conduct (Contini, Roach Anleu and Rottman 2014). In general, JPE focusses on individual judicial skills, capacities and practices assessed against an abstract normative model of a good or proper judge (Roach Anleu and Mack 2014). While the model or criteria against which performance is evaluated may not be expressed in terms of judicial emotion or emotion work, such capacities are important to achieve the standards set.

JPE can be implemented through informal processes, as part of professional self-regulation, or more formally through external processes. In Australia, there is very little formal or structured JPE (Bryant 2014; Law Reform Commission of Western Australia 2012; but see Wallace, Roach Anleu and Mack 2015). Australian courts have performance indicators (Australian Government Productivity Commission 2020; International Consortium for Court Excellence 2013), but individual JPE is voluntary. Use of any findings is for individual professional development and is not available to inform work allocation or discipline. There is no involvement of the public, nor are any findings made available to other members of the judiciary for guidance, let alone publicly. These limits are understood to be a consequence of constitutional guarantees of judicial independence (Hiskey 2002; Lee 2011; Mack and Roach Anleu 2004; Warren 2011).

Some peer observation of judicial courtroom work in Australia has been independently organised among groups of judicial officers, mainly to provide another perspective to stimulate judicial self-reflection on their own practices (Hiskey 2002, 2005). The state of Victoria developed a voluntary 360-degree review system to assist judges to get a more accurate perception of themselves and improve their own work, which some other courts have implemented (Warren 2011, 2014). This programme elicits evaluations from judicial colleagues, court staff and lawyers who regularly interact with the judge being evaluated and who are nominated by that judge. There is some recognition of the importance of interaction and emotion among the dimensions of judicial work considered, including verbal and non-verbal communication, listening and interpersonal skills, as well as organisation and planning. Specific qualities include '[t]reats others with respect and courtesy' and '[e]ffectively manages the stresses and demands of the role' (Warren 2014: 964). An independent professional moderator gathers and analyses the ratings and then provides the information to the judge in confidence, in a way that does not associate evaluators with their ratings.

In the USA and in many European countries, JPE is more formal, often taking place within official programmes conducted by a court or in association with judicial education bodies or the local legal profession (Brody 2008–2009; Contini and Mohr 2008; Fabri 2016; Kourlis 2010; McIntyre 2014; Roach Anleu and Mack 2014). Purposes may include improving the performance of individual judicial officers and the judiciary as a whole; informing voters in judicial retention elections in US states; contributing to professional development programmes; assigning judges to appropriate roles within a court and determining suitability for promotion to a higher court, especially in European countries (Berch and Bass 2014; Elek, Rottman and Cutler 2014; McIntyre 2014; Riedel 2014).

Formal JPE programmes in the USA are well established (ABA 2005b; Colbran 2006; Gill and Oganesyan 2016; National Center for State Courts 2017; Woolf and Yim 2011). Many states use some version of the ABA model surveys (ABA 2005a) completed by attorneys and court staff; surveys may also be distributed to litigants, jurors and witnesses. The criteria draw on the qualities articulated in the ABA *Code*, and so potentially regulate judicial emotion and emotion management. Assessment of impartiality includes 'treating all people with dignity and respect' (Guideline 5.2.2). Evaluation of 'professionalism and temperament' includes 'a dignified manner' (Guideline 5.4.1), 'courtesy' (Guideline 5.4.2), 'patience and self-control' (Guideline 5.4.3) and 'dealing with pro-se [unrepresented] litigants fairly and effectively' (Guideline 5.4.4). In these surveys, attorneys and other courtroom participants are asked directly, for example, whether the judge 'treats people with courtesy', 'acts with patience and self-control', and 'acts in a dignified manner'. These and other items, such as 'maintains control of the courtroom' and 'presents a neutral presence from the bench', may potentially capture elements of performance related to emotion experience and emotion management (Elek, Rottman and Cutler 2014).

Some types of data from US JPE processes are publicly available, including aggregate survey results (for example, Arizona Supreme Court 2020; State of California Commission on Judicial Performance 2020; Utah Judicial Performance Evaluation Commission 2020). Making some of the data available is seen as appropriate, as a guide for professional development of other judicial officers and for the public in relation to judicial elections (Gill and Oganesyan 2016; Woolf and Yim 2011). This information could potentially provide a better picture of the meaning and regulatory power of the general language in formal guidelines, rules or norms of the ABA *Code*. However, there are concerns about these surveys. Research finds that the standard surveys used in the USA are systematically biased against women and minority judges (Elek and Rottman 2014; Gill, Lazos and Waters 2011).

One jurisdiction that undertakes a wider approach is Utah, where a 'full evaluation' of a judge draws on information gathered by surveys, public comments and courtroom observations, as well as judicial disciplinary records (Utah Judicial Performance Evaluation Commission 2020; also see Woolf and Yim 2011). The Utah evaluation programme, especially the court observation phase, is directed towards procedural justice 'principles of neutrality, respect and voice' (Woolf and Yim 2011: 87) and so could capture elements of judicial emotion and emotion work. The survey asks respondents to choose from a list of positive and negative attributes or qualities that describe their experience of the judge being reviewed. Some adjectives in both the positive and the negative categories imply emotion or emotion work, such as 'calm', 'attentive', 'patient', 'defensive', 'flippant' or 'impatient'. While some judges received 98 percent positive adjectives, compared with others who received 72 percent positive adjectives, no distinct emotion-related patterns were discerned.

Very few emotion-specific comments can be found in the qualitative court observation comments. In one example, a court observer described a judge's tone during sentencing as 'tough and caring, with no anger or condescension' (Utah Judicial Performance Evaluation Commission 2014: 12). This comment was positive about this judge, though it may imply having seen anger or condescension in other judicial officers.

While there may be considerable value for individual judges in the JPE information provided, in particular the adjective choice section and the specific comments from court observers, this material does not provide a systematic basis to identify the demarcation between appropriate, acceptable and undesirable judicial emotion. This finding echoes a more general conclusion about the Utah programme: that there is very little variation in the JPE survey results, providing little distinction among the judges and so 'precious little actionable feedback' (Gill and Oganesyan 2016: 91).

Another facet of JPE and judicial emotion regulation is the relation of JPE to other regulatory or disciplinary processes. In the USA, there is a strong view that JPE should not be linked to discipline, as this would be inconsistent with providing good feedback for individual judicial developmental purposes (Elek, Rottman and Cutler 2014).

Other professional guidance

Judicial officers learn the norms applicable to emotion and judging and acquire skills of emotion management as part of court craft. For some in the judiciary, informal processes can be preferable to other forms of regulation or guidance, as one judge comments:

> That kind of ability to look around and pick up what others are doing and see what the, not the lowest common denominator, not the highest common factor, but what generally is happening and try and put yourself in there at the people that you trust or the people you admire or the things that resonate with you and make you think, you know, that's how I want to be seen, that's how I would want to practice and so on, and I think that's how we do it so it's quite protean and quite amorphous I suppose and that's probably a good thing—although one day I suspect we'll get a judicial commission of some kind and that will lay down rules and you know we'll all have to abide by those. The dangers of those is that you work to the rules rather than absorb the self-discipline that is appropriate for being a judge. (I 11)[13]

This judge emphasises the importance of self-discipline as essential to an independent professional judiciary.

Significant informal professional resources include judicial education or development programmes, benchbooks, legal literature, especially judicial speeches and writing about judging and emotion and role models, court culture and shared experience with judicial peers.

Judicial education

Judicial officers in Anglo-American common law systems are not specifically trained to become judicial officers before appointment. The assumption is that many years of legal practice, especially courtroom work, is sufficient preparation (Doyle 2005; Warren 2014). As a result, judicial education is focussed on post-appointment programmes. Professional development can come from a wide range of national, state-based and local sources, from courts themselves or independent providers, offering different types of events in a range of online and face-to-face formats (Judicial College of Victoria [JCV] 2019; see, for example, National Judicial College of Australia [NJCA] 2019; National Judicial College [NJC] (USA) 2020b).

Education programmes address some aspects of judicial emotion management, such as wellness, stress or resilience, suggesting awareness of and

13 This quote is from a judicial officer interviewed as part of the *Courts, the Judiciary and Social Change* project funded by an Australian Research Council (ARC) Discovery Project grant (DP 1096888). The interviews were conducted in 2012–2013. The data is indicated by the code 'I ##' in which the letter I identifies this as interview data and ## is the number assigned to the individual interviewee. Quotations are used verbatim and have not been edited to correct grammar or reduce infelicities of spoken language, but retain qualities of natural, everyday speech reflecting the narrative quality of the interviews. All identifying, or potentially identifying, details have been deleted. For more information on this phase of the research, see the Appendix.

concern about judging and emotion in terms of demands on the judicial officer (JCV 2019; NJCA 2019; NJC (USA) 2020a). Education about secondary trauma can identify emotion management practices such as mindfulness, as well as more concrete strategies for judicial emotion work (Maroney and Gross 2014; Jaffe, Crooks, Dunford-Jackson et al. 2003; see, for example, Casey, Burke and Leben 2012; Schrever 2018). The JCV offers a Communication in the Courtroom workshop as part of its Court Craft programme. Judges preside in an interactive simulated court proceeding, receiving feedback from others present in the simulation and can review a video of the process later (Warren 2014). Programmes in the USA on procedural justice and therapeutic jurisprudence may provide judicial officers with greater awareness of, and insight into, emotional dimensions of their work, including better awareness of the emotion needs of court users and positive aspects of emotion regulation (Hora 2011; Leben 2019; NJC (USA) 2020a).

A different kind of resource is the *Judicial Excellence* report, providing a framework for judicial education based on the views of judicial officers about judicial excellence (Elek, Rottman and Spacek Miller et al. 2017). Insight into emotion and emotion management forms an important dimension of the findings of the report, with some judges valuing qualities such as interpersonal communication and emotion management, while also noting significant variation of judicial views.

Some US judges interviewed for the *Judicial Excellence* project recommend that emotion management be taught early in a judicial career, even within judicial orientation (Elek, Rottman and Spacek Miller et al. 2017: 5). In Australia, the National Judicial Orientation Program impliedly recognises the need for judicial emotion work through topics such as courtroom control which cover the ways language, voice, conduct and body can communicate respect for other participants, and more generally how judicial demeanour can impact on proceedings (NJCA 2019). Elsewhere in Australia, judicial education programmes address topics such as 'Resilience, wellbeing and mindfulness', 'Family & domestic violence' and 'Contempt in the face of the court' (NJCA 2019), 'Bullying and harassment in the court room' and 'Dealing with unrepresented litigants in lengthy and complex trials' (JCNSW 2019).

However, it is rare for programmes to explicitly frame this material as emotion awareness or emotion work, though that is in effect what is being addressed. This is especially so in relation to aspects of judicial practice and interaction with court participants that might be included within a programme on court craft.

A useful role for some of the disciplinary materials reviewed above might be in a structured educational setting, where an instructor has reviewed and selected illustrative cases. These could provide opportunities for judges to discuss practical problems of judicial emotion and management, to bring home the mundane reality of emotion challenges judges may face, and to help judges better anticipate and avoid potential emotion issues.

Benchbooks

Benchbooks can be a valuable source of guidance for judicial officers in Australia and the USA on a range of aspects of judicial work (see, for example, Atkinson, Boddice and Henry 2016; Douglas and Chapple 2019; JCNSW 2007; King 2009). They may contain scripts for court proceedings, procedural details or key points of substantive law.

One example of a benchbook providing guidance in relation to emotion in judicial work is the *Victorian Criminal Proceedings Manual* which specifically addresses emotion as an aspect of poor or improper judicial conduct potentially evincing bias. It notes that 'mere ... bad temper' is insufficient to show bias (JCV 2014: [6.1.2] at [14]) and that a 'short ... emotional exchange will not necessarily demonstrate' loss of impartiality (JCV 2014: [6.1.2] at [15]). Another possible circumstance for emotion and judicial bias is a judge who has been a victim of a crime or experienced personal 'trauma' (JCV 2014: [6.1] at [83]).

More explicit attention to emotion as part of judicial work is found in benchbooks on family, domestic or sexual violence (see, for example, Office of Court Administration (Texas) 2010; Panella 2015). The Australian *National Domestic and Family Violence Bench Book* describes the emotion abuse perpetrators inflict and stresses the importance of a respectful judicial demeanour towards victims (Douglas and Chapple 2019).

These benchbooks appear to treat emotion as an obstacle or challenge for judicial officers. In contrast, some benchbooks provide more positive examples of emotion in judging. In Australia, the *Solution-Focused Judging Bench Book* (King 2009) discusses more interactive approaches to judicial work such as therapeutic jurisprudence and procedural justice. These have the potential to improve processes and outcomes and provide satisfaction for judicial officers, but they also require substantial judicial emotion awareness and engagement (Chase and Hora 2009). The *Procedural Fairness Bench Card* for judges developed by the American Judges Association and the Center for Court Innovation and NCSC provides concrete practical guidance for positive emotion work (American Judges Association, Center for Court Innovation, NCSC et al. 2017).

Judicial writing and speeches

Speeches and writings from judicial officers can be important sources of information about experiences, practices or informal norms supporting professional socialisation and regulation of emotion (see, for example, Kirby 1995, 2013). An interviewee described reading a judge's biography which tells of 'agony over … the head and the heart' which resonated with his own struggles to do justice as required by the oath when it might appear to differ from what the law requires in a particular case (I 11). Remarks by judges at swearing-in ceremonies or special court sitting for judicial retirements can also provide insights into emotion and judging (Moran 2018; Roberts 2012).

Perhaps the most important example of Australian judicial writing underpinning professional socialisation and regulation of judicial emotion is *Judicial Ethics in Australia*, written by James Thomas, a former judge of the Queensland Court of Appeal, published in three editions, each increasing in scope and detail (Thomas 1988, 1997, 2009). This text draws on standards set by a variety of international organisations and other nations. Though it has no official standing and does not systematically enunciate guiding principles, it has been influential in Australia, including being considered as part of a disciplinary inquiry (In re Burns 2018). In contrast to the AIJA *Guide*, which mainly describes aspirational qualities, Thomas's approach is less abstract. The author relates many anecdotes and examples, nearly always of inappropriate judicial behaviour, enlivened with the author's personal opinions (Ehlers 2010). *Judicial Ethics* frequently uses explicit language of emotion to characterise judicial behaviour, describing impatience, frustration, aggression or hostility, but does not generate or articulate a systematic analysis of emotion or emotion work.

Role models, shared experience and court culture

In spite of the isolation which can be a feature of judicial work, learning from colleagues, older and younger, can be a valuable source of guidance (Thomas 2017; Warren 2014; Young 2018). One Australian judge describes her approach:

> I modelled my umm judicial demeanour on the judge that I worked for who was a male and very much from a privileged elite but his style was, I think, similar to the style of most women judges which is … he was calm, he spoke respectfully and polite, politely to people and he was able to defuse emotion in the courtroom terribly well as a result because he, he expected, he modelled the behaviour he expected back and he got it and umm so when I was appointed to my first judicial position which was as a umm, as a tribunal member, I thought, 'oh how do I do this, argh', I'll—and I just naturally followed his style. But I think, I think that's a style that if, umm, if I think about my colleagues on the [intermediate court] who are females it's pretty much their style too. (I 37)

Another aspect of professional socialisation in relation to emotion is legal practice before becoming a judge. One interviewee suggests that judicial officers who have limited experience of clients, especially criminal defendants, may lack empathy (I 34, quoted in Chapter 3).

Court culture (Ostrom, Ostrom and Hewitt et al. 2003) can be especially influential in judicial emotion and related conduct, including the emotional climate of the work context itself. As one senior court official in Australia points out:

> Well, I think that the culture is that people don't express, um, unhappiness because it's a very hard-working culture and it's a—and a culture of—which is respectful essentially of the role of the Registrar, so people generally don't complain. And they might, privately, think 'why am I getting all this crime?' and they might privately, or they might on occasion say that to me—some have—but, um, they wouldn't—yeah, as I say, it's a hard-working non-complaining culture. (W 13)[14]

A different judicial officer links improved judicial communication to generational change and to greater emphasis on efficiency:

> The necessity for court processes to be efficient and for judges to be involved in making sure that cases do get on and disposed of as quickly as possible, just necessitates a more interventionist approach but that also requires, you know, a greater ability to communicate and to listen and to make sure that you really are deciding the right issues. (W 01)

On the other hand, one judge who agrees that the emotional atmosphere of the courtroom is now different, regards the 'current breed of judges … as far more tolerant and understanding and approachable than certainly when I started in the law' (I 10). He suggests that the threat of judicial wrath may have improved preparation by legal practitioners: 'I would never have gone into court unprepared for a lot of reasons but one of them was that you would, you would incur the wrath very severely of a judge …' (I 10). This judge indicates that a court culture which supports the ability to generate an emotional atmosphere of fear or embarrassment can have a positive effect on practitioner performance.

Professional socialisation in its many forms can be an effective

[14] This interview data comes from the *Judicial Officers and Workload Allocation* project supported by an Australian Research Council (ARC) Linkage Project grant (LP 0669168), undertaken in collaboration with Professor Anne Wallace. The quotations used are verbatim based on transcription of the audio-recorded interviews. Any identifying information has been deleted. This data is indicated by the code 'W ##' in which the letter W identifies this interview data from the Workload project and ## is the number assigned to an individual interviewee, whether a judicial officer or court administrator/staff. For more information on this phase of the research, see the Appendix.

communicator of informal norms regulating judicial emotion and emotion work. Values and norms conveyed in these ways can be difficult to discern as, by definition, they are not systematically compiled, written or shared, and may not be equally accessible to all judicial officers. Nonetheless, informal norms can be more powerful than formal regulatory mechanisms (Murray, Murray and Tulich 2020; Wendel 2001).

Conclusion

Regulation of judicial emotion requires assessing judicial emotion or related conduct as appropriate or inappropriate, according to regulatory standards (Roach Anleu, Mack and Tutton 2014). Such standards generally expect patience, courtesy, dignity and decorum, presented as a judicial demeanour, whether or not accompanied by a congruent internal emotional state. These qualities presuppose a detached, emotionless, impersonal judicial officer who embodies a particular notion of impartiality. The display of other feelings, such as impatience, aggression or anger will ordinarily violate these standards (Maroney 2012; Thomas 2009).

Examining the various regulatory processes for insight into the place of emotion in judicial work confirms the 'pluralist nature' of professional regulation (Haller 2010: 227). Regulation includes general, abstract or aspirational statements contained in the ABA *Code*, *Bangalore Principles*, AIJA *Guide* or *Guide* (E & W), JPE, discipline regimes which identify and respond to inappropriate emotion displays or management, and elaboration of implicit norms and management strategies through professional development programmes or other informal socialisation processes.

Available regulatory approaches usually consider only individual conduct (Abbott 1983) and rarely pay sufficient attention to context as part of the emotional environment within which judicial officers work. As one analysis of judging points out that:

> beginning with a definition of a good judge or good judging causes us to focus too much on the qualities or characteristics of [individual] judges, and not enough on the nature of the context or environment in which they make decisions (Wistrich 2010: 257).

Desirable or undesirable qualities or behaviour may be characterised as personal, as reflected in the AIJA *Guide* which describes qualities such as patience and courtesy as 'personal attributes' (p. 19). This formulation lacks a sense of the various episodes, moments and situations that judicial officers encounter, participate in or create through their interactions and responses to other participants (Roach Anleu and Mack 2017).

Even though these regulatory sources and processes are rarely framed in emotion terms, a key insight from the analysis in this chapter is that emotion matters, but there is a lack of fit between the lived emotion experience of judicial practice and the various regulatory regimes and standards. Regulatory processes that deal mainly with extreme cases meriting discipline show clearly how failures of judicial emotion self-regulation can lead to public sanctions for judicial misconduct. However, they have a limited capacity to delineate the boundaries between acceptable and unacceptable judicial emotion and display. To establish the line between appropriate and inappropriate judicial emotion, it is necessary to have details about conduct which does breach the rules as well as conduct which approaches but does not breach boundaries. Such information needs to be reasonably accessible, sufficiently detailed and concrete, and consistent with concerns about confidentiality. Professional socialisation has an important regulatory function in relation to norms governing judicial emotion, especially informal norms, and judicial practice, but is unsystematic and uneven in its reach.

Regulation which adequately addresses the considerable variety and intensity of judicial emotion, and occasions for emotion management, will require engaging many elements of the ethical and regulatory infrastructure to reflect the realities of judicial practice and culture. Ultimately judicial officers individually and collectively must delineate the judicial role and regulate their own conduct in the face of practical interpersonal demands and competing abstract regulatory expectations about judging and emotion, anchored by the core value of impartiality. In this way, the judiciary itself constitutes the applicable norms as well as being constrained by them. The experiences and insights of judicial officers themselves, as revealed through the research presented in this book, provide an essential resource to guide regulation of judicial emotion work.

References

Abbott, Andrew, 1983, 'Professional Ethics', *American Journal of Sociology 88*: 855–885.

Abbott, Andrew, 1988, *The System of Professions: An Essay on the Division of Expert Labor*. Chicago, IL: University of Chicago Press.

American Bar Association 2005a, *Black Letter Guidelines for the Evaluation of Judicial Performance*. Retrieved 9 May 2020, from https://www.americanbar.org/content/dam/aba/publications/judicial_division/jpec_final.authcheckdam.pdf.

American Bar Association 2005b, *Guidelines for the Evaluation of Judicial Performance with Commentary*. Retrieved 9 May 2020, from http://www.americanbar.org/content/dam/aba/publications/judicial_division/aba_blackletter-guidelines_jpe_wcom.authcheckdam.pdf.

American Bar Association 2011, *ABA Model Code of Judicial Conduct*. Retrieved 9 May 2020, from http://www.americanbar.org/groups/professional_responsibility/publications/model_code_of_judicial_conduct.html.

American Judges Association, Center for Court Innovation, National Center for

State Courts and National Judicial College 2017, 'Procedural Fairness/Procedural Justice: A Bench Card for Trial Judges', *Court Review 53*: 189–190.

Appleby, Gabrielle and Suzanne Le Mire 2014, 'Judicial Conduct: Crafting a System That Enhances Institutional Integrity', *Melbourne University Law Review 38*: 1–67.

Appleby, Gabrielle and Suzanne Le Mire 2016, 'The Australian Judiciary: Resistant to Reform?'. In *Regulating Judges: Beyond Independence and Accountability*, eds. Richard Devlin and Adam Dodek, 35–54. Cheltenham and Northampton, MA: Edward Elgar.

Appleby, Gabrielle and Suzanne Le Mire 2019, 'Ethical Infrastructure for a Modern Judiciary', *Federal Law Review 47*: 335–357.

Appleby, Gabrielle, Suzanne Le Mire, Andrew Lynch and Brian Opeskin 2019, 'Contemporary Challenges Facing the Australian Judiciary: An Empirical Interruption', *Melbourne University Law Review 42*: 299–369.

Arizona Supreme Court 2020, 'JPR Process'. Retrieved 9 May 2020, from https://www.azcourts.gov/jpr/About-JPR/JPR-Process.

Arkfeld, Louraine C., 2007, 'Ethics for the Problem-Solving Court Judge: The New ABA Model Code', *Justice System Journal 28*: 317–323.

Atkinson, Roslyn G., David Boddice and James D. Henry, eds. 2016, *Equal Treatment Benchbook*. Retrieved 10 May 2020, from https://www.courts.qld.gov.au/__data/assets/pdf_file/0004/94054/s-etbb.pdf.

Australasian Institute of Judicial Administration 2015, *Suggested Criteria for Judicial Appointments*. Melbourne: Australasian Institute of Judicial Administration.

Australian Government Productivity Commission 2020, *Report on Government Services, Part C, Section 7, Courts, Context*. Retrieved 9 May 2020, from https://www.pc.gov.au/research/ongoing/report-on-government-services/2020/justice/courts.

Berch, Rebecca White and Erin Norris Bass 2014, 'Judicial Performance Review in Arizona: A Critical Assessment', *Oñati Socio-Legal Series 4*: 927–952.

Breen, Jacqueline, 2019, 'NT Chief Judge Elizabeth Morris Finalises Investigation into Complaint against Judge Greg Borchers', *Australian Broadcasting Corporation*. 11 December. Retrieved 29 February 2020, from https://www.abc.net.au/news/2019-12-11/nt-chief-judges-investigates-complaint-against-greg-borchers/11784300.

Brody, David C., 2008–2009, 'The Use of Judicial Performance Evaluation to Enhance Judicial Accountability, Judicial Independence, and Public Trust', *Denver University Law Review 86*: 115–156.

Bryant, Diana, 2014, 'Court Excellence and the Perfect Storm', paper presented at the *International Association for Court Administration 7th International Conference*, Sydney, 24 September. On file with authors.

Canadian Judicial Council 2004, *Ethical Principles for Judges*. Ottawa: Canadian Judicial Council. Retrieved 9 May 2020, from https://cjc-ccm.ca/sites/default/files/documents/2019/news_pub_judicialconduct_Principles_en.pdf.

Casey, Pamela, Kevin Burke and Steve Leben 2012. *Minding the Court: Enhancing the Decision-Making Process*. 1 October. White Paper of the American Judges Association, Retrieved 9 May 2020, from https://lajudicialcollege.org/wp-content/uploads/2014/08/AJA-White-Paper-10-1-2012.pdf.

Chambliss, Elizabeth, 2012, 'Whose Ethics? The Benchmark Problem in Legal Ethics Research'. In *Lawyers in Practice: Ethical Decision Making in Context*, eds. Leslie

C. Levin and Lynn Mather, 47–62. Chicago, IL and London: University of Chicago Press.

Chambliss, Elizabeth and David B. Wilkins 2002, 'Promoting Effective Ethical Infrastructure in Large Law Firms: A Call for Research and Reporting', *Hofstra Law Review 30*: 691–716.

Chase, Deborah J. and Peggy Fulton Hora 2009, 'The Best Seat in the House: The Court Assignment and Judicial Satisfaction', *Family Court Review 47*: 209–238.

Colbran, Stephen, 2006, 'A Comparative Analysis of Judicial Performance Evaluation Programmes', *Journal of Commonwealth Law and Legal Education 4*: 35–67.

Contini, Francesco and Richard Mohr 2008, *Judicial Evaluation: Traditions, Innovations and Proposals for Measuring the Quality of Court Performance*. Germany: VDM Publishing.

Contini, Francesco, Sharyn Roach Anleu and David B. Rottman 2014, 'Evaluating Judicial Performance: Editors' Introduction', *Oñati Socio-Legal Series 4*: 839–842.

Council of Chief Justices of Australia and New Zealand 2017, *Guide to Judicial Conduct*. 3rd ed. Melbourne: Australasian Institute of Judicial Administration. Available from https://aija.org.au/publications-introduction/guidelines/guide-to-judicial-conduct/.

Courts and Tribunals Judiciary 2020, *Guide to Judicial Conduct*. 30 March. Retrieved 9 May 2020, from https://www.judiciary.uk/publications/guide-to-judicial-conduct/.

Devlin, Richard and Adam Dodek 2016, 'Regulating Judges: Challenges, Controversies and Choices'. In *Regulating Judges: Beyond Independence and Accountability*, eds. Richard Devlin and Adam Dodek, 1–34. Cheltenham and Northampton, MA: Edward Elgar.

Douglas, Heather and Kate Chapple 2019, *National Domestic and Family Violence Bench Book*. July. Retrieved 9 May 2020, from http://dfvbenchbook.aija.org.au/contents.

Doyle, John, 2005, 'How Do Judges Keep up to Date?', paper presented at Lawasia Downunder, Queensland, 21–22 March. Retrieved 9 May 2020, from https://njca.com.au/wp-content/uploads/2017/12/How-do-Judges-keep-up-to-date-Doyle-CJ.pdf.

Ehlers, Ashley, 2010, 'Book Review: *Judicial Ethics in Australia*', *Queensland University of Technology Law & Justice Journal 10*: 140–145.

Elek, Jennifer K. and David B. Rottman 2014, 'Methodologies for Measuring Judicial Performance: The Problem of Bias', *Oñati Socio-Legal Series 4*: 863–879.

Elek, Jennifer K., David B. Rottman and Brian L. Cutler 2014, 'Judicial Performance Evaluation in the States: A Re-Examination', *Judicature 98*: 12–19.

Elek, Jennifer K., David B. Rottman, Shelley Spacek Miller and Lydia Hamblin 2017, *Elements of Judicial Excellence: A Framework to Support the Professional Development of State Trial Court Judges – Project Final Report*. Williamsburg, VA: National Center for State Courts.

Fabri, Marco, 2016, 'Clash of Visions: Regulating Judges and Prosecutors in Italy'. In *Regulating Judges: Beyond Independence and Accountability*, eds. Richard Devlin and Adam Dodek, 245–261. Cheltenham and Northampton, MA: Edward Elgar.

Geyh, Charles Gardner, James J. Alfini, Steven Lubet and Jeffrey M. Shaman 2013, *Judicial Conduct and Ethics*. 5th ed. Newark, NJ: Lexis.

Gill, Rebecca D., Sylvia R. Lazos and Mallory M. Waters 2011, 'Are Judicial Performance Evaluations Fair to Women and Minorities? A Cautionary Tale from Clark County, Nevada', *Law & Society Review 45*: 731–759.

Gill, Rebecca D. and Rafael Oganesyan 2016, 'The Ideal Judge: How Implicit Bias Shapes Assessment of State Judges', *Revista Forumul Judecatorilor*, 75–98.

Gray, Cynthia, 2007, 'How Judicial Conduct Commissions Work', *Justice System Journal 28*: 405–418.

Gray, Cynthia, 2009, *Ethical Standards for Judges*. Des Moines, IA: American Judicature Society. Retrieved 9 May 2020, from https://www.ncsc.org/__data/assets/pdf_file/0026/17594/ethical-standards-for-judges.pdf.

Gray, Cynthia, 2019, 'State Judicial Discipline in 2018', *Judicial Conduct Reporter 40*: 2–4. Retrieved 9 May 2020, from https://www.ncsc.org/__data/assets/pdf_file/0016/15550/jcr_winter_2019.pdf.

Green, Bruce A. and Rebecca Roiphe 2008, 'Regulating Discourtesy on the Bench: A Study in the Evolution of Judicial Independence', *New York University Annual Survey of American Law 64*: 497–558.

Haller, Linda, 2010, 'Regulating the Professions'. In *The Oxford Handbook of Empirical Legal Research*, eds. Peter Cane and Herbert M. Kritzer, 216–233. Oxford and New York: Oxford University Press.

Hiskey, Garry Francis, 2002, 'Mutual Observation, Reflection and Discussion and Professional Development for Magistrates', *Journal of Judicial Administration 12*: 39–56.

Hiskey, Garry Francis, 2005, 'Mutual Observation, Reflection and Discussion and Professional Development for Magistrates: Further Developments', *Journal of Judicial Administration 15*: 107–121.

Hora, Peggy Fulton, 2011, 'Courting New Solutions Using Problem-Solving Justice: Key Components, Guiding Principles, Strategies, Responses, Models, Approaches, Blueprints and Tool Kits', *Chapman Journal of Criminal Justice 2*: 7–52.

In re Betts 2011, *Report of an Inquiry by a Conduct Division of the Judicial Commission of NSW in Relation to Magistrate Jennifer Betts*. 21 April. Report by C. Simpson, D. H. Lloyd and K. Moroney, Retrieved 9 May 2020, from https://www.judcom.nsw.gov.au/complaints/conduct-division-reports/.

In re Burns 2018, *Report of an Inquiry by a Conduct Division of the Judicial Commission of NSW in Relation to Magistrate Dominique Burns*. 21 December. Report by Anthony Payne, Roger Dive and K. Moroney, Retrieved 9 May 2020, from https://www.judcom.nsw.gov.au/complaints/conduct-division-reports/.

In re Maiden 2019, *Report of an Inquiry by a Conduct Division of the Judicial Commission of NSW in Relation to Judge Peter Maiden SC*. 26 March. Report by Robert Macfarlan, Arthur Emmett and Ken Moroney, Retrieved 9 May 2020, from https://www.judcom.nsw.gov.au/complaints/conduct-division-reports/.

In re Maloney 2011, *Report of the Conduct Division to the Governor Regarding Complaints against His Honour Magistrate Brian Maloney*. 6 May. Report by Michael Campbell, Jane Mottley and M. Jabour, Retrieved 9 May 2020, from https://www.judcom.nsw.gov.au/complaints/conduct-division-reports/.

International Consortium for Court Excellence 2013, *International Framework for Court Excellence*. 2nd ed. Retrieved 9 May 2020, from http://www.courtexcellence.com/Resources/The-Framework.aspx.

Jaffe, Peter G., Claire V. Crooks, Billie Lee Dunford-Jackson and Michael Town 2003, 'Vicarious Trauma in Judges: The Personal Challenge of Dispensing Justice', *Juvenile and Family Court Journal 54*: 1–9.
Judicial College of Victoria 2014, *Victorian Criminal Proceedings Manual*. Retrieved 10 May 2020, from http://www.judicialcollege.vic.edu.au/eManuals/VCPM/index.htm.
Judicial College of Victoria 2019, *Annual Report 2018/19*. Retrieved 9 May 2020, from https://www.judicialcollege.vic.edu.au/sites/default/files/2019-11/JCV_Annual%20Report%202018-2019_FINAL_web.pdf.
Judicial Commission of New South Wales 2007, *Sexual Assault Trials Handbook*. Sydney: Judicial Commission of New South Wales. Retrieved 9 May 2020, from https://www.judcom.nsw.gov.au/sexual_assault/.
Judicial Commission of New South Wales 2017, *Annual Report 2016-17*. Retrieved 9 May 2020, from https://www.judcom.nsw.gov.au/annual-report-2016-2017/.
Judicial Commission of New South Wales 2018, *Annual Report 2017-18*. Retrieved 9 May 2020, from https://www.judcom.nsw.gov.au/annual-report-2017-2018/.
Judicial Commission of New South Wales 2019, *Annual Report 2018-19*. Retrieved 9 May 2020, from https://www.judcom.nsw.gov.au/annual-report-2018-2019/.
Judicial Commission of New South Wales n.d., *Complaint Statistics*. Retrieved 9 May 2020, from https://www.judcom.nsw.gov.au/complaints/complaint-statistics/.
Judicial Conduct Investigations Office 2016, *Statement from the Judicial Conduct Investigations Office (27/16)*. 12 July. On file with authors, Retrieved 4 May 2017, from https://judicialconduct.judiciary.gov.uk/disciplinary-statements/2016/.
Judicial Conduct Investigations Office 2018, *Statement from the Judicial Conduct Investigations Office (53/18)*. 12 Decembet. On file with authors, Retrieved 24 April 2020, from https://judicialconduct.judiciary.gov.uk/disciplinary-statements/2019/.
Judicial Conduct Investigations Office 2019a, *Annual Report 2018-19*. Report, London.
Judicial Conduct Investigations Office 2019b, *Statement from the Judicial Conduct Investigations Office (01/19)*. 3 January. On file with authors, Retrieved 24 April 2020, from https://judicialconduct.judiciary.gov.uk/disciplinary-statements/2019/.
Judicial Conduct Investigations Office n.d., *Magistrates Complaints*. Retrieved 29 February, from https://judicialconduct.judiciary.gov.uk/contact-an-advisory-committee/.
Judicial Conference of Australia, 2010, *Reports of the Complaints against Judicial Officers Committee*. 22 January 2020, Retrieved from http://www.jca.asn.au/wp-content/uploads/2013/10/JCA-Reports-of-the-Complaints-Against-Judicial-Officers-Committee.pdf.
King, Michael, 2009, *Solution-Focused Judging Bench Book*. Melbourne: Australasian Institute of Judicial Administration.
Kirby, Michael, 1995, 'Judicial Stress', *Australian Bar Review 13*: 3–42.
Kirby, Michael, 2003, 'Judicial Accountability in Australia', *Legal Ethics 6*: 41–54.
Kirby, Michael, 2013, 'Judicial Stress and Judicial Bullying', *Australian Law Journal 87*: 516–527.
Kourlis, Rebecca, 2010, 'Judicial Performance Evaluation', *Wayne Law Review 56*: 765–769.

Law Reform Commission of Western Australia 2012, *Complaints against Judiciary*. Project 102, Final Report 102. Law Reform Commission of Western Australia: Perth. Available at https://www.lrc.justice.wa.gov.au/_files/P102-JudiciaryFR.pdf.

Leben, Steve, 2019, 'Exploring the Overlap between Procedural-Justice Principles and Emotion Regulation in the Courtroom', *Oñati Socio-Legal Series 9*: 852–864.

Lee, H. P., 2011, 'Appointment, Discipline and Removal of Judges in Australia'. In *Judiciaries in Comparative Perspective*, ed. H P Lee, 22–45. Cambridge: Cambridge University Press.

Lens, Vicki, 2016, 'Against the Grain: Therapeutic Judging in a Traditional Family Court', *Law & Social Inquiry 41*: 701–718.

Local Court of the Northern Territory 2019, *Judicial Complaints Protocol*. 16 July. Retrieved 9 May 2020, from https://localcourt.nt.gov.au/resources-support/judicial-complaints-protocol.

Mack, Kathy and Sharyn Roach Anleu 2004, 'The Administrative Authority of Chief Judicial Officers in Australia', *Newcastle Law Review 8*: 1–22.

Mack, Kathy and Sharyn Roach Anleu 2006, 'The Security of Tenure of Australian Magistrates', *Melbourne University Law Review 30*: 370–398.

Maroney, Terry A., 2012, 'Angry Judges', *Vanderbilt Law Review 65*: 1207–1284.

Maroney, Terry A., 2020, '(What We Talk About When We Talk About) Judicial Temperament', *Boston College Law Review 61*: 2085–2153

Maroney, Terry A. and James J. Gross 2014, 'The Ideal of the Dispassionate Judge: An Emotion Regulation Perspective', *Emotion Review 6*: 142–151.

McIntyre, Joe, 2014, 'Evaluating Judicial Performance Evaluation: A Conceptual Analysis', *Oñati Socio-Legal Series 4*: 898–926.

McIntyre, Joe, 2019, *The Judicial Function*. Singapore: Springer.

Moran, Leslie J., 2018, 'What's a Box of "Bakewell Tarts" Got to Do with It? Performing Gender as a Judicial Virtue in the Theatre of Justice'. In *Judges, Judging and Humour*, eds. Jessica Milner Davis and Sharyn Roach Anleu, 211–240. Cham: Palgrave Macmillan.

Murray, Sarah, Ian Murray and Tamara Tulich 2020, 'Court Delay and Judicial Wellbeing: Lessons from Self-Determination Theory to Enhance Court Timeliness in Australia', *Journal of Judicial Administration 29*: 101–117.

National Center for State Courts 2017, *Judicial Performance Evaluation: Resource Guide*. 18 October, retrieved 9 May 2020, from http://www.ncsc.org/Topics/Judicial-Officers/Judicial-Performance-Evaluation/Resource-Guide.aspx.

National Center for State Courts 2020, *Center for Judicial Ethics*. Retrieved 9 May 2020, from https://www.ncsc.org/cje.

National Judicial College (USA) 2020a, *2020 Courses*. On file with authors, Retrieved 9 May 2020, from https://www.judges.org/wp-content/uploads/courses_at_a_glance2020_Jan20_r.pdf.

National Judicial College (USA) 2020b, *NJC Courses*. Retrieved 25 January 2020, from https://www.judges.org/current-courses/.

National Judicial College of Australia, 2019, *Annual Report 2018-2019*. Retrieved 9 May 2020, from https://njca.com.au/about-us/annual-reports/.

Office of Court Administration (Texas) 2010, *Texas Family Violence Benchbook*.

December. Retrieved 10 May 2020, from http://www.ncdsv.org/images/OfficeCourtAdm_TXFVBenchbook_12-2010Edition.pdf.

Office for Judicial Complaints 2013, *Statement from the Office for Judicial Complaints (34/13)*. 4 July. On file with authors, Retrieved 4 May 2017, from https://judicialconduct.judiciary.gov.uk/disciplinary-statements/2013/.

Ostrom, Brian J., Charles W. Ostrom, William E. Hewitt, Neal B. Kauder, Robert C. LaFountain, Matthew Kleiman and Brenda Otto 2003, *Minnesota Judicial Workload Assessment, 2002*. Report, National Center for State Courts, Williamsburg, VA.

Panella, Jack A., 2015, *Pennsylvania Crimes of Sexual Violence Benchbook* (Third Edition). 2015. Retrieved 9 May 2020, from http://www.pacourts.us/assets/files/setting-3008/file-723.pdf.

Parker, Christine, 2004, 'A Critical Morality for Lawyers: Four Approaches to Lawyers' Ethics', *Monash University Law Review 30*: 49–74.

Parker, Christine, Adrian Evans, Linda Haller, Suzanne Le Mire and Reid Mortensen 2008, 'The Ethical Infrastructure of Legal Practice in Larger Law Firms: Values, Policy and Behaviour', *University of New South Wales Law Journal 31*: 158–185.

Richmond, Douglas R., 2012, 'Bullies on the Bench', *Louisiana Law Review 72*: 325–360.

Riedel, Johannes, 2014, 'Individual Evaluation of Judges in Germany', *Oñati Socio-Legal Series 4*: 974–992.

Roach Anleu, Sharyn, Jennifer Elek and Kathy Mack 2021, 'Researching Judicial Emotion and Emotion Management'. In *The Edward Elgar Research Handbook on Law and Emotions*, eds. Susan Bandes, Jody Madeira, Kathryn Temple and Emily Kidd White. Cheltenham and Northampton: Edward Elgar.

Roach Anleu, Sharyn and Kathy Mack 2014, 'Judicial Performance and Experiences of Judicial Work: Findings from Socio-Legal Research', *Oñati Socio-Legal Series 4*: 1015–1040.

Roach Anleu, Sharyn and Kathy Mack 2017, *Performing Judicial Authority in the Lower Courts*. London: Palgrave.

Roach Anleu, Sharyn, Kathy Mack, Jennifer Elek and David Rottman 2020, 'Judicial Ethics, Everyday Work and Emotion Management', *Journal of Law and Courts 8*: 127–150.

Roach Anleu, Sharyn, Jennifer Elek and Kathy Mack 2019, 'Judicial Conduct Guidance and Emotion', *Journal of Judicial Administration 28*: 226–239.

Roach Anleu, Sharyn, Kathy Mack and Jordan Tutton 2014, 'Judicial Humour in the Australian Courtroom', *Melbourne University Law Review 38*: 621–665.

Roach Anleu, Sharyn, David Rottman and Kathy Mack 2016, 'The Emotional Dimension of Judging: Issues, Evidence, and Insights', *Court Review 52*: 60–71.

Robbennolt, Jennifer K., 2015, 'Behavioral Ethics Meets Legal Ethics', *Annual Review of Law and Social Science 11*: 75–93.

Roberts, Heather, 2012, '"Swearing Mary": The Significance of the Speeches Made at Mary Gaudron's Swearing-in as a Justice of the High Court of Australia', *Sydney Law Review 34*: 493–510.

Sackville, Ronald, 2015, 'Judicial Ethics and Judicial Misbehaviour: Two Sides of the One Coin?', *Australian Law Journal 89*: 244–259.

Salyzyn, Amy and Richard Devlin 2020, 'Judges Need Ethics Rules, Not Just Ethical

Guidance', *Slaw*. 28 January. Retrieved 9 May 2020, from http://www.slaw.ca/2020/01/28/judges-need-ethics-rules-not-just-ethical-guidance/.

Schneyer, Ted, 1991, 'Professional Discipline for Law Firms?', *Cornell Law Review 44*: 1–46.

Schneyer, Ted, 1998, 'A Tale of Four Systems: Reflections on How Law Influences the Ethical Infrastructure of Law Firms', *South Texas Law Review 39*: 245–277.

Schrever, Carly, 2018, 'Sentencing Stress and Vicarious Trauma' presentation at the *NJCA and ANU Sentencing Conference*, Australian National University, Canberra, 3 March 2018. Retrieved 9 May 2020, from https://njca.com.au/wp-content/uploads/2018/03/Sentencing-Stress-Carly-Schrever-slides-3.1-MB.pdf.

Shetreet, Shimon, 2014, 'The Status of Codes of Judicial Conduct in Comparative Perspectives'. In *The Culture of Judicial Independence Rule of Law and World Peace*, ed. Shimon Shetreet, 292–297. Neiden: Koninklijke Brill.

State of California Commission on Judicial Performance 2020, *How to File a Complaint*. Retrieved 9 May 2020, from https://cjp.ca.gov/file_a_complaint/.

Supreme Court of Western Australia 2019, *Feedback and Complaints*. 1 May. Retrieved 9 May 2020, from https://localcourt.nt.gov.au/resources-support/judicial-complaints-protocol.

Tenbrunsel, Ann E. and Kristin Smith-Crowe 2008, 'Ethical Decision Making: Where We've Been and Where We're Going', *The Academy of Management Annals 2*: 545–607.

Tenbrunsel, Ann E. Kristin Smith-Crowe and Elizabeth E. Umphress 2003, 'Building Houses on Rocks: The Role of the Ethical Infrastructure in Organizations', *Social Justice Research 16*: 285–307.

Thomas, Cheryl, 2017, *2016 UK Judicial Attitude Survey: Report of Findings Covering Salaried Judges in England & Wales Courts and UK Tribunals*. 7 February. Report by the University College London Judicial Institute, London, Retrieved 9 May 2020, from https://www.judiciary.gov.uk/wp-content/uploads/2017/02/jas-2016-england-wales-court-uk-tribunals-7-february-2017.pdf.

Thomas, James, 1988, *Judicial Ethics in Australia*. Sydney: Law Book Company.

Thomas, James, 1997, *Judicial Ethics in Australia*. 2nd ed. Sydney: LBC Information Services.

Thomas, James, 2009, *Judicial Ethics in Australia*. 3rd ed. Chatswood: LexisNexis Butterworths.

Treviño, Linda Klebe, Niki A. den Nieuwenboer and Jennifer J. Kish-Gephart 2014, '(Un)Ethical Behavior in Organizations', *Annual Review of Psychology 65*: 635–660.

United Nations Office on Drugs and Crime 2002, *The Bangalore Principles of Judicial Conduct*. Retrieved 9 May 2020, from https://www.unodc.org/pdf/crime/corruption/judicial_group/Bangalore_principles.pdf.

Utah Judicial Performance Evaluation Commission 2014, *The Honourable David Hamilton: Judicial Performance Evaluation Commission Report: Retention 2014*. Retrieved 9 May 2020, from http://digitallibrary.utah.gov/awweb/awarchive?type=file&item=70576.

Utah Judicial Performance Evaluation Commission 2020, *Full Evaluation Details*. Retrieved 9 May 2020, from https://judges.utah.gov/process/full-time-evaluation-details/.

Victor, Bart and John B. Cullen 1988, 'The Organizational Bases of Ethical Work Climates', *Administrative Science Quarterly 33*: 101–125.

Wallace, Anne, Sharyn Roach Anleu and Kathy Mack 2015, 'Evaluating Judicial Performance for Caseload Allocation', *Monash University Law Review 41*: 445–468.
Warren, Marilyn, 2011, 'Enhancing Our Self-Perception: 360-Degree Feedback for Judicial Officers', *Journal of Judicial Administration 21*: 3–7.
Warren, Marilyn, 2014, 'From Evaluation to Improvement: A Chief Justice's Perspective', *Oñati Socio-Legal Series 4*: 953–973.
Wendel, W. Bradley, 2001, 'Nonlegal Regulation of the Legal Profession: Social Norms in Professional Communities', *Vanderbilt Law Review 54*: 1955–2055.
Wilensky, Harold L., 1964, 'The Professionalization of Everyone?', *American Journal of Sociology 70*: 137–158.
Wistrich, Andrew, 2010, 'Defining Good Judging'. In *The Psychology of Judicial Decision Making*, eds. David Klein and Gregory Mitchell, 249–268. Oxford and New York: Oxford University Press.
Woolf, Nicholas H. and Jennifer M. J. Yim 2011, 'The Courtroom-Observation Program of the Utah Judicial Performance Evaluation Commission', *Court Review 47*: 82–91.
Young, Ronald, 2018, *Judicial Mentoring Toolkit*. November. Prepared for the Federal Court of Australia and published by New Zealand Ministry of Foreign Affairs and Trade, Retrieved 9 May 2020, from https://www.fedcourt.gov.au/__data/assets/pdf_file/0006/58389/Online-Version-Judicial-Mentoring-Toolkit.pdf.

Cases

Alvares v The Queen [2011] NSWCCA 33. Available from http://www.austlii.edu.au/cgi-bin/viewdoc/au/cases/nsw/NSWCCA/2011/33.html.
Ford v The Queen [2016] NSWCCA 69. Available from www.austlii.edu.au/cgi-bin/viewdoc/au/cases/nsw/NSWCCA/2016/69.html.
Galea v Galea (1990) 19 NSWLR 263.
Long v Mayger [2004] WASCA 41. Available from http://www.austlii.edu.au/cgi-bin/viewdoc/au/cases/wa/WASCA/2004/41.html.
Michael v Western Australia [2007] WASCA 100. Available from http://www.austlii.edu.au/cgi-bin/viewdoc/au/cases/wa/WASCA/2007/100.html.
Nguyen v The Queen [2019] NSWCCA 209. Available from http://www.austlii.edu.au/cgi-bin/viewdoc/au/cases/nsw/NSWCCA/2019/209.html.
Percival v The Queen [2015] VSCA 200. Available from http://www.austlii.edu.au/cgi-bin/viewdoc/au/cases/vic/VSCA/2015/200.html.
Piccolotto v The Queen [2015] VSCA 143. Available from http://www.austlii.edu.au/cgi-bin/viewdoc/au/cases/vic/VSCA/2015/143.html.

Legislation

Constitution Act 1902 (NSW)
Federal Court of Australia Act 1976 (Cth)
Judicial Commission of Victoria Act 2016 (Vic)
Judicial Commissions Act 1994 (ACT)
Judicial Conduct Commissioner Act 2015 (SA)
Judicial Officers Act 1986 (NSW)

Chapter 7

Conclusion

Introduction

Judging and Emotion establishes that emotion is a much larger part of everyday judicial work than conventionally acknowledged. Judicial emotion, often understood as spontaneous and/or uncontrollable, is usually denied, challenged as problematic or regarded as a source of stress. This book articulates a broader conception of emotion, as a social practice emerging from interaction, and demonstrates how judicial officers undertake emotion work and use emotion as a resource to achieve impartiality. Judicial officers manage their experience and performance of emotions, and they anticipate, interpret, elicit, manage or suppress feelings or emotional displays in others. They are aware of, interpret and apply formal requirements, implicit norms and feeling rules governing emotional experience and display, including powerful expectations of judicial dispassion and detachment.

Judicial perception and experience of emotion

Judicial officers sometimes anticipate emotion, and they experience emotion arising from specific situations or from the general events of the day. This felt emotion can occur in the moment or later, inside or outside the courtroom, even beyond the courthouse. While their institutional role and the courtroom context constrain judicial capacity to express diverse emotions, some display of emotion demonstrates human facets of the judge as more than the embodiment of impersonal, dispassionate law. As one judge points out: 'you're not human if you can't express some emotion' (I 11).[1] Underpinning this reflexivity is a strong

1 This quote is from a judicial officer interviewed as part of the *Courts, the Judiciary and Social Change* project funded by an Australian Research Council (ARC) Discovery Project grant (DP 1096888). The interviews were conducted in 2012–2013. The data is indicated by the code 'I ##' in which the letter I identifies this as interview data and ## is the number assigned to the individual interviewee. Quotations are used verbatim and have not been edited to correct grammar or reduce infelicities of spoken language, but retain qualities of

demarcation of the amount and quality of emotion that can and should be displayed: 'we do express emotions, but in a more restrained way' (I 11).

Judicial officers rely on their own feelings, for example, anger or sympathy, as a barometer or warning sign of potential bias or loss of impartiality, inappropriate to the judicial role. They then act to manage or regulate their feelings (Roach Anleu and Mack 2019a). In these ways, emotion and emotion awareness are tools or resources to help judicial officers perform their impartial judicial role (Craciun 2016).

Judicial officers also anticipate, observe and interpret others' behaviour, actions or speech, either in relation to their own feelings and display or as indicators of emotion. This emotion perception, experience and management can take place in advance, in the moment, or may occur later, suggesting the spillage of emotion and emotion work into other domains.

Judging and emotion work

Strategies to manage a judicial officer's own and others' feelings and display are embedded in the interrelations that constitute judicial work, especially in the courtroom, and rely on interaction and communication. Classifying emotion work as either relating to the judicial self or to others artificially separates them, as they are often fused in one interaction. These strategies are multi-functional and can be deployed simultaneously. They enable judicial officers to manage their own feelings, conforming to the dominant feeling rule of emotionlessness, and they can serve to manage the emotions of others. Emotion management involves self-talk, demeanour, humour, engaging other resources and recognising a place for empathy.

Self-talk

Several judicial officers describe a practice of self-talk—a conversation between the judge as ordinary person and the judge *qua* judge. This strategy can be deployed in advance of anticipated emotion, in the moment or later. Self-talk is a conscious effort that can parallel the judicial officer's transition from chambers (private) to the courtroom (public), recalling Goffman's distinction between 'front and back regions' (1959: 123). Self-talk can be an important component of the performance of impartiality. It may include a reminder of the judicial oath and the parameters of the judicial role. Judicial officers rely on metaphors of keeping an open mind and putting aside bias, as though bias is a discrete thing that can be identified then removed. This

natural, everyday speech reflecting the narrative quality of the interviews. All identifying, or potentially identifying, details have been deleted. For more information on this phase of the research, see the Appendix.

recurring emphasis on the judicial role and function is a way of moving away from the private or personal self, where emotion is allowed, towards the judicial or professional self, where emotion is disavowed.

Demeanour

Judicial demeanour is an important component of communication to different audiences, conveying information to legal representatives, the prosecution, the defendant, litigants, victims, witnesses and other courtroom participants. Judicial officers deploy their demeanour—through body movement, facial expression, tone of voice—to induce certain feeling states and behaviours among participants and in themselves. A calm and courteous demeanour, regardless of a judicial officer's own feelings, reduces emotion displays deemed inappropriate and enables accomplishment of work tasks. Displays of calmness, patience and courtesy set an emotional climate and serve to delineate and convey feeling rules.

A demeanour that evokes patience can allow another's emotion to be acknowledged, perhaps displayed, even if somewhat intense. Bodily work is a key facet of judicial demeanour, comprising actions such as putting hands on the bench as a calming action or biting the tongue to avoid saying something that might cause regret or embarrassment. Then, 'letting the silt settle' (I 31) can prepare the judicial officer for making or delivering the decision and the litigants (and others) for receiving it. This is akin to Booth's (2012) use of Goffman's concept of 'cooling out' (1952: 462) to explain how judges manage victims' disappointment, grief and resentment so that these negative feelings do not flood out, disrupt legal proceedings or potentially jeopardise impartiality.

Judicial officers strategically display emotion in ways that might suggest feelings of compassion, sympathy, sadness, distress, disgust or happiness and pleasure, perhaps shared or overlapping with the emotion of some other court users. Visible markers of emotion might include tears, body movements like leaning forward, or tone of voice. Such displays will shape the emotion and emotion display of other court participants and can foster trust, enhance legitimacy or confidence in legal processes or be a strategy to humanise impersonal, formal legal proceedings. Alternatively, such displays may undermine confidence through departure from institutional norms and feeling rules.

Judicial demeanour can be a didactic tool which conveys feeling rules to others, as well as confirming impartiality. Displaying required or desired demeanours can entail surface acting, managing the outward expression of affect and suppressing actual feelings to conform with the situational feeling rules. Alternatively, it can involve deep acting where individuals actually generate the internal subjective experience of the institutionally expected feelings.

Humour

Occasionally, judicial officers use humour as a strategy to manage their own and others' feelings. An expression of humour might indicate shared emotion with courtroom participants: jurors, witnesses, defendants, family members or professional participants, including legal representatives. Judicial officers sometimes rely on humour along with other emotion displays to reinforce interprofessional boundaries, to distinguish judicial work, including emotion work, from the tasks of other occupations (Bergman Blix and Wettergren 2018a; Roach Anleu and Mack 2018). Such emotion displays can enhance rather than detract from judicial authority and legitimacy. Outside the courtroom, judicial officers report sharing humour with associates, court staff or other judicial officers, including what is sometimes termed 'gallows' or black humour (Obrdlik 1942: 799).

Other resources

Strategies involving other resources include relying on courtroom formality, input from other personnel, adjournment and debriefing with colleagues or family members and friends. Reminding participants (especially those without legal representation) of the formal court procedures, by using the everyday notion of turn-taking, can reassure these court users that they will have the opportunity to speak. This can quell potential frustration, impatience and anxiety.

Judicial officers also seek input from other courtroom personnel in the quest to manage moments of emotion. This may entail asking a lawyer to speak to their client or requesting court staff provide tissues or a glass of water to a distressed witness. This delegation of emotion work draws boundaries between the role of the judicial officer and that of other participants, limits the sharing of emotion, or defines situations and locations in which judicial emotion can be shared.

Adjournment or taking a break provides time and space for emotion management and an opportunity for debriefing for all in the courtroom. An adjournment to manage an emotionally dense situation is a demarcation between the scope and nature of the judicial officer's emotion work and that performed by other participants (lay and professional). During the adjournment, legal professionals and other courtroom participants may engage in their own emotion work which is embedded in their professional interrelations. It also creates an opportunity for emotion work to be performed by those to whom the judicial officer might turn for debriefing and emotion management, which cannot be undertaken within the formal proceedings or location of the courtroom.

Emotion sharing, a key form of emotion work, occurs off-stage, out of court, in chambers or the private sections of the court building where judicial officers seek and provide reciprocal emotion support with colleagues, while also expecting or accepting non-reciprocal support from court staff. These strategies further delineate the judicial role in line with hierarchical occupational expectations about demanding and providing emotion work.

Empathy

Managing the felt and displayed emotions of others, and the strategies used, depends on which others and which emotions the judicial officer perceives and how they are assessed. Notably, this can require empathy, a capacity with cognitive and affective elements. Empathy gives insight into others' experiences, including their feelings, but is perceived as presenting a risk to impartiality, especially if it is selectively deployed. Judicial officers perform empathy in a variety of ways, including the words they use, their demeanour or the substantive decision. A decision may be couched in legal language, but the result might convey empathy for the circumstances or special needs of a person before the court. Empathy can determine judicial emotion display or suppression. One magistrate comments:

> On occasions I have to say that I haven't completely controlled my emotions and I don't know that that is a bad thing. I have cried a couple of times in court … and I don't think that that hurt, that I showed that I was emotional … I don't think it hurt for them [the litigants] to understand that it was, that it's hard for the court too. (I 32)

This judicial officer suggests that displaying how she felt in court could foster valuable feelings in others, especially in circumstances where they may feel angry, hostile and distrustful. Some sharing of emotion may reassure litigants their concerns have been heard and enhance their appreciation of legal requirements, thus minimising emotional outbursts that would breach courtroom feeling rules. She also seeks empathy from the litigants. Here, emotion is central to the maintenance of judicial authority and legitimacy.

These strategies imply a conception of emotion as potentially dangerous or risky and requiring control, though on some occasions judicial officers allow their own or another's emotion expression. Whatever strategies are used, judicial officers seek to implement a concept of the judicial role as detached and impersonal (Remiche 2015). Invoking this image is itself an important emotion management tool, an anchor for the judicial officer against which to recalibrate and manage emotion. The conventional judicial role that disavows emotion becomes a touchstone for judicial officers' reflexive monitoring of the myriad emotions they experience. It refines the scope for emotion, the kind of emotion, and the situations or circumstances in which emotion and its display are appropriate or helpful.

Emotion work: Interconnections and boundaries

Such simple descriptors—emotion and emotion work—cannot encompass the multiple dimensions of judicial emotion and emotion management. Emotion work can be conceptualised as cascading, a ripple effect or as chains of emotion work, rather than embedded or located only in one interaction, or interrelationship or situation. Emotion work may not have a clear beginning or end, and the nature of emotion work for the judiciary is shaped by the physical and symbolic separation between the front stage (courtroom) and back stage (chambers, court building) and beyond in personal or private spaces. While some limits are 'embedded in the environment, as opposed to created by atomized individuals' (Lamont and Molnár 2002: 171), a judicial officer's performance of judicial work sets professional boundaries, distinguishing judicial work from non-judicial work (cf Gieryn 1983).

The many judicial emotion management strategies demonstrate that institutional requirements of emotionless judging do not completely determine judicial practice. In this regard, judicial officers may have more autonomy in performing emotion work than other occupational groups. Not all judicial officers approach or think (or feel) about their work in the same ways. Neither do they understand impartiality identically, nor experience and display identical emotions when aspiring to be impartial. For some in the judiciary, emotion and emotion work can be a burden or source of stress, compromising judicial performance and wellbeing and perhaps undermining impartiality (Schrever, Hulbert and Sourdin 2019). Boundaries regarding the scope and nature of emotion as a tool to accomplish tasks mean that the shape of emotion and emotion work as a positive resource for judicial work is situationally and individually dependent.

Feeling rules and regulation

Judges' and magistrates' reflections on their emotion experiences and emotion work all suggest conscious effort to comply with the norms regulating felt and displayed emotion. These feeling rules are guidelines for assessing emotion in particular situations. A judicial officer's comment implies recognition of the force of feeling rules and the contours of appropriate judicial emotion and display: 'you have to be conscious of guarding against your own emotional reaction … you have to be the calming one in the situation' (I 32).

Judicial officers constantly evaluate emotion as appropriate, reasonable, allowable or not. This research demonstrates the ways they actively constitute the feeling rules against which their own conduct and that of courtroom participants is assessed. Institutional and organisational obligations broadly define appropriate felt and displayed emotion, but the situational and relational nature of judicial work makes the limits of these feeling rules difficult to predict. Feeling rules have a significant degree of flexibility and can apply differently to different court participants. Those whose emotions the judicial officer assesses as 'fair enough' (I 21) or a result of 'the strains that people are under' (I 15) are treated differently than those defined as 'difficult people' (I 09, I 24).

At times, judicial officers allow themselves and others some emotion display, though they remain mindful of strong institutional limits on emotion in court. Even so, the available ethical guidance or formal regulation of judicial officers' emotion work is limited (Roach Anleu, Mack and Elek et al. 2020). Current approaches to judicial conduct guidance and ethics in Australia and elsewhere provide primarily abstract or aspirational precepts (Council of Chief Justices of Australia and New Zealand 2017). Discipline processes, judicial performance evaluation and judicial education tend to concentrate on managing the extreme conduct of individual judicial officers. These approaches do not sufficiently acknowledge the fundamentally interactive or social nature of much judicial work.

Judicial officers themselves increasingly recognise the emotional aspects of their work, and their experiences and insights can provide concrete direction which assists with the judicial work of managing emotions. Translating these experiences and insights into effective guidance is challenging. Greater insight into the occasions for judicial emotion work is needed to address the considerable variety and intensity of judicial emotions and demands for emotion management, while recognising that an individual judge is part of a self-regulating profession.

Emotion work, gender and judging

The initial conceptualisation of emotional labour (Hochschild 1979, 1983) spawned considerable research on interactive service work in several largely feminised, often low status, occupations such as flight attendant, hairdresser, nurse, sales assistant, supermarket checkout operator and table waiter or food server (Grandey, Diefendorff and Rupp 2012; Grandey and Gabriel 2015; Wharton 2009). Even where women work in traditionally male-dominated professions such as law or medicine, they may experience gendered expectations regarding their capacity and willingness to provide emotion work to others, including colleagues (Lively 2002; Froyum 2018; Pierce 1995; Polletta and Tufail 2016; Tufail and Polletta 2015). This perhaps partly reflects the long-standing tight social and cultural association of women with emotion and 'deep-rooted stereotypes about which gender is best suited for particular kinds of jobs' (Wharton 2009: 149). Nonetheless, gender and emotion work are not correlated perfectly (Lively 2019).

While there is an extensive literature on gender and judging generally (see, for example, Schultz and Shaw 2013), there is little empirical consideration of gender, judging, emotion and emotion work (Douglas, Bartlett, Luker et al. 2014). The imagery of the judiciary points to 'the ever-present image of "the judge" as male' and the consequent displacement of women and disavowal of the feminine (Thornton 1996: 207–208; also see Bartlett and Douglas 2018; Moran 2009; Resnik and Curtis 2011). This image is congruent with the disavowal of emotion in judging. However, some of the usual formal markers of gendered job inequality—differences in pay, authority and responsibilities—are less present in the judiciary. Men and women at the same court level undertake the same kinds of work, exercise the same formal legal authority and receive the same salary and benefits. These structural imperatives suggest that emotion and emotion work in the judiciary may not be completely gendered. Given the complexities of gender and of emotion, it would be inappropriate to infer from an interview quote that women in the judiciary are more attuned to emotion and emotion work than their male colleagues. Male and female judicial officers reflected on their emotion experiences and emotion work in the interviews reported in this book. The findings suggest that different approaches to emotion in judicial work do not always align with binary gender expectations (Darwin 2017; West and Zimmerman 1987). Nonetheless, some differences deriving from gender stereotypes persist. Interviewees report that male judges sometimes display emotions—for example, anger or tears—that women could not, as they would be at greater risk of negative evaluation or loss of perceived authority.

A detailed study of emotion and the Swedish judiciary reports that 'the preliminary impression of our findings rather suggests that women and men are as likely to embrace, and to problematize, the ideal of non-emotional justice' (Bergman Blix and Wettergren 2018b: 4). Australian national survey data identifies few differences between men and women judicial officers in terms of emotion and emotion work (Roach Anleu and Mack 2017). Women in the judiciary value some emotional capacities such as empathy, compassion and patience, more intensely than their male counterparts, though this may be confounded by court level as the demand for emotion work may be greater in lower courts where women judicial officers are disproportionately located (Roach Anleu and Mack 2005, 2019b). About half of women and men judges in the higher (jury) trial and appeal courts assess managing the emotions of court users as essential or very important in their everyday work (Roach Anleu and Mack 2017). In contrast, among Australian magistrates, a greater proportion of women (79 percent) than men (58 percent) consider managing the emotions of court users to be essential or very important in their daily work. The different attitudes of men and women in magistrates courts, compared with the similarity of attitudes between men and women in the higher courts, confirm the complexity of gender as a single explanation and reinforces the importance of context for understanding judicial emotion and emotion work.

Conclusion

Judging and Emotion adopts an expansive and composite conception of emotion, recognising emotion as an outcome of social interactions, embedded in interpersonal and interprofessional relations, rather than as a primarily individual or personal phenomenon. This departs significantly from the implicit legal and judicial understanding of emotion as spontaneous, uncontrollable and dangerous. Reconceptualising emotion in this way enables recognising emotion as a significant resource for everyday judicial practice. Judicial officers demonstrate considerable reflexivity regarding the emotion dimensions of their work, engaging in a complex interpretation of their own and others' emotion and display, acknowledging the interactive nature of emotion and emotion work (Burkitt 2012; Holmes, 2010, 2015).

At the same time, judicial officers are wary of emotion, deploring emotional outbursts in court, rude legal representatives and visible expressions of anger, distress, frustration or sadness. They distinguish appropriate from inappropriate display of emotion, actively constituting feeling rules. This might suggest that judicial officers perceive emotions in their judicial work as negative. However, this research establishes that emotion is a positive resource to accomplish everyday work, especially in the courtroom.

Despite the prevalence of emotion in judicial work, judicial officers rarely frame their work in emotion terms. Not surprisingly, they use legal language to talk about their daily practices, even when experiencing and managing emotion. When judicial officers describe projecting a calm, neutral or unemotional demeanour, in contrast to an intense emotion they may be feeling, they tend to characterise this as an expression of judicial impartiality, a legal norm, and as performing their judicial role. Nonetheless, projecting and maintaining an unemotional demeanour entails emotion work. In this way, when judicial officers talk about their performance of everyday judicial tasks and activities, they are implicitly describing emotion and emotion work, though often without recourse to emotion language.

Whether emotions are valorised, recognised, managed or denied, the judiciary's obligation to be impartial remains. Understanding how emotion intersects with impartiality is central to a new conceptualisation of the judicial role and judging. All judicial officers are committed to the core value of impartiality, but the ways this value is performed varies with different court contexts and individual judicial officers. At the same time, variations in judicial approach are not entirely personal or outside law.

Judging and Emotion demonstrates how institutional requirements do not completely determine the emotion dimensions of judicial work. Judicial officers' experiences and expressions of emotion are subject to feeling and display rules, professional regulation and, perhaps most powerfully, conceptions of impartiality as dispassion. Through their everyday work, judicial officers themselves constitute these norms and so construct and maintain the boundaries of an impartial judicial role which necessarily incorporates emotion and emotion work.

References

Bartlett, Francesca and Heather Douglas 2018, '"Benchmarking" a Supreme Court and Federal Court Judge in Australia', *Oñati Socio-Legal Series 8*: 1355–1385.

Bergman Blix, Stina and Åsa Wettergren 2018a, 'Humour in the Swedish Court: Managing Emotions, Status and Power'. In *Judges, Judging and Humour*, eds. Jessica Milner Davis and Sharyn Roach Anleu, 179–210. Cham: Palgrave Macmillan.

Bergman Blix, Stina and Åsa Wettergren 2018b, *Professional Emotions in Court: A Sociological Perspective*. Abingdon: Routledge.

Booth, Tracey, 2012, '"Cooling out" Victims of Crime: Managing Victim Participation in the Sentencing Process in a Superior Sentencing Court', *Australian & New Zealand Journal of Criminology 45*: 214–230.

Burkitt, Ian, 2012, 'Emotional Reflexivity: Feeling, Emotion and Imagination in Reflexive Dialogues', *Sociology 48*: 458–472.

Council of Chief Justices of Australia and New Zealand 2017, *Guide to Judicial Conduct*. 3rd ed. Melbourne: Australasian Institute of Judicial Administration. Available from https://aija.org.au/publications-introduction/guidelines/guide-to-judicial-conduct/.

Craciun, Mariana, 2016, 'The Cultural Work of Office Charisma: Maintaining Professional Power in Psychotherapy', *Theory and Society 45*: 361–383.

Darwin, Helana, 2017, 'Doing Gender Beyond the Binary: A Virtual Ethnography', *Symbolic Interaction 40*: 317–334.

Douglas, Heather, Francesca Bartlett, Trish Luker and Rosemary Hunter 2014, 'Introduction: Righting Australian Law'. In *Australian Feminist Judgments: Righting and Rewriting Law*, eds. Heather Douglas, Francesca Bartlett, Trish Luker and Rosemary Hunter, 1–18. Oxford and Portland OR: Hart Publishing.

Froyum, Carissa, 2018, 'Gender and Emotion Management'. In *Handbook of the Sociology of Gender*, eds. Barbara J. Risman, Carissa M. Forum and William J. Scarborough, 417–429. Cham: Springer.

Gieryn, Thomas F., 1983, 'Boundary-Work and the Demarcation of Science from Non-Science: Strains and Interests in Professional Ideologies of Scientists', *American Sociological Review 48*: 781–795.

Goffman, Erving, 1959, *The Presentation of Self in Everyday Life*. New York: Doubleday Anchor.

Grandey, Alicia A. and Allison S. Gabriel 2015, 'Emotional Labor at a Crossroads: Where Do We Go from Here?', *Annual Review of Organizational Psychology and Organizational Behavior 2*: 323–349.

Grandey, Alicia A., James Diefendorff and Deborah Rupp, eds. 2012, *Emotional Labor in the 21st Century: Diverse Perspectives on Emotion Regulation at Work*. New York and London: Routledge.

Hochschild, Arlie Russell, 1979, 'Emotion Work, Feeling Rules and Social Structure', *American Journal of Sociology 85*: 551–575.

Hochschild, Arlie Russell, 1983, *The Managed Heart: Commercialization of Human Feeling*. Berkeley, CA: University of California Press.

Holmes, Mary, 2010, 'The Emotionalization of Reflexivity', *Sociology 44*: 139–154.

Holmes, Mary, 2015, 'Researching Emotional Reflexivity', *Emotion Review 9*: 61–66.

Lamont, Michèle and Virág Molnár 2002, 'The Study of Boundaries in the Social Sciences', *Annual Review of Sociology 28*: 167–195.

Lively, Kathryn J., 2002, 'Client Contact and Emotional Labor: Upsetting the Balance and Evening the Field', *Work and Occupations 29*: 198–225.

Lively, Kathryn J., 2019, 'Sociological Approaches to the Study of Gender and Emotion in Late Modernity: Culture, Structure and Identity'. In *Emotions in Late Modernity*, eds. Roger Patulny, Alberto Bellocchi, Rebecca E. Olson, Sukhmani Khorana, Jordan McKenzie and Michelle Peterie, 69–82. Abingdon and New York: Routledge.

Moran, Leslie J., 2009, 'Judging Pictures: A Case Study of Portraits of the Chief Justices, Supreme Court of New South Wales', *International Journal of Law in Context 5*: 295–314.

Obrdlik, Antonin J., 1942, '"Gallows Humour"—a Sociological Phenomenon', *American Journal of Sociology 47*: 709–716.

Pierce, Jennifer, 1995, *Gender Trials: Emotional Lives in Contemporary Law Firms*. Berkeley, CA and Los Angeles, CA: University of California.

Polletta, Francesca and Zaibu Tufail 2016, 'Helping without Caring: Role Definition and the Gender-Stratified Effects of Emotional Labor in Debt Settlement Firms', *Work and Occupations 43*: 401–433.

Remiche, Adélaïde, 2015, 'When Judging Is Power', *Journal of Law and Courts 3*: 95–114.

Resnik, Judith and Dennis E. Curtis 2011, *Representing Justice: Invention, Controversy, and Rights in City-States and Democratic Courtrooms*. New Haven, CT and London: Yale University Press.

Roach Anleu, Sharyn and Kathy Mack 2005, 'Magistrates' Everyday Work and Emotional Labour', *Journal of Law and Society 32*: 590–614.

Roach Anleu, Sharyn and Kathy Mack 2017, *Performing Judicial Authority in the Lower Courts*. London: Palgrave.

Roach Anleu, Sharyn and Kathy Mack 2018, 'Judicial Humour and Inter-Professional Relations in the Courtroom'. In *Judges, Judging and Humour*, eds. Jessica Milner Davis and Sharyn Roach Anleu, 141–178. Cham: Palgrave Macmillan.

Roach Anleu, Sharyn and Kathy Mack 2019a, 'Impartiality and Emotion in Everyday Judicial Practice'. In *Emotions in Late Modernity*, eds. Roger Patulny, Alberto Bellocchi, Rebecca E. Olson, Sukhmani Khorana, Jordan McKenzie and Michelle Peterie, 253-266. Abingdon and New York: Routledge.

Roach Anleu, Sharyn and Kathy Mack 2019b, 'A Sociological Perspective on Emotion Work and Judging', *Oñati Socio-Legal Series 9*: 831–851.

Roach Anleu, Sharyn, Kathy Mack, Jennifer Elek and David Rottman 2020, 'Judicial Ethics, Everyday Work, and Emotion Management', *Journal of Law and Courts 8*: 127–150.

Schrever, Carly, Carol Hulbert and Tania Sourdin 2019, 'The Psychological Impact

of Judicial Work: Australia's First Empirical Research Measuring Judicial Stress and Wellbeing', *Journal of Judicial Administration 28*: 141–168.
Schultz, Ulrike and Gisela Shaw 2013, *Gender and Judging*. Oxford and Portland, OR: Hart Publishing.
Thornton, Margaret, 1996, *Dissonance and Distrust: Women in the Legal Profession*. Melbourne: Oxford University Press.
Tufail, Zaibu and Francesca Polletta 2015, 'The Gendering of Emotional Flexibility: Why Angry Women Are Both Admired and Devalued in Debt Settlement Firms', *Gender & Society 29*: 484–508.
West, Candace and Don H. Zimmerman 1987, 'Doing Gender', *Gender & Society 1*: 125–151.
Wharton, Amy S., 2009, 'The Sociology of Emotional Labor', *Annual Review of Sociology 35*: 147–165.

Appendix

Research design and data

The empirical data in this book directly investigates how judicial officers understand, experience, display, manage and deploy emotions, their own and others, as part of their everyday work, especially in court. All this data collection was undertaken as part of the Judicial Research Project (JRP) at Flinders University.[1] Since 2000, the JRP has investigated many dimensions of the everyday work of the judiciary[2] including job satisfaction, skills, work allocation and the changing demands of and approaches to judicial work (Roach Anleu and Mack 2017). Each of the empirical studies undertaken has been approved by the Flinders University Social and Behavioural Research Ethics Committee. The major empirical research projects and studies that provide the data for this book are:

- the *National Court Observation Study*, including transcriptions of court proceedings, 2004–2005;
- the *National Survey of Australian Magistrates* 2007;
- the *National Survey of Australian Judges* 2007;
- interviews with judges, magistrates and court staff conducted as part of the *Judicial Officers and Workload Allocation* project, 2007–2012;
- interviews with judges and magistrates undertaken nationally as part of the *Courts, the Judiciary and Social Change* project, 2012–2015; and
- materials relating to judicial ethics, discipline and performance

[1] The Judicial Research Project has been funded primarily by several grants from the Australian Research Council, with additional financial and in-kind support from courts, government, judicial professional associations and other organisations as well as Flinders University internal competitive grants and infrastructure. See the Preface for further detail.

[2] Within Australia, the term 'magistrate' refers to members of the judiciary who preside in the lower state or territory courts, while 'judge' refers to those who preside in the intermediate or higher state, territory or national courts. (Except in the Northern Territory where the Magistrates Court was renamed the Local Court in 2016, magistrates are now called 'judge'.) In this book, the term 'judicial officer' is used generically to refer to any member of the judiciary, regardless of court level or type.

evaluation in Australia and the USA collected as part of the *Changing Judicial Performance: Emotion and Legitimacy* project, 2015–2020.

Interviews

Researchers often choose interviews as the most appropriate method to investigate participants' experiences of emotion and perceptions of emotion work, as they allow scope for reflexivity and opportunities for probing (Atkinson and Silverman 1997; Holmes 2015). While interview methodology can enable a far-reaching flow of consciousness, some interviewees are more reflexive than others. Some judicial officers may regard questions about emotion difficult (Bergman Blix and Wettergren 2019). It might be impossible for the interviewer (researcher) to discern whether judicial officers are reticent to talk about emotion or whether they lack the tools to do so, especially as the judicial framework is primarily cognitive and behavioural. Judicial work is valorised as thinking and reasoning, not feeling.

A feature of interviews and their analysis as a research strategy is their temporal nature. An interview occurs and is recorded at one point in time. Later it is transcribed, and much later analysed, perhaps several times in different ways. The interview as narrative or conversation becomes text, and the interactive nature shifts from interviewee and interviewer to the researcher(s), not necessarily the interviewer, who interprets the interview transcript, identifies themes and codes the text (Strauss and Corbin 1998). The research process becomes more akin to historical research that scrapes insight about emotion from documents where '[t]he feeling itself is long gone' (Matt 2014: 41; also see Barclay 2017).

Interviews were undertaken in two JRP projects—*Courts, the Judiciary and Social Change* (ARC DP 1096888) and *Judicial Officers and Workload Allocation* ARC (LP 0669168). As part of the *Courts, the Judiciary and Social Change* project, interviews investigated judicial officers' views regarding new roles for and expectations about judges and courts in a changing social, economic and policy context; their understandings of core judicial values; and the role of emotion in their work. Between August 2012 and December 2013, Sharyn Roach Anleu conducted open-ended, face-to-face interviews with 38 judicial officers—17 magistrates, 21 judges; 19 men and 19 women—in state courts throughout Australia. The average length of the interviews was 53 minutes (median 51 minutes), and they ranged from 25 minutes to one hour and 33 minutes. Most interviews took place in the judicial officer's chambers. All interviewees consented to note-taking, and all but two agreed to audio recording. Handwritten notes were fully written up after each interview. The interviews were double coded by Sharyn Roach Anleu and a research assistant (Miles, Huberman and Saldaña 2020; Saldaña 2016).

This data is indicated by the code 'I ##' in which the letter I identifies this as interview data and ## is the number assigned to the individual interviewee. Quotations are used verbatim and have not been edited to correct grammar or reduce infelicities of spoken language, but retain qualities of natural, everyday speech reflecting the narrative quality of the interviews. All identifying, or potentially identifying, details have been deleted.

Undertaking the interviews is followed by interpreting and analysing the material (James 2012; Mason 2002; Silverman 2013). One researcher conducted all of the interviews benefitting from the 'contextual experience—the being-there-ness of the researcher—for the process of data analysis' (James 2012: 565). The other researcher (Kathy Mack) was able to question any taken-for-granted assumptions. 'Such collaborative exchanges can help with the process of interpretation' (James 2012: 565; also see Roach Anleu, Bergman Blix and Mack 2015). The interview transcripts were coded into nodes relating to emotion, anticipation, interpretation, experience and management of emotion on the part of the judicial officer and other court participants, within and beyond the courtroom, then analysed using NVivo 10. This text was carefully read several times to identify any further emergent subthemes and patterns. As the interviews were often a flow of consciousness, imposing too many categories may unnecessarily truncate them and depart from the narrative quality of the interview.

In the *Judicial Officers and Workload Allocation* project, semi-structured interviews were undertaken with judges, magistrates and court officers involved in workload allocation from four magistrates courts, two intermediate and two higher courts between 2007 and 2012. In total, nine judicial officers and 14 court officers or court administrators were interviewed. Each interview was conducted by two researchers, usually Anne Wallace[3] and Sharyn Roach Anleu; five were conducted by Anne Wallace and Kathy Mack. One interview with an intermediate court involved four people at once, two judicial officers and two court staff. Most interviews lasted between one and one and a half hours. This data is indicated by the code 'W ##' in which the letter W identifies this interview data from the Workload project and ## is the number assigned to an individual interviewee, whether a judicial officer or court administrator/staff. The question format was structured, to gather similar information from all courts and to enable comparison of practices and attitudes across the interviewees, though questions were generally open-ended. Interview questions sought background information about the court context, including the volume and nature of work undertaken, details of the process and method of workload allocation, and information on principles, values or goals that guide workload allocation. All these interviews were recorded and transcribed. Interviews were analysed thematically to identify views of a range of interviewees on an issue, such as specialisation or fairness.

3 At the time of this research collaboration, Professor Anne Wallace was Associate Dean (Education) in the Faculty of Business, Government and Law at the University of Canberra. She is currently Adjunct Professor at La Trobe Law School.

National Court Observation Study

The transcripts of court proceedings used in this book were obtained as part of the *National Court Observation Study* undertaken within an ARC Linkage Project Grant: *The Changing Role of the Magistrates Court* (LP 0210306). The study provided data on interactions between magistrates and other major participants—prosecutors, defence representatives and defendants—as well as with some less frequent actors, such as court staff, social welfare, probation or corrections staff.

This research involved observing 27 magistrates conducting a general non-trial criminal list in 30 different court sessions in 20 different locations, including all capital cities, five suburban, and four regional locations in Australia between August 2004 and July 2005. To enhance reliability and limit subjectivity, two researchers undertook the court observations (Mitteness and Barker 2004; Roach Anleu, Bergman Blix, and Mack et al. 2015). With few exceptions, these were Kathy Mack and Sharyn Roach Anleu together; one was always an observer.

Most observation sessions ($n = 22$) covered the same magistrate in one courtroom for the entire day. The study produced data on 1287 matters. A 'matter' was when each defendant's case was called, regardless of whether the defendant appeared. The magistrates observed include men and women of a range of ages and judicial experience.

In each session, the two observers took detailed notes on standardised pre-printed templates or forms. Observers noted and coded many dimensions of the courtroom interaction, including magistrates' demeanours towards other court participants (mainly prosecutors, defendants and defence representatives) using five demeanour categories: welcoming or good natured; patient or courteous; routine, businesslike or impersonal; impatient, rushed, inconsiderate or bored; harsh, condescending or rude.

In 27 of the 30 sessions observed, court-prepared transcripts or audio records of the proceedings were made available. (Three sessions were not audio-recorded.) Where audio records were provided, research project staff prepared transcriptions. The transcribed text includes 27 sessions, 24 magistrates and 1111 matters, comprising almost 2000 typed pages.

All transcript excerpts have been given a consistent format rather than retaining the relevant court's local formatting. M indicates magistrate; DR indicates a defence representative; P indicates a prosecutor; D indicates defendant. Names have been changed, and, on occasion, other details such as dates or location have been removed if they potentially identify a location or participant. As part of the anonymisation process each individual magistrate was assigned a code number from 1 to 27, and each matter allocated a discrete number (from 1 to 1287).

Sharyn Roach Anleu and a research assistant coded this textual data, identifying any instance or kind of emotion, broadly defined. After coding in parallel, the two coders discussed their codes and made changes or additions. This coding process noted specific words or phrases magistrates used to describe their own feelings and their observations and inferences about the emotions of others, such as the defendant, the prosecutor, the defence representative or any other court participants. Magistrates' actions or conduct could also convey or suggest emotion such as compassion or empathy by referring to feelings of the defendant or victims present in the courtroom. Instances of humour which suggest emotion management strategies were also noted.

Surveys

As well as interviews, surveys are another method to ask judicial officers about emotion. A major focus of the JRP has been an ambitious national survey programme, beginning with a survey sent to all Australian magistrates in 2002 (undertaken as part of an ARC Linkage Project Grant: *The Changing Role of the Magistrates Court* [LP 0210306]), followed by a survey of all Australian judges in 2007, and a second survey of all Australian magistrates in 2007 (Roach Anleu and Mack 2017). The 2007 surveys were undertaken as part of an ARC Discovery Grant: *The Australian Judiciary: A National Socio-Legal Analysis* (DP 0665198).

Using the 2002 magistrates survey as the starting point, the two authors developed, pilot-tested then mailed the *National Survey of Australian Judges* to all 566 judges throughout Australia in March 2007 with a response rate of 55 percent. The 2007 *National Survey of Australian Magistrates* was mailed to all 457 state and territory magistrates throughout Australia, with a response rate of 53 percent. The respondents are generally representative of the judiciary, in terms of gender, age and time on the bench. The surveys used a mix of closed and open-ended questions relating to current position, career background and education, everyday work, job satisfaction and demographic information.

Some of the questions directly address the role of emotion in judicial officers' everyday work. One question asked survey respondents to rate the importance of several qualities or skills including compassion, courtesy, empathy, patience and managing the emotions of court users as essential, very important, important, somewhat important or not important. Other questions addressed stress-related dimensions of judicial work such as 'my work is emotionally draining' and 'difficult decisions keep me awake at night' with the response categories of always, often, sometimes, rarely and never. Response choices for 'making decisions is very stressful' were strongly agree, agree, neutral, disagree, strongly disagree. Open-ended questions asking judicial officers to reflect on their judicial careers also generated information about emotion.

Surveys and interviews provide complementary data. Surveys collect the same kind of information from many people, and responses can be aggregated and compared. Interviews enable more in-depth exploration of responses. However, it is important to note that data from the JRP surveys and interviews is not cross-linked. Surveys were anonymous; there was no identification or tracking of survey booklets or respondents. It is impossible to know who did or did not respond, so the interviewees were not and could not be cross-referenced in any way with the survey participants and their responses, who remain anonymous.[4]

Publicly available information and analysis

Several chapters draw upon publicly available statistical information on Australian courts published by the courts or court administration bodies (such as annual reports), Australian government bodies (in particular the Australian Government Productivity Commission and the Australian Bureau of Statistics) and the Australasian Institute for Judicial Administration. Other publicly available information is used most notably in Chapter 6. This includes published court judgments and materials related to disciplinary proceedings involving judicial officers in the USA, England and Wales, and Australia and produced by regulatory or judicial bodies such as the Judicial Commission of New South Wales, the Judicial Conduct Investigations Office (England and Wales), the Arizona Commission on Judicial Conduct and the Utah Judicial Performance Evaluation Commission.

References

Atkinson, Paul and David Silverman 1997, 'Kundera's Immortality: The Interview Society and the Invention of the Self', *Qualitative Inquiry 13*: 304–325.
Barclay, Katie, 2017, 'Performance and Performativity'. In *Early Modern Emotions: An Introduction*, ed. Susan Broomhall, 14–17. Abingdon and New York: Routledge.
Bergman Blix, Stina and Åsa Wettergren 2019, 'The Emotional Interaction of Judicial Objectivity', *Oñati Socio-Legal Series 9*: 726–746.
Holmes, Mary, 2015, 'Researching Emotional Reflexivity', *Emotion Review 9*: 61–66.
James, Allison, 2012, 'Seeking the Analytic Imagination: Reflections on the Process of Interpreting Qualitative Data', *Qualitative Research 13*: 562–577.
Mason, Jennifer, 2002, *Qualitative Researching*. 2nd ed. London: SAGE Publications.
Matt, Susan J., 2014, 'Recovering the Invisible: Methods for the Historical Study of the Emotions'. In *Doing Emotions History*, eds. Susan J. Matt and Peter N. Stearns, 41–53. Urbana, IL: University of Illinois Press.

[4] It is not possible for the researchers to know if any of the interviewees responded to either of the surveys, though only some interviewees would have been in judicial office at the time of the surveys. Any interviewee first appointed to the judiciary after 2007 would not have received a survey.

Miles, Matthew B., A. Michael Huberman and Johnny Saldaña 2020, *Qualitative Data Analysis: A Methods Sourcebook*. 4th ed. Los Angeles, CA: SAGE Publications.

Mitteness, Linda and Judith C. Barker 2004, 'Collaborative and Team Research'. In *Qualitative Research Practice*, eds. Clive Seale, Giampietro Gobo, Jaber F. Gubrium and David Silverman, California: SAGE Publications.

Roach Anleu, Sharyn, Stina Bergman Blix and Kathy Mack 2015, 'Researching Emotion in Courts and the Judiciary: A Tale of Two Projects', *Emotion Review 7*: 145–150.

Roach Anleu, Sharyn, Stina Bergman Blix, Kathy Mack and Åsa Wettergren 2015, 'Observing Judicial Work and Emotions: Using Two Researchers', *Qualitative Research 16*: 375–391.

Roach Anleu, Sharyn and Kathy Mack 2017, *Performing Judicial Authority in the Lower Courts*. London: Palgrave.

Saldaña, Johnny, 2016, *The Coding Manual for Qualitative Researchers*. 3rd ed. London and Thousand Oaks, CA: SAGE Publications.

Silverman, David, 2013, *Doing Qualitative Research*. 4th ed. London: SAGE Publications.

Strauss, Anselm and Juliet Corbin 1998, *Basics of Qualitative Research: Techniques and Procedures for Developing Grounded Theory*. 2nd ed. Thousand Oaks, CA: SAGE Publications.

Index

For Product Safety Concerns and Information please contact our EU representative GPSR@taylorandfrancis.com
Taylor & Francis Verlag GmbH, Kaufingerstraße 24, 80331 München, Germany

www.ingramcontent.com/pod-product-compliance
Ingram Content Group UK Ltd.
Pitfield, Milton Keynes, MK11 3LW, UK
UKHW020007200926
475702UK00015B/2528
9780367678685